FOOD LOVERS' SERIES

FOOD LOVERS'
GUIDE TO®
MASSACHUSETTS

The Best Restaurants, Markets
& Local Culinary Offerings

Third Edition

Patricia Harris and David Lyon

Guilford, Connecticut

This book is dedicated to hungry travelers everywhere.

Copyright © 2014 by Morris Book Publishing, LLC

Project editor: Lynn Zelem
Layout artist: Mary Ballachino
Text design: Sheryl Kober
Illustrations by Jill Butler with additional art by Carleen Moira Powell and
  MaryAnn Dubé
Maps: Melissa Baker © Morris Book Publishing, LLC

ISSN 1544-7405
ISBN 978-0-7627-9203-0

Printed in the United States of America
10 9 8 7 6 5 4 3 2 1

Contents

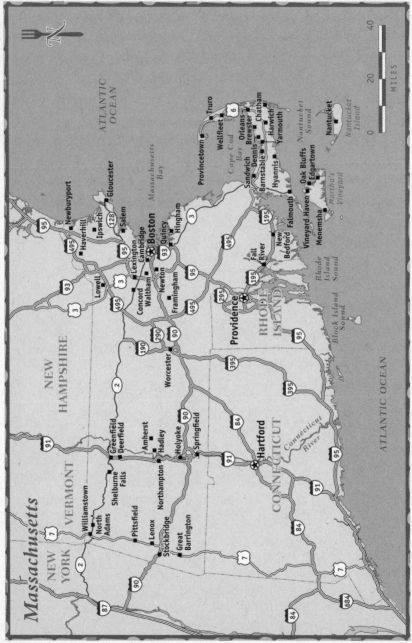

Massachusetts

NEW YORK

VERMONT

NEW HAMPSHIRE

ATLANTIC OCEAN

Massachusetts Bay

RHODE ISLAND

CONNECTICUT

Connecticut River

Rhode Island Sound

Block Island Sound

ATLANTIC OCEAN

Williamstown
North Adams
Pittsfield
Lenox
Stockbridge
Great Barrington
Shelburne Falls
Greenfield
Deerfield
Amherst
Hadley
Northampton
Holyoke
Springfield
Worcester
Lowell
Concord
Waltham
Lexington
Cambridge
Newton
Framingham
Boston
Quincy
Hingham
Salem
Ipswich
Gloucester
Haverhill
Newburyport

Hartford
Providence

Fall River
New Bedford
Falmouth
Vineyard Haven
Oak Bluffs
Edgartown
Menemsha
Martha's Vineyard

Provincetown
Truro
Wellfleet
Orleans
Brewster
Chatham
Harwich
Yarmouth
Dennis
Barnstable
Hyannis
Sandwich
Cape Cod
Cape Cod Bay

Nantucket
Nantucket Island
Nantucket Sound

Atlantic Ocean

N

0   20   40

MILES

Recipes, 283

Appendices, 311

Index, 339

About the Authors

Patricia Harris and David Lyon are coauthors of Globe Pequot Press's *The Meaning of Food, Food Lovers' Guide to Boston, Food Lovers' Guide to Montreal, Food Lovers' Guide to Vermont & New Hampshire,* and *Food Lovers' Guide to Rhode Island*. They have written about Vermont cheese, Belgian beer, Tahitian *poisson cru,* Rhode Island hot dogs, Neapolitan pizza, Maine lobster, Louisiana bayou crawfish, and Spanish elvers for such publications as the *Boston Globe, The Robb Report, Westways,* and *Cooking Light*. They chronicle their travel adventures and culinary explorations on Hungry Travelers.com.

Acknowledgments

We would like to thank everyone in the food business in Massachusetts whose tireless work year after year has made Massachusetts such a great place to eat. We are especially grateful to the cooks and chefs who shared their recipes for this volume. We offer a memorial salute to the late Laura Strom for conceiving the Food Lovers' series, and thank Amy Lyons for letting us take such an active role in the much-expanded series that she envisioned and made happen. We also want to thank project editor Lynn Zelem for shepherding this edition of *Food Lovers' Guide to Massachusetts* to publication.

Introduction: Massachusetts— The Line-Caught, Field-Grown, Craft-Brewed Revolution Continues

When we researched the first edition of this book more than a decade ago, we were surprised by the depth and intensity of the flavors in our own state. If anything, its riches have grown. This third edition of *Food Lovers' Guide to Massachusetts* celebrates how far we have come—and how well we can eat.

Some things, of course, never change. The land and the sea endure. The drumbeat of "local, local, local" has created new markets for farmers and fishermen. Many restaurants used to get all their foodstuffs off a single truck, but these days a growing number of chefs cultivate relationships with farmers and foragers who deliver the freshest product to the restaurant's back door. As a result, Massachusetts menus have a striking seasonality—from the green pea risotto of spring to the braised parsnips and pork belly of winter. This edition features greatly expanded coverage of restaurants. Whether the chef is offering Portuguese seafood stew, Italian *insalata caprese,* or roasted prime rib, the ingredients likely came from a boat or farm not far away.

The proliferation of farmers' markets has made it easier for home cooks to partake of the bounty of local fruits and vegetables, honey, farmstead cheeses, locally raised meats, and even great breads.

In the height of the harvest season, farmers are setting up dinner tables in the fields to dramatically shorten the distance from farm to fork. But all is not lost when the temperature drops. Winter farmers' markets are springing up, belying the notion that there is no local food when there is snow on the ground in Massachusetts.

Another trend we love is the flowering of the food truck movement. A far cry from the lunch wagons of yesteryear, today's food trucks put restaurant creativity on wheels. Look for them in city plazas and wherever people gather at summer outdoor events.

That ingenuity and inventiveness plays out all across the foodscape. Charcuterie is no longer the province of a few French chefs. Artisanal sausages, mousses, and terrines and smoked and salted meats can be found in country stores, delis, and smokehouses. Farmstead cheeses are popping up all over the state wherever farmers tend a small herd of Jersey cattle or Saanen goats. The styles range from fresh chèvre to aged Alpine cheeses to pungent blues.

The Bay State's fledgling wine industry continues to grow as more small vintners have learned to cultivate European wine grapes and make quality wines in our challenging climate. At no time since Prohibition have so many small distilleries plied their trade in Massachusetts. Several of them make clear spirits (vodka and gin), a few produce American whiskies, and several make that most New England of hard drinks, rum.

But the real revolution is among the makers of craft ales. Some producers are so small that they qualify as nanobreweries. Others have been so successful that they have moved into the ranks of microbreweries. It's not enough to make a pale ale, an IPA, and a porter anymore. Every brewer has a signature saison.

All this ferment makes Massachusetts food truly exciting. We have written this book for hungry travelers everywhere. We hope it will introduce you to some of the characters, products, and dishes of the Bay State and lead you to gastronomic discoveries all your own.

How to Use This Book

Massachusetts runs the gamut from extremely rural to unrelentingly urban. We have divided the state into eight cultural and agricultural slices. Metropolitan Boston gets its own chapter, and the immediate suburbs of the city fill another chapter. Western Massachusetts is divided into the distinctly different growing areas of the Berkshires and the Connecticut River Valley. The communities surrounding Worcester—roughly from the Quabbin Reservoir east to I-495—constitute the Central Massachusetts chapter. Our divisions into Northeast and Southeast are made along the lines of the Massachusetts Turnpike. Cape Cod and the Islands (that is, Nantucket and Martha's Vineyard) are self-explanatory.

Each chapter includes a map of the region, which can help you plan trips to do your own exploring. While you're on the road, be sure to check chapters for adjacent areas—a terrific surprise might await just a few miles away. Farm stands and farm stores are seasonal by nature, and we've done our best to identify when they're open. Still, it's always a good idea to call ahead.

We have listed entries in the eight regions under the following categories:

Foodie Faves

These are restaurants that represent some of the best dining in the region.

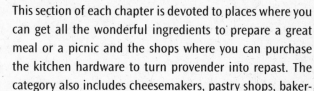

Specialty Stores, Markets & Producers

This section of each chapter is devoted to places where you can get all the wonderful ingredients to prepare a great meal or a picnic and the shops where you can purchase the kitchen hardware to turn provender into repast. The category also includes cheesemakers, pastry shops, bakeries, bakery cafes, breweries, coffee roasters, wineries, and fishmongers.

Farm Stands & PYOs

Farm stands can range from a card table and a hand-lettered sign at the end of a driveway to a year-round store that offers honey, jam, pickles, breads, and maybe even flowers in addition to fresh fruits and vegetables. We could not possibly include every farm selling a few cucumbers from a table by the mailbox, but we have tried to include many that are open for longer seasons. Pick-your-own produce and fruit operations are included in this category, as are dairies and livestock farms that offer points of sale for their milk and meat. Look to this section for maple sugar shacks as well.

Farmers' Markets

Many Massachusetts farms have been in the same families for generations, and farmers' markets are essential venues for meeting the people behind your dinner. Farmers selling at the markets often feel they must offer something special—something you cannot get from the local grocery store. That may be an heirloom fruit or vegetable, an unusual ethnic varietal, or the assurance that the food you buy is free of chemicals. Because the number of farmers' markets continues to proliferate, it's always a good idea to double-check times and locations on the website of the Massachusetts Department of Agriculture: mass.gov/agr/massgrown/farmers_markets.htm.

Price Code

Each restaurant carries a price code to give you a rough approximation of what you will spend. We chose to base the code on dinner entree prices. As a general rule, double the figure to estimate the cost of a three-course meal with a glass of wine. The codes represent the majority of dinner entrees; most restaurants will have a few dishes that are less expensive and a few that are more expensive. Note that some fish dishes (lobster, especially) vary with the price of the market. The cost of lunch is almost always lower.

$	**under $15**
$$	**$15 to $25**
$$$	**$25 to $40**
$$$$	**more than $40 or prix fixe**

Keeping Up with Food News

Not surprisingly, the lively Massachusetts food scene has attracted a lot of opinion mongers who are only too happy to put in their two cents' worth. Here are some information sources that may have an opinionated point of view but speak with authority.

Edible Berkshires, Edible Boston, Edible Cape Cod

Chances are that it won't be news by the time these quarterly magazines publish, but their feature coverage of restaurants, growers, and producers tends to be insightful and sometimes thought-provoking. The magazines are given away free at foodie locations, and can be found online at ediblecommunities.com.

Boston Globe

Restaurant reviews and "cheap eats" reviews of casual spots are published in the Wednesday G section. About a year of these reviews are archived on the free *Globe* website at Boston.com. Many years of reviews are archived on the *Globe*'s pay site, BostonGlobe.com.

The Restaurant Hub

You can find news about chefs and restaurant openings and closings in the *Globe*'s Sunday Arts in a column called "Tables." More extensive coverage is available online at boston.com/blogs/ae/restaurants/the-restaurant-hub.

Dishing

This free column by *Boston Globe* staff appears on the Boston.com website. Many of the posts are devoted to recipes and cooking news. Many others are behind-the-scenes notebook pieces by some of the reviewers. Restaurant news also appears frequently on Dishing. Here's the URL: boston.com/lifestyle/food/dishing.

BostonChefs.com

Almost all the news of interest about the Boston restaurant scene appears on BostonChefs.com. Track all the events, find out about soft openings, and see where the jobs are. (When a place is advertising for a head chef, you might want to eat elsewhere.)

Boston Magazine

Boston's city lifestyle magazine may be best known for bestowing Best of Boston awards, but it also features good restaurant criticism that represents a distinct point of view. For lively, contemporary dish on the dining scene by talented younger writers, see *Boston*'s dining blog, Chowder, at blogs.bostonmagazine.com/chowder.

Eater Boston

Eater is a national network of local blogs that cover bar and restaurant news. Most of eastern Massachusetts is covered by the Boston office. To their credit, Eater often gets the inside scoop on who is opening next, which chef is in and which one is out, and where the foodies in the know are trending. Getting that information means cultivating sources, so there's also a lot of fluff. Not every new restaurant can be the second coming of Nobu. Check it out at boston.eater.com.

Zagat.com

While the standard reviews are compilations of user comments, the Boston office publishes regular features. Although some just repackage old Zagat reviews under a theme, features with staff descriptions of new restaurants are often very sharp. Check zagat.com/boston.

The Berkshires

To much of the world, the Berkshires are a summer place where the Boston Symphony Orchestra plays on the broad lawns of Tanglewood, Shakespeare & Company electrifies audiences with the evergreen plays of the Bard, and Manhattanites carry on a rarefied social life in castle-like cottages and oh-so-quaint antiques shops. Long, rolling vistas greet the eye—verdant valleys interrupted by the piney Berkshire Hills and the bald-headed majesty of Mount Greylock. From Independence Day until Labor Day, the region becomes an idyll of performing arts in a country setting.

But even during the summer hubbub, you need only turn off traffic-clogged Route 7 to find yourself on a Berkshire back road where every third house, it seems, has set up a card table with the fruits and vegetables that mark the subseasons of summer, from peas and strawberries to blackberries and peaches. While the cellists are tuning up and the actors are running throat exercises, Berkshire farmers and gardeners are weeding and hoeing, thinning and harvesting. When the hot-weather idyll ends and the summer folk go back to the city, the land remains and the work goes on. Above all, Berkshire County is an intensely agricultural region of small holdings where farmers cultivate bramble and tree fruits, gather maple sap for syrup, and raise livestock.

The urban sophisticates and the country farmers find common ground in their love of good food, and that's led to the creation of Berkshire Grown, one of the state's most active and effective agricultural support groups. The organization brings together chefs, farmers, retailers,

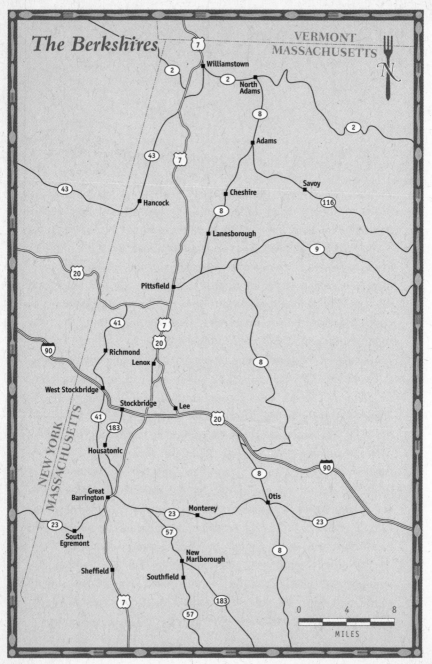

The Berkshires

VERMONT
MASSACHUSETTS

N

Williamstown

North Adams

Adams

Hancock

Cheshire

Savoy

Lanesborough

Pittsfield

Richmond

Lenox

West Stockbridge

Stockbridge

Lee

Housatonic

Great Barrington

Monterey

Otis

South Egremont

Sheffield

New Marlborough

Southfield

NEW YORK
MASSACHUSETTS

0   4   8

MILES

and the interested public in an effort to promote local agriculture and maintain the highest standards for good eating. Shop or dine anywhere the Berkshire Grown emblem is displayed and you'll know you're dealing with people who care where your food came from and how it's been treated.

Foodie Faves

Allium Restaurant + Bar, 42–44 Railroad St., Great Barrington, MA 01230; (413) 528-2118; alliumberkshires.com; New American/Vegetarian; $$–$$$. This sister restaurant to Mezze (see p. 9) shares its commitment to sourcing almost everything on the menu from local growers and producers. Bright salads and house charcuterie figure heavily on the appetizer list and the entrees are simple comfort food—a great burger, tagliatelle with braised duck ragout, roasted free-range chicken with fregola and braised greens. Daily specials include vegetarian options. Craft beer drafts change often, and the bar also offers a selection of nice, good-value wines by the glass or bottle.

Alta Restaurant & Wine Bar, 34 Church St., Lenox, MA 01240; (413) 637-0003; altawinebar.com; New American; $$–$$$. With a French chef who is clearly in touch with the adjoining cuisines of the Italian and Spanish coasts, Alta features dishes rarely found on most wine bar menus. Think trout with a white wine and caper sauce, or tomato and fennel linguine with artichokes and black olives. Even North African influences creep in with dishes like a lamb tagine with pomegranate molasses. Even better, Alta has the wine list to match. This is not the home of simpering Sauvignon Blancs or muddy Merlots. Inexpensive choices might run to Guigal's Côtes du Rhône or a Pinot Grigio from the Veneto, while serious wine aficionados might opt for bottles of Newton Unfiltered Chardonnay or a nice old-vines

Gevrey-Chambertin Burgundy. Two dozen wines are available by the glass, and bargain three-course dinners are offered weeknights in the winter and early spring.

Barrington Brewery & Restaurant, 420 Stockbridge Rd., Great Barrington, MA 01230; (413) 528-8282; barringtonbrewery .net; Brewery; $–$$. Although brewmaster Andrew Mankin had been an enthusiastic homebrewer for a dozen years, he apprenticed at the Vaux Brewery in Sunderland, England, before going pro here in 1995. Not surprisingly, the signature Barrington Brown Ale achieves a rich, nutty, English style—a nice middle ground between the Hopland Pale Ale (very lively with Pacific Northwest hops) and the dark and creamy, deeply roasted Black Bear Stout. Mankin also makes three to four additional seasonal beers. Sampler flights are available. The midday menu emphasizes burgers, sandwiches, and sausages. In fact, the best lunch is probably the sausage on a roll—choice of bratwurst, bauernwurst, or kielbasa—steamed in beer and served with sauerkraut. In the evening, the restaurant offers more substantial plates of steak, chicken, and pastas—not to mention its dreamy **Chocolate Stout Cake** (see recipe on p. 306).

Bell & Anchor, 178 Main St., Great Barrington, MA 01230; (413) 528-5050; New American; $$–$$$. Chef-Owner Mark Firth made his name cooking in Brooklyn, but he has fond memories of growing up in South Africa. So he named this farm-to-table restaurant after his favorite pub in Cape Town, which might explain what a nautical name is doing in the Berkshires. Firth buys whole locally raised animals through the **Meat Market** (see p. 18), and offers a burger that locals swear by. He also makes creative use of less-than-obvious cuts. For example, a salad might have "croutons" of lamb neck meat formed into patties and fried to a crisp. The staff also makes its own charcuterie and sausages—just as if they were working in a French *bouchon*. Most dishes are surprisingly reasonable—except for those that feature the very top cuts of meat. Rib eye, for example, is justifiably expensive. Firth builds his menus around the proteins, but vegetarians can make do with dishes like a plate of spaghetti, cauliflower, leeks, Kalamata olives, and Parmesan cheese. Desserts are limited but superb; the chocolate caramel tart is a beauty to behold and even better to eat.

Bistro Zinc, 56 Church St., Lenox, MA 01240; (413) 637-8800; bistrozinc.com; French; $$–$$$. With its dented pressed-tin ceiling, sleek zinc bar, and framed photographs, Zinc has a sophisticated and urban look and stays open until 1 a.m.—making it one of the few spots that hop when concerts are over and curtains fall at the theaters. For Francophiles, the menu is like a roster of comfort food, starting with an appetizer list that includes steamed mussels, oysters on the half shell, lump crab toasts, and French onion soup. Classicism also rules the main dishes with such choices as coq au vin, *steak-frites, boeuf bourguignon,* and pork cassoulet. Only the wine list defects to other nations to bring in some Californian, Spanish, Argentine, Australian, and Italian selections. Zinc also has Lenox's best selection of cognac and Armagnac.

Blantyre, 16 Blantyre Rd., Lenox, MA 01240; (413) 637-3556; blantyre.com; Continental; $$$$. This stunning 19th-century property, modeled on a Scottish country estate, puts on a lavish spread fit for the robber barons who first made the Berk-
shires their rustic hideaway more than a century ago. The fixed-price menu, which changes with the season, is as luxurious as the property. You might start with a few caramelized scallops or Hudson Valley *foie gras* with a potato confit, move on to boneless rack of lamb with morel sauce, and wrap up with a cheese sampler or a small plate of vanilla crème brûlée, sticky toffee pudding, and yogurt ice cream. The wine list is deep and broad, emphasizing Bordeaux and Burgundy but spiced by the addition of some memorable New World wines. Diners are expected

to dress for dinner, with jacket and tie *de rigueur* for gentlemen. Reservations essential.

Church Street Cafe, 65 Church St., Lenox, MA 01240; (413) 637-2745; churchstreetlenox.com; New American; $$–$$$. The porch is *the* place in Lenox to be seen dining before an evening concert or play. The town's most enduring American bistro (since 1981) keeps up with the times, serving its roasted rib eye with a side of mac and cheese and smoky bacon and adding a lamb curry to the mix. At lunch, the best bets are the flatbread-style pizzas. The Parma is topped with a combination of prosciutto, figs, summer greens, and roasted garlic. The wine list, while not as extensive as at sister restaurant **Alta** (see p. 3), does offer good choice and value.

Firefly New American Bistro, 71 Church St., Lenox, MA 01240; (413) 637-2700; fireflylenox.com; New American; $$–$$$. Chef-Owner Laura Shack studied for three years under the great James Beard, and she brings some of his no-nonsense gusto to this Lenox fixture known for its first decade as Roseborough Grill. The grill still features strongly in the Firefly menu, but who can complain about a grilled rack of lamb? Or even grilled rainbow trout? Shack continues to feature some marvelously homey dishes like panfried chicken livers  with caramelized onions, raisins, and a port wine drizzle as an appetizer. She also makes an excellent Angus burger that comes with hand-cut fries. Berkshire Blue cheese or applewood-smoked bacon are extra. Firefly sometimes offers a bargain menu for two on weeknights. Whatever you order, save room for the jumble berry pie with an all-butter crust.

Gould Farm Roadside Store & Cafe, Route 23, Monterey, MA 01245; (413) 528-2633; gouldfarm.org; Casual American; $.

Since 1913, Gould Farm has offered a therapeutic refuge for persons with disabilities. The Roadside Store & Cafe is one of the cottage industries that help support the community. Bounteous breakfasts include huge pancakes with the farm's own maple syrup. In fact, much of the food is made with Gould Farm products, including organic vegetables and herbs, dairy items, meat, maple syrup, and cheese. Many of these items are also available for sale. Open for breakfast and lunch Wed through Sun. On weekends only, Gould Farm's Harvest Barn Bakery offers fresh baked goods as well as other farm products, including fresh produce in season.

Gramercy Bistro, 87 Marshall St., North Adams, MA 01247; (413) 663-5300; gramercybistro.com; New American; $$-$$$. Chef-Owner Alexander "Sandy" Smith has always served inspired bistro food with an international palate and a Berkshires provenance. Now that his bistro has moved into a former factory building at the Massachusetts Museum of Contemporary Art (Mass MoCA), he can feed museum goers who work up an appetite tromping the miles of cavernous galleries. Smith's sensibilities mash up New England seacoast with the desert southwest in dishes like seared scallops with a southwestern hash and poblano chile sauce. He can do an about-face with a country French coq au vin, or go Moroccan with sweetbreads in brown butter with preserved lemon. The sunny dining room is also a great spot for Sunday brunch, with the usual Benedict suspects and the truly unexpected rabbit pot pie. Like so many of the ingredients, sunny-side-up eggs in the breakfast tart (with goat cheese, bacon, chives, and puff pastry) hail from a nearby farm.

Gypsy Joynt Cafe, 293 Main St., Great Barrington, MA 01230; (413) 644-8811; gypsyjoyntcafe.net; Casual American; $. The Weller tribe runs this truly funky cafe (as well as the used clothing store up the street), and they seem to have stepped directly out of Alice's Restaurant into the 21st century. At least one member is a musician, so Gypsy Joynt has live acoustic music on weekends with an open mic midweek. All day long you can eat really huge cookies, brownies, soups, sandwiches, and hummus with veggies, while the evening supper fare concentrates on heavily sauced pasta (spaghetti, fettuccine Alfredo, mac and cheese). The most over-the-top supper dish is probably the Sleazy Mac and Cheese, with crawfish, bacon, asparagus, sun-dried tomatoes, jalapeño peppers, fresh basil, avocado, and bread crumbs. It's drizzled with truffle oil. Hard liquor, craft beer, and a limited choice of wines are available, which is why the Wellers moved to Great Barrington from North Carolina in the first place. (Their landlord believed alcohol was a sin.)

Jack's Hot Dog Stand, 12 Eagle St., North Adams, MA 01247; (413) 664-9006; jackshotdogstand.com; Casual American; $. When somebody says "they don't make 'em like they used to," send them to this marvelously historic 12-stool lunch counter. It was opened in 1917 by Jaffros Levanos, the Greek grandfather of the current chief cook and owner, Jeff Levanos. The hot dogs—only about a buck each to the astonishment of out-of-towners—are made specially for the restaurant and are only available here. They have a nice spiciness unusual in Massachusetts dogs—a bite that can be slightly enhanced by ordering a chili dog. Jack's also serves hamburgers, pepper steak, fries, and onion rings. The dogs are the draw, though. According to a sign on the wall, the all-time consumption record is 25 hot dogs in one hour.

Jae's Asian Bistro, 55 Pittsfield Rd., Lenox, MA 01240; (413) 637-9777; jaeslenox.com; Asian; $$. Located at the entrance to the Lenox Country Shops about halfway between Lenox and Pittsfield, Jae's is the Berkshires toehold of Jae Chung, the Korean-American restaurateur who first brought healthy Pan-Asian menus to both Boston and western Massachusetts. (The menu still carries his motto: "Eat at Jae's, live forever.")

The rice or noodle platters are among the most popular on the extensive menu. Choose the type of noodle or rice, and then add chicken, beef, shrimp, seafood, or vegetables and a choice of Asian sauces. Kids are always charmed when their meal arrives in a bento box.

John Andrews/A Farmhouse Restaurant, 224 Hillsdale Rd., South Egremont, MA 01258; (413) 528-3469; jarestaurant.com; New American; $$–$$$. No one named John Andrews is associated with this paragon of locavore dining. Chef Dan Smith and Susan Bianchi run the place, and they walk the walk when it comes to supporting local agriculture. Each evening features a different cut of Lila's Mountain Lamb (raised by Lila Berle on a 400-acre Great Barrington sheep farm), some version of local grass-fed beef, Pigasso Farm's pork, and veggies from all up and down the Housatonic and Hudson Valleys. In fact, Smith and Bianchi work with more than 30 area farms all year for everything from greens and berries to foraged and cultivated mushrooms to maple syrup. The diners who come here tend to be pretty sophisticated, even though the restaurant occupies a rural farmhouse with creaky floorboards. About the only things on the menu that aren't local are the fish dishes, the coffee, the wines, and the chocolate in the desserts. Even the booze is made at Berkshire Mountain Distillers.

Mezze Bistro + Bar, 777 Cold Spring Rd. (Route 7), Williamstown, MA 01267; (413) 458-0123; mezzerestaurant.com; New American; $$–$$$$. Japanese-American chef Joji Sumi cooks inspired farm-to-table dishes that reflect his classical training and his commitment to local producers. More than 70 local farms supply almost everything from grass-fed local beef to hand-crafted artisan cheeses to salad vegetables. The spacious dining rooms in this woodsy retreat overlooking Sheep Hill south of town are a great place to spread out and enjoy *chitarra* pasta with a house version of Bolognese that uses local mutton, pork, and Italian sausage—or an Amish chicken roulade with buttermilk spaetzle. Desserts such as the olive oil cake with sweetened ricotta, orange marmalade, and honey rosemary gelato show unusual sophistication and restraint.

Nudel Restaurant, 37 Church St., Lenox, MA 01240; (413) 551-7183; nudelrestaurant.com; New American; $–$$. Chef-Owner Bjorn Somlo is something of a rock star chef, having been nominated repeatedly for James Beard awards. But he modestly calls Nudel an "American pasta bar." In truth, he is the guy who always comes up with a creative dish when a grower comes in and laments that he has an overstock of something. A surplus of broccoli? Somlo makes a spicy peanut butter soup with broccoli florets. The menu always includes three pasta dishes along with lots of small plates and a handful of entrees like maple-poached Canadian duck. But it's never really clear what's for dinner until Somlo posts the menu outside at 5 p.m. each day. If you love the dish, remember it. It may not come around again until next growing season.

Old Inn on the Green, 134 Hartsville–New Marlborough Rd., New Marlborough, MA 01230; (413) 229-7924; oldinn.com; New American; $$–$$$$. This circa-1760 stagecoach inn doesn't exactly overdo the electric lights—the dining rooms are lit entirely by romantic candlelight, which is only a problem for scrutinizing the menu. Chef and co-owner Peter Platt is a big booster of local farms, so his highly seasonal menus tend to reflect the Berkshire harvest. While the Saturday fixed-price dinner is a rather formal affair of multiple courses, Platt offers a la carte meals and bargain midweek and Sunday three-course fixed-price menus. A midweek meal might start with carrot ginger soup, move on to braised Angus short ribs, and finish up with a triple-fudge chocolate brownie. The facility is also an inn, with cozy historic rooms and modernized suites in the original inn building and an equally ancient Thayer House next door on the village green.

Red Lion Inn, 30 Main St., Stockbridge, MA 01262; (413) 298-5545; redlioninn.com; New American; $$–$$$$. The chefs of this historic inn, which serves food in both a cozy tavern and formal dining rooms, were among the founders of the Berkshire Grown network that began promoting local food years before Slow Food got up off its Italian couch and started agitating in America. Current chef Brian Alberg continues the good work, offering a range of menu choices from traditional New England country fare to contemporary New American dishes—all of them leaning heavily on local farms and orchards. Even for a starter salad, he might source the greens, goat cheese, and maple vinaigrette from three different local farms, and the field-grown vegetables from Equinox Farm often feature in side dishes or as vegetarian entrees. One of the tastiest starters in the spring is a ramp risotto topped with braised local mountain lamb. For the Red Lion Inn's recipe for **Berkshire Apple Pancake**, a favorite on the breakfast menu, see p. 285.

Rouge Restaurant, 3 Center St., West Stockbridge, MA 01266; (413) 232-4111; rougerestaurant.com; French/Spanish; $$$. Chef William Merelle spent his formative years in the Pyrenees region, so his nominally French cooking speaks with a strong Spanish accent. He is one of the few chefs in Massachusetts we trust to make a paella that wouldn't be out of place in Valencia, yet his duck cassoulet (using free-range duck, a rarity, and traditional French beans) would be right at home in the dish's native Languedoc. Merelle draws extensively from the Berkshire countryside for his meat, dairy, and produce, but he prepares his dishes with a wonderful combination of French panache (quail with prune and bacon) and Spanish soul (calamari in squid ink). If you'd rather eat small plates, Rouge also serves an extensive list of tapas that range from warm chèvre with a baguette to a single lamb chop with Parmesan and a red wine shallot sauce.

Southfield Store, 163 Main St., Southfield, MA 01259; (413) 229-5050; southfieldstore.com; New American; $–$$. The hamlet of Southfield is so small that many maps don't even show it, but it's one of the prettiest little villages in the high southern Berkshires. The town's erstwhile general store, now owned by Peter Platt and Meredith Kennard of the **Old Inn on the Green** (see p. 10), functions as a convenience store for local hill country folks (mostly gourmet cheeses, cured meats, beer, and wine) and as a cafe that serves great pastries, granola, and a few egg dishes for weekday breakfasts, a nice array of sandwiches at lunchtime, and a pull-out-the-stops prix-fixe Sunday brunch.

From May into December, the store also serves dinner on weekends. Appetizers might include a local fresh mozzarella on baby greens, an heirloom tomato salad, or a gazpacho of Berkshire tomatoes and peppers. Meats also come from nearby farms in the Berkshires and over the line into neighboring New York.

Spice Dragon, 297 North St., Pittsfield, MA 01201; (413) 443-1234; eatatspicedragon.com; Asian/Vegetarian; $–$$. Exactly the right spot to grab a bite before or after a production at Barrington Stage, which is more or less around the corner, this gigantic eatery looks a little like the owners got too good a deal on Chinese New Year decorations. Yet at heart, it's a Vietnamese-Thai-Cambodian restaurant, and the Vietnamese-style spring rolls are one of the best items on the menu. The broad selection of vegetarian dishes is a plus for non-meat eaters, and there are even some American comfort food options (like a hamburger, truffled fries, or flatbread-style pizzas) for diners who don't do chopsticks.

Barrington Coffee Roasting Company, 165 Quarry Hill Rd., Lee, MA 01238; (413) 243-3008; barringtoncoffee.com; Coffee. Barrington Coffee's owners, Barth Anderson and Gregg Charbonneau, and staff are true java junkies. They lovingly hand-roast single-origin coffees by color and aroma to accentuate the special characteristics of each crop—the delicate blueberry note in Ethiopian Harrar, bright toasted peanut in Indian Mysore, the hint of nutmeg in Kauai. Ten or fifteen additional seconds of roasting can make a radical difference in the flavor, so while roasting "seems like a scientific process," says roaster Christine Stanton, "we have an artistic approach." Barrington Coffee has been up and running since 1993, and the coffee is available in whole-bean bags in select regional markets and at Charbonneau's coffee shop, **Lenox Coffee** (52 Main St., Lenox; 413-637-1606). You are also welcome to stop by the roasting facility to pick up a few bags.

Berkshire Mountain Bakery, 367 Park St. (Route 183), Housatonic, MA 01236; (413) 274-3412; berkshiremountainbakery .com; Bakery. Richard Bourdon has been fermenting and baking amazing sourdough loaves in Housatonic for about three decades and fortunately shows no signs of letting up. In addition to traditional European whole-wheat sourdoughs, Bourdon and his staff of more than a dozen bakers also make spelt breads, pizza dough, and even wholesome sprouted grain cookies. For the broadest choice, visit the bakery; some breads are also available in area markets.

Catherine's Chocolate Shop, 260 Stockbridge Rd., Great Barrington, MA 01230; (800) 345-2462; catherineschocolates.net; Chocolatier. Stop by Catherine's on your way to a play or a concert for a small "Theater Box" of assorted chocolates. You might want to return

ART OF THE TANGLEWOOD PICNIC

When the Tanglewood Music Festival put on its first outdoor concerts in 1937, rainstorms drenched the patrons, leading the Boston Symphony Orchestra to construct the open auditorium with overhead roof now known as The Shed. But the real pleasure of Tanglewood is braving the elements to spread a blanket with a sumptuous picnic repast on the grassy lawn.

When preparing a picnic, keep in mind that it's a significant hike from the parking lot to the lawn, so don't burden yourself with more than you'll want to carry. If you lack the time, patience, or skill to assemble your own picnic, **Nejaime's Wine Cellars,** which has delis at all three of its locations, has the art of the Tanglewood picnic down to a science. They offer three popular combinations: the Berkshire Summer Classic (hummus, tabouli salad, roasted salmon, fresh chèvre, sesame lo mein salad, cookies, and a baguette), French Country (Brie, chicken liver pâté with truffles, smoked chicken breast, pasta salad, roasted eggplant, and a fruit pie), and Mediterranean (Brenta cheese, dry Italian sopressata, curried chicken salad, stuffed grape leaves, tabouli salad, lentil salad, and baklava). Nejaime's also has a superb wine selection. If you remember to bring a corkscrew, you'll meet lots of absentminded people at Tanglewood who didn't.

Nejaime's Wine Cellars, 3 Elm St., Stockbridge, MA 01262; (800) 946-3987; 60 Main St., Lenox, MA 01240; (800) 946-3978; 444 Pittsfield/Lenox Rd., Lenox, MA 01240; (800) 946-3988; nejaimeswine.com.

later for some of the homemade fudge, truffles, chocolate-dipped fruit, or chocolate Florentine cookies. The shop is best known for its sumptuous "butterkrunch," made from a recipe that was first developed by a family member in the 1920s. This signature confection consists of butter, sugar, cashews, and "other natural ingredients" cooked to 300°F, rolled on a cool marble slab, covered with dark chocolate, and coated in crushed cashews.

Charles H. Baldwin & Sons, 1 Center St., West Stockbridge, MA 01266; (413) 232-7785; baldwinextracts.com; Grocery. Five generations of Baldwins have been making flavor extracts in tiny West Stockbridge since 1888. The street-level shop is jammed with baking supplies, spices, country store candy, and Baldwin products, including semi-exhausted vanilla beans useful mostly for potpourri. The vanilla extract is made in the basement, according to Jackie Moffatt, whose husband, Earl Baldwin Moffatt, represents that fifth generation. "Everything else is made up here," she says, referring to the shop's back room, where anise, 'lemon, orange, spearmint, peppermint, and almond extracts are produced. For the company's signature vanilla, Moffatt uses Bourbon vanilla beans from Madagascar and ages the extract in 100-year-old oak barrels to produce a dark, rich flavor. The small shop also produces its own Worcestershire sauce from a recipe that Earl and Jackie found wadded up in Earl's grandfather's rolltop desk. Many locals favor Baldwin's Table Syrup, a maple blend developed in the 1920s as a tasty but less expensive alternative to pure maple syrup. For Baldwin's recipe for **Easy Vanilla Wafers,** see p. 304.

Chocolate Springs Cafe, Lenox Commons, 55 Pittsfield-Lenox Rd. (Route 7), Lenox MA 01240; (413) 637-9820; chocolatesprings .com; Chocolatier. Joshua Needleman is the quintessential contemporary chocolatier. He's not content to simply produce exquisite bonbons and truffles. Each one has to have a special twist. His "champagne" bonbon, for example, has Pop Rocks in it to make it fizz. The cafe also serves drinks (including an achingly decadent hot chocolate) as well as specialty individual cakes like the all dark chocolate mousse cake (dark chocolate mousse on dark chocolate sponge cake). And in true patisserie fashion, Needleman also makes a few flavors of classic macarons.

Cricket Creek Farm, 1255 Oblong Rd., Williamstown, MA 01267; (413) 458-5888; cricketcreekfarm.com; Cheese. This historic small farm milks Jersey and Brown Swiss cows and makes several artisanal cheeses. They include Maggie's Round, a semisoft aged raw-milk cheese similar to *toma* cheeses from the Italian Alps; Tobasi, a semisoft raw-milk cheese with an edible washed rind; and Berkshire Bloom, a Camembert-style cheese made with pasteurized milk. Visitors are welcome to observe the cows being milked and to stop in the farm store for all the cheeses along with Cricket Farms' pasture-raised beef, whey-fed pork, raw milk, maple syrup, honey, and other products.

Different Drummer's Kitchen, 374 Pittsfield Rd., Lenox, MA 01240; (413) 637-0606; differentdrummerskitchen.com; Housewares. You might feel that you need your passport when you walk into this roadside store where you can buy a tortilla press and taco-shell pans; the complete Joyce Chen line of woks and Chinese cooking utensils; Emile Henry custard cups, quiche pans, and terrines; enameled cast-iron Le Creuset pots and pans; or stainless steel and copper pots from Germany, England, and even the good old USA. While some of the goods are upscale enough to make you think about a home equity loan, there are also dozens of inexpensive but essential trifles, like cutters for making filled linzer cookies and carriers for every size of picnic.

Furnace Brook Winery/Hilltop Orchards, 508 Canaan Rd. (Route 295), Richmond, MA 01254; (413) 698-3301; furnace brookwinery.com; Wine, Beer & Spirits. Some of the trees in John Vittori's orchard date back a full century and include heirloom apples rarely seen even at specialist orchards, such as Wealthy and Milton. He puts the fruit to good use for two very different hard ciders: an American/British-style Johnny Mash made from a blend of Northern Spy and McIntosh apples, and an exquisite and nuanced French *cidre*, a Normandy-style cider that is fermented on the skins and aged in oak. The winery makes a number of wines as well, but the grapes are purchased from other regions. Among the best is the sparkling muscato, a sweet wine that goes very well with spicy Asian food and with certain more delicate New England cheeses. The hilltop property is a great place to visit in any season, and staff encourage visitors to stroll through the orchards or follow hiking paths across the property. Apple picking is available in the fall. We like to return in winter to snowshoe through the orchards and then warm up with a glass of cider and an apple cider doughnut in front of the big fireplace in the tasting room.

Guido's Quality Fruit & Produce, 1020 South St., Pittsfield, MA 01201; (413) 442-9912; 760 S. Main St., Great Barrington, MA 01230; (413) 528-9255; guidosfreshmarketplace.com; Grocery. Guido's resembles a farm stand on steroids—lots of local produce as well as the culinary essentials you'd find in a supermarket. Guido's gathers the best seasonal produce from the farms of the Berkshires (and adjacent New York) into one place where you can stand paralyzed by the choices of exquisite foodstuffs. Look here for such local treats as Berkshire Blue and Monterey Chèvre cheeses, Barrington Coffee, Country Hen organic eggs, and Prima Pasta (made at Guido's). For the recipe for **Guido's Gazpacho,** see p. 287.

Haven Cafe & Bakery, 8 Franklin St., Lenox, MA 01240; (413) 637-8948; havencafebakery.com; Bakery Cafe. We like to think of Haven as the place where folks from Williamsburg (Brooklyn), the Upper East Side (Manhattan), and Housatonic (the Berkshires) all sit down together in an all-organic version of the Peaceable Kingdom that smells like fresh croissants. Breakfast here is always popping, and the order taker at the counter doesn't bat an eyelash at requests for all egg whites on that breakfast burrito, and, oh, hold the spinach but could I have some extra avocado? It might be the only place we've ever encountered gluten-free french toast. (There's a croissant version of French toast for diners without dietary restrictions.) Burgers, sandwiches, and quesadillas rule at lunch—along with cocktails mixed with spirits from Berkshire Mountain Distillers.

The Meat Market, 389 Stockbridge Rd., Great Barrington, MA 01230; (413) 528-2022; themeatmarketgb.com; Butcher. Most of the farms that raise the livestock for this classic butcher shop, which opened in 2011, are located less than 40 miles away. The ability to source local meat, make sure it's properly aged, and then cut to customers' specifications sets The Meat Market, frankly, a cut above the rest. Owner Jeremy Stanton, who trained at the Culinary Institute of America, oversees the charcuterie personally, and offers a menu of prepared, smoked, cured, and pickled foods in addition to the fresh meats. Stop in to watch the butchers working their magic at their wooden blocks—or just to pick up an English-style meat pie to pop in the oven later on.

Monterey General Store, 448 Main Rd., Monterey, MA 01245; (413) 528-5900; monterey-general-store.com; Grocery. This building has been the hill town's village store since 1780, and remains an integral part of the community, stocking grocery staples along with maple syrup, honey, cheese, and vegetables from local farms. It's a great place to catch up on local gossip over breakfast or lunch. Sandwiches range from simple country fare such as roast turkey with lettuce, tomato, and mustard to more Manhattan-tinged offerings such as Scottish smoked salmon with cream cheese, red onion, capers, tomato, and cucumber.

Otis Poultry Farm, 1570 N. Main Rd., Otis, MA 01253; (413) 269-4438; otispoultryfarm.com; Grocery. If you find the road, you can't miss the store: It's a huge red building with two giant white chickens holding a sign that reads WELCOME TO OTIS POULTRY FARM out front. Another sign proclaims, WE HAVE 23,000 EMPLOYEES WHO PRODUCE CUSTOM-LAID EGGS. The organic eggs begin at extra-large (white or brown) and keep going through jumbo (white or brown). You can even buy double yolks. Otis also sells fresh free-range chicken, frozen soup chickens, chicken croquettes, nuggets, hot wings, tenders, and turkey and chicken potpies (with and without vegetables). Some other products include fresh peanut butter, jellies and preserves, salad dressing, mustard, spreading cheeses, and fudge. You can order sandwiches (from bread baked on the premises) at a deli counter. The farm prides itself on being the "home of the famous chicken gicken fertilizer—your garden's best friend."

Rawson Brook Farm, New Marlborough Road, Monterey, MA 01245; (413) 528-2138; Cheese. Visitors are welcome to drop in at Susan Sellew's goat farm and cheese operation at 5 p.m. any evening from mid-April to mid-November to watch her milk her herd of 50 droopy-eared Nubian, white Sanaan, and French and American Alpine goats. The farm produces plain Monterey Chèvre and several versions with added herbs. The most popular contains chives and garlic. Each goat yields about a gallon of milk per day, which is enough to make one pound of cheese. Between mid-March and early January, Sellew produces 350 to 400 pounds per week, keeping back some stock in the freezer to have a supply throughout the year. The cheeses are available at some Berkshire markets as well as at the farm.

Rubiner's Cheesemongers & Grocers, 264 Main St., Great Barrington, MA 01230; (413) 528-0488; rubiners.com; Cheese. When chefs from as far away as Napa, California, want a special cheese, they call Matt Rubiner. When the *Wall Street Journal* wants a pithy quote on American farmstead cheese, they call Matt Rubiner. When hungry folk in Great Barrington get a hankering for cheese (or cured meats and fish), they visit Rubiner's or pop into Rubi's Cafe in the back for salads, cheese and meat boards, and sandwiches—including a divinely simple grilled cheese with sliced cornichons. The shop carries spectacular artisanal and farmstead cheeses from all over the world.

Tunnel City Coffee Roasters, 100 Spring St., Williamstown, MA 01267; (413) 458-5010; Coffee. Tunnel City roasts its own coffees on the premises, including exotic varieties such as Ethiopian Longberry Harrar. But what sets the shop apart is a vast array of French and Viennese pastries that range from delicate raspberry-filled butter cookies to a drop-dead-beautiful tall chocolate cake filled with alternating layers of raspberry cream and vanilla buttercream.

Wohrle's Food Warehouse, 1619 East St., Pittsfield, MA 01202; (413) 442-2411; wohrlesfoods.com; Grocery. No one ever said Wohrle's hot dogs and sausages were gourmet fare, but this food warehouse has been stuffing casings since 1921, and their franks are the dog of choice for roasting on a stick at a state park grill. There's a definite ethnic twist to the sausages, which include bratwurst, kielbasa links, kielbasa rings, sweet and hot Italian sausages, and breakfast patties and links. This is also the place to pick up food-service-size canned foods for a giant family reunion—a gallon jar of maraschino cherries, an 8-pound can of Hershey's chocolate syrup, or 50-ounce cans of Campbell's soups.

Bartlett's Orchard, 575 Swamp Rd., Richmond, MA 01254; (413) 698-2559. Ron and Rick Bartlett grow 18 varieties of apples on the premises (including some experimental types such as Stars and Stripes) and make natural apple cider that's sterilized with ultraviolet light, instead of the traditional heat pasteurization, to preserve the cider's natural flavors. The farm store also offers a huge variety of produce—local whenever possible—including the Bartletts' own old-fashioned tomatoes: Mountain Spring, Pik Rite, Jet Star, Prime Time, Market Pride, Brandywine, and Sun Gold cherry tomatoes. During corn season, they pick several times a day to ensure absolute freshness.

The Good Shepherd Farm, 142 Griffin Hill Rd., Savoy, MA 01256; (413) 743-7916. Located well out in the sticks, near the Windsor State Forest, Good Shepherd suddenly appears out of the woods as a broad expanse of fenced mountain meadows where Pat and Tom Sadin's herd of registered Romney sheep graze. The Sadins have been raising sheep and selling lamb since the late 1980s. Unlike imported lamb, which can be up to two years old, Good Shepherd lambs are slaughtered at six to eight months, ensuring maximum tenderness and mild flavor. "They eat only grass, their mothers' milk, and our own hay," Pat says. Good Shepherd takes orders in August, on a first-come, first-served basis, for pickup of freezer packages in October. The Sadins also sell yarn, tanned sheepskins, hand-knit wool hats, and brown and white fleece for hand spinners. Call ahead before visiting, as the farm is well off the beaten path.

IOKA Valley Farm, 3475 Rte. 43, Hancock, MA 01237; (413) 738-5915; iokavalleyfarm.com. Don and Judy Leab's 600-acre farm in the sweeping valley near Jiminy Peak Ski Resort used to be a dairy operation, but Don converted the old milking parlor into a state-of-the-art facility for canning the maple syrup that he still boils down the old-fashioned way over a wood fire. The Leabs serve pancake meals on weekends from mid-February through early April and sell their own maple syrup, maple cream, maple butter, maple sugar, and maple lollipops. But there are plenty of reasons to visit this fun and welcoming place throughout the growing season. Pick-your-own strawberries are available during late June and early July and you can return in September and October for PYO pumpkins. The Leabs maintain a petting zoo called "Uncle Don's Barn Yard" that is open from late June through Labor Day. The farm also raises (and sells) all-natural hormone-free beef.

Lakeview Orchard, 94 Old Cheshire Rd., Lanesborough, MA 01237; (413) 448-6009; lakevieworchard.com. Lakeview has a long season of sweet fruits that begins in July with red and black raspberries, continues with sweet cherries, and then segues into red currants, plums, and finally apples. You can pick some fruit yourself or take it easy and buy them in the store, along with shallots, Walla Walla onions, sweet cider pressed on site, and honey from the farm's own hives. "What we grow—or the neighboring farm grows—is what we sell," says Judy Jurczak. Baked goods include chocolate and pumpkin whoopie pies (a local favorite, for which everyone has a secret recipe), fruit turnovers, and delicious cider doughnuts that roll off an ingenious cooker called the "Donut Robot." Open May through Oct.

Mountain View Farm, Old Cheshire Road, Lanesborough, MA 01237; (413) 445-7642. The southeast-facing hillside above the Cheshire Reservoir moderates Mountain View's microclimate to provide the extra warmth and sun needed for bounteous tomato harvests. The season opens in late June with pick-your-own strawberries and continues with blueberries, tomatoes, and pumpkins. Throughout the growing season, you can also select from a variety of already picked vegetables including broccoli, cauliflower, early and late cabbage, and corn. By the way, if you get carried away with your strawberry picking, the proprietors suggest freezing some to enjoy later. Hull the berries right away, remove any dirt with a damp cloth, place them in one layer on a cookie sheet, and freeze for about an hour. The frozen berries can then be stored in a container until you have a craving for a taste of summer on a cold or rainy day. Open June through Oct.

Taft Farms, 119 Park St. N., Great Barrington, MA 01230; (413) 528-1515 or (800) 528-1015; taftfarms.com. Dan and Martha Tawczynski and their sons Keith and Paul offer more than 400 produce items at the store, along with freshly laid organic eggs. Although Taft Farms field-grown produce is not certified organic (if you want to learn the complex politics of relatively meaningless USDA certification, just ask), the Tawczynskis are local leaders in promoting organic practices, alternative planting techniques, and soil building to eliminate the need to spray or dust. Taft bakes its own pies, cakes, cookies, and breads and makes soups with homegrown produce. You'll also find their own applesauce, chowchow, and a line of jams, jellies, and preserves. In addition to the farm's own products, the store stocks maple syrup, jams and jellies, breads and cookies, fresh pasta, and local eggs and milk from other Berkshires producers. Pick your own strawberries in June and pumpkins in Sept and Oct.

Whitney's Farm Market, Route 8, Cheshire, MA 01225; (413) 442-4749; whitneysfarm.com. Just a short distance north of the Berkshire Mall, the Whitney family has been selling produce and landscaping plants since 1940. Eric and Michelle Whitney's farm offers pick-your-own blueberries and pumpkins, while the store has a broad range of produce, both local and from distributors, including the farm's own sweet corn. Like most area farm stands, the store makes every effort to provide local products, whether it's the cheeses from

SHAKER YOUR PLATE

From 1783 to 1960, members of the United Society of Believers in Christ's Second Appearing occupied a model farm community just west of Pittsfield. The Shakers, as they were better known, were widely hailed for their agriculture and animal husbandry, and the museum of Hancock Shaker Village carries on the tradition in a reduced way. Food lovers tend to be fascinated by the heirloom vegetable and herb gardens and by the heritage breeds of livestock. But, as the old saying goes, the proof is in the pudding. On a couple of weekends in the fall, the village offers Shaker Suppers. They begin with hors d'oeuvres and specialty ciders served in the historic Brick Dwelling by hosts in mid-19th-century costume. A candlelight buffet dinner in the Believers' Dining Room follows, and then a program of Shaker music. The menu is drawn from *The Best of Shaker Cooking*, written by the founder of Hancock Shaker Village, Amy Bess Miller. In keeping with Shaker tradition, you should take only what you will eat—and be sure to eat it all. That's called "shakering your plate."

The village is open from early April through October. Call or visit the website for details on Shaker Suppers.

Hancock Shaker Village, 1843 W. Housatonic St. (Routes 20 and 41), Pittsfield, MA 01201; (413) 443-0188; hancockshaker village.org.

farmstead cheesemakers, coffee from Barrington Coffee Roasting, or frozen potpies from Otis Poultry. The large deli makes excellent sandwiches and sells cookies and other sweets baked on the premises. Kids enjoy the small petting zoo with pigs, goats, and various poultry. Open from Easter through late Dec.

Windy Hill Farm, 686 Stockbridge Rd., Great Barrington, MA 01230; (413) 298-3217; windyhillfarminc.com. Located on the Great Barrington–Stockbridge town line, Windy Hill's retail operation is devoted principally to landscaping and bedding plants, with great masses of petunias and impatiens in the spring and equally vast collections of chrysanthemums starting in August. The garden center also sells a wide variety of landscape decorations—birdbaths, cast-concrete garden animals, and the like. But they also offer pick-your-own blueberries and from mid-August through late October, the hillside behind the garden center is one of the most convenient pick-your-own apple orchards around. All trees are on dwarf stock, obviating the need for ladders. Open Apr through Dec.

Farmers' Markets

Adams Farmers' Market, 60 Columbia St., Adams. Fri from noon to 6 p.m., late May through Oct.

Berkshire Farmers' Market, 398 Stockbridge Rd., Great Barrington. Sat from 10 a.m. to 2 p.m., mid-June through Sept.

Great Barrington Farmers' Market, Community Health Programs, 422 Stockbridge Rd., Great Barrington. Thurs from 4 to 7 p.m., June through Aug.

Great Barrington Farmers' Market, historic train station behind Town Hall, Great Barrington. Sat from 9 a.m. to 1 p.m., May through Oct.

Lanesborough Farmers' Market, Berkshire Mall parking lot, Route 8 at Sears, Lanesborough. Wed and Sat, 8 a.m. to 2 p.m., May through Nov.

Lee Farmers' Market, Lee Post Office, Lee. Fri from 10 a.m. to 1 p.m., early May through early Oct.

Lenox Farmers' Market, Shakespeare and Co., 70 Kemble St., Lenox. Fri from 1 to 5 p.m., late May through early Oct.

North Adams Farmers' Market, St. Anthony municipal parking lot, Marshall and Center streets, North Adams. Sat from 8 a.m. to noon, July through Oct.

Otis Farmers' Market, 2000 E. Otis Rd., Otis. Sat from 9 a.m. to 1 p.m., May through early Oct.

Pittsfield Farmers' Market, First Street parking lot, Fenn and Eagle streets, Pittsfield. Sat from 10 a.m. to 2 p.m., May through Sept.

Sheffield Farmers' Market, Old Parish Church, 340 S. Main St., Sheffield. Fri from 2:30 to 6:30 p.m., early May to early Oct.

West Stockbridge Farmers' Market, Harris St. and Merritt Way, West Stockbridge. Thurs from 3 to 7 p.m., late May through mid-Oct.

Williamstown Farmers' Market, Spring Street parking lot, Williamstown. Sat from 8 a.m. to noon, late May through Oct.

Connecticut Valley

If representatives from the culinary subcultures of the Connecticut River Valley all sat down to a barbecue, the menu might be tofu kielbasa with a side of organic sauerkraut, washed down by a microbrewed beer spiked with fair-trade coffee, and followed by a pint of super-premium maple ice cream with rain forest nuts smooshed in.

Preposterous fusions aside, the people of the Connecticut Valley cultivate diversity as surely as they grow pumpkins next to bitter melons, asparagus a field away from lemongrass, and Silesian cabbage cheek by jowl with bok choy. The bottomlands along the Connecticut River are some of the richest agricultural soils in the Northeast and arguably some of the most beautiful.

Despite the presence of industrial Springfield, the Connecticut River flows through a largely bucolic valley populated with small towns. Northampton, Amherst, and South Hadley are the homes of Smith, Amherst, Hampshire, and Mount Holyoke Colleges as well as the behemoth flagship campus of the University of Massachusetts. These institutions provide the yeast of youth and the leavening effects of urban sophistication to an otherwise rural countryside. Yet at the same time that urban exiles tool around the valley in their Audis, the villages in the Berkshire foothills west of the valley still echo with the cannon shots of the 1960s cultural revolution, and Polish-American farmers along the river hold fast to their Old World traditions. Where else can you get a pierogi or a kielbasa sandwich when you stop to buy sweet corn?

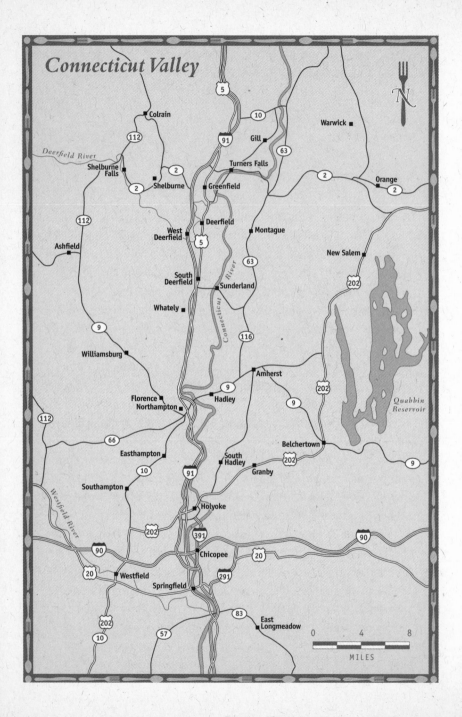

Connecticut Valley

N

Colrain

Warwick

112

Deerfield River

Gill

Shelburne
Falls

Turners Falls

Orange

Shelburne

Greenfield

Deerfield

West
Deerfield

Montague

Ashfield

New Salem

South
Deerfield

Sunderland

Whately

Connecticut River

Williamsburg

Amherst

Florence
Northampton

Hadley

Quabbin
Reservoir

Easthampton

South
Hadley

Belchertown

Southampton

Granby

Westfield River

Holyoke

Chicopee

Westfield

Springfield

East
Longmeadow

0   4   8

MILES

All this cultural diversity makes the Connecticut Valley a fascinating place for food lovers. The extraordinary vegetables of the Sunderland, Whately, and Hadley truck farms dominate the summer menus of haute-cuisine restaurants and highway diners alike—and they're often for sale at makeshift stands on the side of the road. You'll find farm boys and frat boys side by side at the bar, quaffing IPAs and bitters and chowing down on quesadillas stuffed with black beans and goat cheese.

The penchant for polemics so characteristic of the Five College area necessarily makes eating a political act. Local farming is promoted by a group that calls itself Community Involved in Sustaining Agriculture (CISA), which celebrated its 20th anniversary in 2013. But we have to agree: Real food should come from one's own backyard whenever possible, and CISA identifies the farmers of Franklin, Hampshire, and Hampden Counties as "Local Heroes." It offers a comprehensive list of farm stands, farmers' markets, and community-supported farms, as well as an agricultural calendar of events and a detailed farm products list (go to buylocalfood.org).

Foodie Faves

Amanouz Cafe, 44 Main St., Northampton, MA 01060; (413) 585-9128; amanouz.com; Mediterranean; $. There are smatterings of Italian, French, Turkish, and Lebanese dishes on the menu here, but you'd be doing yourself a disservice not to concentrate on the Moroccan couscous, tagines, and kebabs. The restaurant is open all day, though the breakfast dishes are mostly variations on eggs. Lunch can be slow (it's a small kitchen) but a lamb shish kebab sandwich on lavash has an authentic taste. The couscous dishes are available in several variations (with or without lentils; with chicken, fish, or lamb), and the restaurant also does a nice fish tagine served over rice. A classic tagine that's sometimes available is the "tagine fez" of lamb stewed with prunes and onions and topped with peas and chopped boiled egg.

Amherst Brewing Company, 10 University Dr., Amherst, MA 01002; (413) 253-4400; amherstbrewing.com; Brewery; $. What started as a 10-barrel brewpub in the heart of Amherst village has grown into a cavernous beer hall—known locally as the ABC—in a strip mall on the edge of the UMass campus near the football stadium. Once you're inside, it's big and dark—which might also describe the Two Sisters Imperial Stout, just one of six year-round brews on tap. Owner John Korpita has always aimed for a broad range of ales in German, English, and Pacific Northwest styles as well as a few lagers. The light Honey Pilsner (a slightly malty lager with hints of honey and crisp German hops) and the North Pleasant Pale Ale (with flowery hops) remain ABC's most popular.

Baker's Oven Bistro, 24 Bridge St.; Shelburne Falls, MA 01370; (413) 489-3110, thebakersovenshelburne.com; New American; $–$$. Michele and Daniel Mojallali used to tote their portable brick oven around to festivals and on catering gigs, so when they decided to set up a storefront restaurant, they called it Baker's Oven. Potential customers mistook them for a bakery, so they added "Bistro" to the name in 2013 to emphasize the dinner entrees (roast wild fish of the night, Wheel View Farms steak of the night, roasted vegetable linguine) that they offer in addition to "farm to table" pizzas.

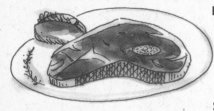

It's a perfect fit for Shelburne Falls, where hill country farmers meet third-generation hippies just steps from the Bridge of Flowers. All the bread doughs, by the way, are whole grain and made on the premises.

Bistro Les Gras, 25 West St., Northampton, MA 01060; (413) 320-4666; bistrolesgras.com; French; $$–$$$. Tucked into a jewel box storefront on West Street across from the Forbes Library, Bistro Les Gras wouldn't look out of place on the Plateau in Montreal or in the Marais in Paris—apart from the foodstuffs almost all grown or raised in the Pioneer Valley (as the Springfield-Greenfield piece of the Connecticut River Valley is sometimes called). This necessarily means a menu that is heavy on meat and root vegetables in the winter and early spring. The chef makes do with what he has preserved, making a mushroom *torchon,* for example, with wild boar lardo and pickled king oyster mushrooms. The menu blossoms like a garden as the season wears on and more and more items are ready for harvest. Fortunately, the menu can be gentle on the wallet, with options like a *croque monsieur* (with "gruyère" from Blythedale Farm in northeast Vermont) and a burger of grass-fed, dry-aged beef from River Rock Farm in Brimfield, Massachusetts.

Brick Wall Bistro, 286 Main St., Greenfield, MA 01301; (413) 475-3880; brickwallbistro.biz; Casual American/Vegetarian; $–$$. Formerly known as Brick Wall Burger, this fixture in the heart of Greenfield expanded the menu and renamed itself accordingly. The burgers are still among the best bargains and greatest dishes, in part because the kitchen grinds the meat fresh every morning. This being Greenfield, vegetarians get some loving consideration too with the black bean burger and a Thai tofu steak. The latter is a firm tofu charred on the grill like any steak and served with a green curry coconut sauce, fresh veggies, and jasmine sticky rice. Lots of sandwiches and salads are available at lunch and dinner, and the front door is often open in the early morning for sales of fresh coffee and doughnuts from **Adams Donuts** (see p. 42).

Buon Appetito, 856 North Rd. (Route 202), Westfield, MA 01085; (413) 568-0002; westfieldbuonappetito.com; Italian; $$. Chef-Owner

Mino Giliberti hails from Puglia, and he proudly champions his home region's cooking at Buon Appetito. Although he offers pizza and grinders as takeout, you really need to sit down to dinner for the full experience. Most of his sauces are lightly cooked—except, of course, the very authentic Bolognese. Since he grew up in the seaside village of Mola di Bari, Giliberti has a special affinity for fish. Ask for a half-serving of pasta (it's not on the menu, but can be requested) as your *primi*, and then order the Rompicapo preparation of salmon—or whatever other fish Giliberti recommends—with broccoli substituting for the farfalle. Several times a year, Giliberti offers cooking classes where he demonstrates an entire five-course dinner—which the students then get to eat. The restaurant has easily the best Italian wine list in the Connecticut Valley.

Champney's Restaurant & Tavern, Deerfield Inn, 81 Old Main St., Deerfield, MA 01342; (413) 772-3087; champneys restaurant.com; Traditional American; $$–$$$. It took Champney's more than a year to get back up and running after the Deerfield flood of 2011, but they figure that the previous flood was in 1938, so all should be good until 2084. Champney's is delightfully devoid of pretension, with a menu that is traditional but hardly hidebound. You might find a bacon and clam chowder or spring parsnip soup with preserved lemon as a starter, for example, followed by a choice of burgers or pizzas, and roasted meats and fish. In season, you can even get bundles of Hadley asparagus wrapped in prosciutto in starter and entree sizes. Hearty eaters might want to split a big dry-aged rib eye steak finished with a sprinkle of sea salt and a side of tarragon-flavored hollandaise.

Chef Wayne's Big Mamou, 63 Liberty St., Springfield, MA 01103; (413) 732-1011; 15 Main St., Williamsburg, MA 01056; (413) 268-8901; chefwaynes-bigmamou.com; Southern; $$. Wayne Hooker cooks with serious spice at Big Mamou, a Louisiana-style restaurant featuring both Cajun and Creole cooking. Among the most popular choices are crawfish, blackened shrimp, and catfish, but a bowl of gumbo and salad combo is available for light eaters. The signature Big Mamou dish is a tangy combo of crawfish tails, shrimp, red peppers, yellow squash, broccoli, and scallions in a lobster and brandy cream sauce, served on puff pastry. Save room for some sweet potato pie or New Orleans bread pudding with whiskey sauce. Hooker was born in Hartford, Connecticut, but he honed his Cajun-Creole cooking through many trips to Louisiana. He says he'll talk to anyone he meets, "and I'm famous for getting myself invited home to dinner." The Springfield location is BYOB, while the Williamsburg location has a full bar.

Chez Albert, 178 N. Pleasant St., Amherst, MA 01003; (413) 253-3811; chezalbert.net; French; $$$. With Chef Paul Hathaway in the kitchen and the smiling visage of Emmanuel Proust in the dining room, Chez Albert conjures up a small-town French bistro in the Pioneer Valley. It's the perfect spot to pop in for a grilled ham and cheese with *frites* for lunch or to luxuriate over a saffron seafood risotto, lamb shanks with couscous, or a chicken fricassee with peas and bacon at dinner. Just make sure you have a reservation or it could be a *very* long wait. No one wants to give up a table when they can dawdle over three courses and a bottle of wine. Chez Albert gets extra points in our book for being a "wireless-free" zone—no phones, no tablets, no computers, no bull.

Coco Restaurant, 95 Main St., Easthampton, MA 01027; (413) 203-5321; New American; $–$$. The decor isn't fancy, and the kitchen is wide open for anyone who stands up to see, but Coco has "it." This is a small restaurant run by people passionate about good food. The menu is equally small and mercurial. (They don't even post it on their Facebook page because it changes so often.) Five small and five larger plates are all the choices, but if you can't be satisfied with the likes of scallops and Meyer lemon with whipped cauliflower or buttermilk fried chicken with garlic mashed potatoes, then Coco might not be for you. The crowd skews young, in part because the prices are low. The beverage choices are limited to nonalcoholic selections, such as homemade ginger lime soda.

Food 101 Bistro, 19 College St. #10, South Hadley, MA 01075; (413) 535-3101; food101bistro.com; New American; $$–$$$. Thanks to Food 101, the Mount Holyoke women and their parents don't have to trek into Northampton for fine dining. The name actually says it all—this is basic New American bistro fare with the requisite first courses of seared ahi tuna, glazed pork belly, and mussels with linguiça steamed in wine. The salads are equally recognizable: roasted beets with goat cheese; arugula, pears, and Gorgonzola; spinach with bacon and mushrooms. Even the main dishes are straight out of the culinary school playbook: roasted rack of lamb, seared salmon with lemon risotto, roasted chicken with garlic mashed potatoes, and a spice-rubbed rib eye steak. It might sound predictable, but it's also very tasty, reasonably priced, and served attentively. Wine choices by the glass are good, if heavily skewed to California.

High Horse Brewing + Wicked Fancy Dining, 24 N. Pleasant St., Amherst, MA 01003; (413) 230-3034; Brewery; $–$$. The beer at this college town brewpub is very, very good and well thought out. The big seller is "Yellow," which is an American-type pale ale made in the style of a German Kolsche. At a mere 5% ABV (alcohol by volume), you could drink it all day. As good as the beer is (and there are more—a witbier, a pink version of a witbier, a couple of IPAs, etc.), the burger is even better. The kitchen grinds all-natural beef every day, bakes perfect brioche buns daily, and even pickles cucumbers. The interior is tiny, which makes it tough during the winter, but the sidewalk spillover in warm weather makes it possible to dine with elbow room. High Horse also offers steaks, as well as a mac and cheese that bubbles with Grafton Village cheddar and comes in a crock topped with golden bread crumbs and a side of roasted broccoli and salad greens. All in all, High Horse has earned its Ph.D. in beer and grub alike.

Hope and Olive, 44 Hope St., Greenfield, MA 01301; (413) 774-3150; hopeandolive.com; New American/Vegetarian; $$–$$$. This locavore favorite proves that farm-centric doesn't have to mean rustic. The menu ranges from homey buttermilk fried chicken to a rather more exotic pumpkin korma with crispy tofu, *saag paneer,* roasted cauliflower, and a pilau of rice with cashews and currants. In between the extremes, you'll find a grilled local lamb burger, cider-braised pork tenderloin, and a vegetable potpie gloriously named "Roots a la King." Diners with daintier appetites or smaller pocketbooks can choose a range of inventive sandwiches such as a BLT with cheese (choice of pork or tempeh bacon), ham and brie with mango chutney, or a lobster Caesar melt.

Magpie Woodfired Pizzeria, 21 Bank Row, Greenfield, MA 01301; (413) 475-3570; magpiepizza.com; Italian/New American; $–$$. Magpie is a pizzeria in the Italian sense—that is, they have some great pizzas, but also serve a lot of baked dishes that make equally good use of the ovens. The 11-inch pizzas make a fine meal for one or appetizer for two. Gluten-free dough is available for an additional charge. You can build your own, but why bother when you can get combos like fennel, arugula, and goat cheese with toasted pine nuts, olives, lemon, and thyme? The daily pastas vary with the cook's whim, but generally include lasagna Bolognese, vegetarian lasagna,

CRAFT BREW BASICS

American beer used to come in three varieties: the brown bottle, the green bottle, and the can. Everything else was just marketing. But the emergence of craft brewing (brewpubs and microbreweries) has proven that there's a lot more to the delectable beverage conjured from mere malted grain, water, yeast, and hops.

Practically speaking, Massachusetts brewers make only two types of beer. Lager beers are fermented with a yeast that resides on the bottom of the vessel. They are usually fermented at temperatures below 50°F and are often aged up to a few months before serving. Ales employ top-fermenting yeasts and warmer temperatures (60–70°F). Lagers tend to be smooth and thin; ales are often thick, cloudy, and full of fruity flavors. We've heard beer aficionados compare the two styles to white and red wines, respectively.

Go to any brewpub, though, and you'll encounter a bewildering number of beers (usually ales) with all sorts of names. Here's a glossary to help sort them out.

Bitter ale: This is another name for pale ale, but a bitter ale usually has a higher hop content and more alcohol than an India Pale Ale (IPA). Extra Special Bitter (ESB) is usually hoppier and even more alcoholic, and it often has a little more body and a redder color. It is generally the beer by which you can judge the skill and style of a brewmaster.

Bock: This dark lager tends to have more than 6 percent alcohol and is often brewed seasonally, around Christmas or the vernal equinox. Doppelbock (a Belgian term) refers to a stronger version.

Brown ale: Popular in England and Scotland, brown ales are less common among Massachusetts craft brewers. They tend to be sweeter and more full-bodied than IPA, ESB, or amber ale. Some have a nutty quality, like toasted hazelnuts.

Oktoberfest lager: At its best, this is a rich, copper-colored, malty beer with a sharp bite of hops—worth celebrating with a fall party.

Pale ale: This is a light-bodied ale fairly low in alcohol—generally the most popular ale among Americans brought up drinking "light" beer. IPA is a variation with more hops in the brew, which gives it a sharper taste. IPAs were created to make ale stable enough to ship on sailing vessels from England to the troops in India, hence the name.

Pilsner lager: Most American commercial beers emulate the Pilsner style, which originated in the town of Pilsen in the Czech Republic. (The original 13th-century brewery still makes Pilsner Urquell.) Pilsner is light and delicately hopped with a gentle, lingering, bitter aftertaste from the use of Czech hops.

Porter: An ale sometimes confused with stout, porter derives a similar dark color from the use of dark malts, not from roasted grain. Porters found in Massachusetts brewpubs tend to be fairly alcoholic and thin-bodied compared to stout. They often have an appealing burnt sugar aftertaste.

Stout: This black ale gets its color from roasted barley added to the brew, which also gives it a creamy body and a certain sharpness. Alcohol content can be quite low, as in the classic Guinness stout, but maltiness makes the drink seem heavier.

Wheat: Wheat beer is brewed by substituting a portion of malted wheat for malted barley. Most Massachusetts wheat beers are light and unfiltered, a style called Hefeweizen. Dark wheat beer is called Dunkelweizen.

linguine and clam sauce, or spaghetti and meatballs. The wine list is short but includes just enough bargain quality wines to go with the food.

Miss Florence Diner, 99 Main St., Florence, MA 01062; (413) 584-3137; missflorencediner.com; Casual American; $. The 1930s Worcester Dining Car Co. diner, about 3 miles west of downtown Northampton, opened in 1941. Except for an addition, little seems to have changed since, making the diner a favorite hangout of NoHo pop-culture vultures. Aim for a seat in the original section so that you can watch the action at the grill. Miss Flo opens at 6 a.m. and serves breakfast all day. The diner fare is ultra-traditional, but don't miss the cream pies—banana, chocolate, and coconut—made fresh on the premises daily.

Northampton Brewery Bar & Grille, 11 Brewster Ct., Northampton, MA 01060; (413) 584-9903; northamptonbrewery .com; Brewery; $$. A pioneer in the Pioneer Valley, this brewpub has been creating classic ales in a former carriage house behind Northampton's downtown parking garage since 1987. The food menu is a bit more ambitious than that of some brewpubs, with several light pastas and roasted meat dishes, but, as with most breweries, eating is a secondary consideration. Many of the ales created here adhere to the philosophy of the Real Ale movement—delicate, perishable, artistic, yet still unpretentious. The best bet is usually the cask-conditioned special (often a bitter), sipped on a warm evening on the rooftop.

Paul & Elizabeth's, Thornes Marketplace, 150 Main St., Northampton, MA 01060; (413) 584-4832; paulandelizabeths.com; New American/Vegetarian; $$–$$$. Vegetarians (and quasi-vegetarians) rejoice! While the Connecticut Valley is full of little places serving indifferent meatless food, Paul & Elizabeth's has elevated the preparation of natural foods to an art. In recent years this Northampton

veteran has refocused its menu to seafood and
tempura, but still offers a number of vegetar-
ian house specialties. A taste of fried organic
tofu and vegetable stir-fry could make you
think twice about relegating soybeans to
mere fodder. Salads are a culinary adventure, especially during the summer, when local farms produce all manner of raw delights.
Even the pies, custards, and puddings are sweetened with honey or
maple syrup instead of white sugar. The restaurant is especially adept
at dealing with special dietary needs or preferences, but it helps to
speak up early—even alerting the staff when you make the reservation.

People's Pint, **24 Federal St., Greenfield, MA 01301; (413) 773-
0333; thepeoplespint.com; Brewery/Vegetarian; $.** Aptly named,
this friendly brewpub captures the spirit of a British or Irish local. The
bar food is very much of the place—that is, more than half vegetarian
and terribly socially conscious. (All the brewpub waste is composted or
recycled; all the food is locally grown if possible.) The pub is unclut-
tered by showy brewing equipment—that whole operation has been
moved to a brewery on Hope Street. Owners Dan Young and Alden
Booth are at their best with substantial, English-style brews. Their Hope
Street Amber ESB (Extra Special Bitter) is aromatic and fruity with a nice
herbal hop snap.

Pulaski Club (Polish American Citizens Club), **13
Norman St., Chicopee, MA 01013; (413) 534-7388; Polish; $.** The
food service at this local community hall is one of the valley's best-
kept secrets, known by locals of Polish descent and by impoverished
students looking for a solid meal at a great price. The traditional
Polish and Polish-American foods are all made from scratch, including golumpki (stuffed cabbage rolls, breaded and fried), pierogi (huge
dumpling pies, big enough to cut), and kielbasa. Open Wed and Fri.

Red Rose Restaurant Pizzeria, 1060 Main St., Springfield, MA 01103; (413) 739-8510; redrosepizzeria.com; Italian/Pizza; $–$$. Back in 1963, Edda Caputo took over an ice cream store and started selling pizza for three tables and takeout. The rest, as they say, is history. "My mom didn't believe in day care, so my two sisters and I grew up under the pizza bench," says Tony Caputo, who joined the business in 1986. Several expansions later, the restaurant, with crystal chandeliers, marble statues, and Bay of Naples murals, seats about 400 and is often full at lunchtime. Pizza is still a mainstay, but Italian-Americans from all over western Massachusetts come for a big Sunday afternoon meal. Diners rise from their tables with substantial doggie bags of shrimp scampi, *arancini* (rice balls), chicken marsala, or the locally famed eggplant rollatini (rolled eggplant filled with ricotta and baked in tomato sauce). The family buys local eggplant in season and slices and freezes it to be able to serve this signature dish all year long.

Seven Sisters Market Bistro, 270 Russell St., Hadley, MA 01035; (413) 582-0007; sevensistersmarketbistro.com; New American; $$–$$$. The Ciaglo family has farmed this land along Route 9 since the early 20th century, but switched to an emphasis on raising bison in 1998. They have converted the old barn into a combination food market and restaurant, serving breakfast, lunch, and dinner and selling a lot of food from other local farms. A special emphasis is placed on dry-aged beef from the consortium known as Northeast Family Farms. The meat case also offers fresh bison. Coolers contain a lot of prepared foods like corn salad with chorizo or smoked chicken wings, and some marinated meats that are ready to cook. At dinnertime the bistro has casual plates of barbecued pork, baby back ribs, and smoked sausages, as well as small plates of meatballs, pork quesadilla, and even vegetarian risotto. The main focus, however, is on grilled meats, especially the Northeast Family Farms beef. On occasion, bison strip and rib eye steaks are also available.

Spoleto, 1 Bridge St., Northampton, MA 01060; (413) 586-6313; spoletorestaurants.com; Italian; $$–$$$. Northampton's pioneer in breezy modern Italian dining left the bustle of Main Street for new digs at the end of 2012. It's a great spot to start off with a glass of Prosecco and antipasti (such as saffron mussels, grilled octopus, or brick-oven meatballs). Pasta courses are considered entrees at Spoleto, but when you're devouring a plate of orecchiette with wild boar sausage, you won't mind that you don't have room for *secondi*. One of the intriguing entrees is essentially a piccata treatment of monkfish, served with ricotta dumplings, preserved lemon, and baby spinach.

Student Prince/The Fort, 8 Fort St., Springfield, MA 01103; (413) 788-6628; studentprince.com; German; $$. If you want to see the movers and shakers of Springfield, make a reservation at the long-reigning king of the city's fine dining. Established in 1935 as the Student Prince Cafe, the complex of rooms also includes the Fort Dining Room. All the rooms are dark and *gemütlich*, and the menu remains resolutely Teutonic, with a few touches of circa-1955 American steakhouse. Best bets include spicy sauerbraten, delicate wiener schnitzel, Hungarian goulash, homemade bratwurst, and the peppery braised rabbit (hasenpfeffer).

30 Boltwood, Lord Jeffery Inn, 30 Boltwood Ave., Amherst, MA 01002; (413) 256-8200; lordjefferyinn.com/amherst-dining; Traditional American; $$$. Sleek, sophisticated, and surprisingly casual for fine dining, 30 Boltwood is the Jay Gatsby of Amherst restaurants. There's no need to apologize for a button-down collar here, but there's also no need to don a school tie and blazer. The menu is a fresh take on classic American grill: a grilled New York sirloin with collard greens, pan-roasted duck breast, pan-seared scallops with fingerling potatoes and asparagus, and roasted rack of lamb with a surprise treat of lamb belly and eggplant puree. Outdoor dining under the gaslit portico takes full advantage of the central Amherst location.

Specialty Stores, Markets & Producers

Adams Donuts, 348 Federal St., Greenfield, MA 01301; (413) 774-4214; adamsdonuts.com; Bakery Cafe. The proliferation of doughnut chains has made most Americans forget what real doughnuts should taste like. At Adams, the cake doughnuts are—what a notion—actual deep-fried cakes, complete with a tender crumb and a range of subtle flavors. The basic old-fashioned plain (which is one of the two yardsticks of doughnut quality) is light and tender and the cake has a faint overtone of nutmeg. You can grasp it with a napkin and never get a grease stain. The glazed doughnut (the other yardstick) is light and full of air pockets, while the glaze is sweet without being sticky. The blueberry cake doughnut—not always available—may be one of the best of its kind. The shop serves breakfast sandwiches and coffee at stools around a horseshoe counter, but most folks come for doughnuts to take away. Arrive early—sometimes the doughnuts are all sold by 10 a.m. (Adams opens at 5 a.m. most days.)

Amherst Farm Winery, 529 Belchertown Rd., Route 9, Amherst, MA 01002; (413) 253-1400; amherstfarmwinery.com; Wine, Beer & Spirits. This compact operation on the road between Amherst and Belchertown occupies a former barn moved from the Quabbin in 1938 before the reservoir waters swallowed the farm there. The winery purchases French-American hybrid grapes from the Finger Lakes in New York to make two whites and two reds that are easy-drinking. It also grows some Marechal Foch, which is used in a light, Beaujolais-style wine called Barn Board Red. In addition, the winemaker crafts a number of fruit wines that retain their characteristic fruit flavors very well.

Bart's Homemade Ice Cream, 103 N. Pleasant St., Amherst, MA 01002; (413) 253-2278; bartshomemade.com; Ice Cream/Yogurt. Valley folk line up for creamy treats at Bart's, where the brass ice-cream-cone knob on the door has been polished smooth by the fingers of the hungry hordes. Scoops, sundaes, shakes, malts, ice cream sodas, and floats are all available in an exhausting list of familiar (and not-so-familiar flavors). Our favorite is Mass Mocha: coffee ice cream with espresso-filled chocolate chunks, semisweet chocolate chunks, and a fudge swirl. Blueberry, strawberry, and peach ice creams made with local fruits are a big hit in season, while Colrain Maple Cream and Colrain Maple Walnut provide local flavor year-round.

Berkshire Brewing Company, 12 Railroad St., South Deerfield, MA 01373; (413) 665-6600; berkshirebrewingcompany.com; Brewery. Berkshire Brewing's signature 22-ounce bottles are available in gourmet and wine shops, and many western Massachusetts pubs have its products on tap. This tiny brewery goes to the trouble of brewing both an American-style and a British-style pale ale (Steel Rail Extra Pale and Berkshire Ale Traditional, respectively). Many small breweries make cautious beers—never very malty, never very sharp with hops, usually light rather than heavy. BBC, on the other hand, is willing to go to extremes, punctuating its wheat beer with strongly spicy hops, for example, or emphasizing the sweet malt of its seasonal porters or Oktoberfest beers. The Saturday afternoon tour includes a tasting.

The Black Sheep, 79 Main St., Amherst, MA 01002; (413) 253-3442; blacksheepdeli.com; Bakery Cafe. The tempting treats of this deli begin with wonderful breads—whole wheat, anadama, rye, six-grain, pumpernickel raisin, oatmeal, etc.—which serve as the base for both traditional and unusual sandwiches. Not only can you order whitefish salad or kippered salmon filling, but you can also get the "East Meets West" of roasted tofu, carrots, red onions, roasted garlic sauce, and peanut hoisin sauce on a baguette. If you have a dinner party in the offing, stop by for a selection of appetizers and entrees, including several different lasagnas. Cakes are high and luscious and include ever-popular carrot cake with cream cheese frosting, Black Forest cake, a lemon-curd white cake, and frosted gingerbread. Pies tend to be seasonal but often include peach, apple, blueberry, pumpkin, and, in late summer, pear mango.

Chase Hill Farm, 74 Chase Hill Rd., Warwick, MA 01378; (978) 544-6327; chasehillfarm.com; **Cheese.** Mark and Jeannette Fellows's cheeses literally begin in the fields where their herd of Normande cows grazes. The French breed is known for the quality of its milk, and all the cheeses are made with raw milk and then aged for at least 60 days. Farmstead, a Colby-style cheese, is particularly suited to grilled cheese sandwiches. The Fellowses also make a tangy cheddar, a natural rind gruyère-type cheese, and an Italian-style aged cheese with a nutty flavor similar to Parmesan. Chase Hill's farmstead cheeses are carried in gourmet shops, delis, and some grocery stores in the Connecticut Valley. They also sell their cheese and raw milk at the farm from March into December.

Chicopee Provision Company, 19 Sitarz St., Chicopee, MA 01014; (800) 924-6328; bluesealkielbasa.com; **Butcher.** Since 1920, this specialist in Polish sausages has absorbed smaller meat packers to emerge as the premier maker of kielbasa in western New England—and even claims to hold the record for manufacturing the world's largest kielbasa (600 pounds). It also produces a full line of hot dogs, sweet and hot sausages, and luncheon meats that are sold in grocery stores and delis throughout New England under the Blue Seal brand. Call for factory store hours.

Different Drummer's Kitchen, 34 Bridge St., Northampton, MA 01060; (413) 586-7978; differentdrummerskitchen.com; House-wares. Not quite as overwhelming as the Lenox store (see p. 16), this trimmed-down version of the one-stop kitchen hardware shop will set you up to make your own pressed terrines (in French terrine pans), stir-fries (in authentic woks), and tortillas (in your very own press). You can also sign up for classes in everything from making French pastry to cooking with fresh herbs or making Vietnamese spring rolls.

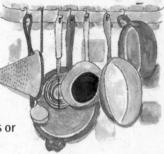

Elmer's Store, 396 Main St., Ashfield, MA 01330; (413) 628-4003; elmersstore.com; Coffee/Grocery. This clapboard building in the center of Ashfield village has been the town store off and on since 1835, but it's unlikely that it was ever the community epicenter that it's become since Nan Parati bought the place in 2005 and actually *asked* everyone in town what they wanted in a store. They wanted breakfast, for one, and Elmer's serves some of the best breakfasts in the Connecticut River Valley and adjoining hill towns. They wanted the crumbly cheddar cheese from a wheel under glass that had been a fixture at Elmer's since the 1930s. They got that, too. And they wanted a community center of sorts where people could post notices or hang out and talk over a fresh cup of coffee. Check. Organic food and basic groceries round out the mix—but Nan Parati's smile is also key.

Frigo's Gourmet Foods, 90 William St., Springfield, MA 01105; (877) 413-7446; 159 Shaker Rd., East Longmeadow, MA 01028; (413) 525-9400; frigofoods.com; Grocery. This stalwart of Springfield's South End Italian neighborhood was launched in 1950 by current owner Joe Frigo's grandfather, an immigrant from the Asiago region in northern Italy. Nonno was a cheesemaker, and though the family sold off the cheese company years ago, cheese is one of the deli's specialties. Joe still sells Asiago made under the Frigo name—after aging it for many months in his cavernous chilled cheese cellar. Custom butchery is another store specialty, but the big business during the day is at lunch, when cops and office workers alike stop at the Springfield shop across from the Mt. Carmel church for sandwiches or hot entrees like spinach lasagna and chicken Florentine. You can order some of the store's specialty products through its website, but nothing beats stopping by in person to sample the subtle differences in flavor between the young and aged Asiago cheeses.

Green Fields Market, 144 Main St., Greenfield, MA 01301; (413) 773-9567; greenfieldsmarket.com; Grocery. This natural foods co-op serving the northern Connecticut Valley community bakes its own breads on a rotating schedule (including an organic rosemary sourdough bread) and offers a striking variety of ready-to-heat meals and grain and vegetable salads prepared on the premises. Attesting to a strong commitment to sustainable agriculture, Green Fields carries many products from local farms, orchards, small dairies, and beekeepers, as well as a full line of locally manufactured soybean-based meat substitutes.

Grub Sandwich Shop, 88 Pleasant St., Northampton, MA 01060; (413) 727-8322; grubsandwichshop.com; Deli/Vegetarian. In the midst of a national burger craze, NoHo's foodies in the know come to Grub for hot dogs with just the right fixings and no unnecessary hype. The Seoul Dog, for example, comes with kimchi, bacon, and spicy mayo, while the Hazmat has roasted chile peppers and melted cheese. (Tofu dogs can be substituted for an extra charge.) A few nifty entree sandwiches are also available at lunch, possibly including a meatloaf with roasted onions and house-made ketchup on baguette. Toward the end of the week, Grub also offers a few dinner entrees that are posted on Wednesday on its website and Facebook page. Unlike most sandwich shops, Grub has a few good wines and a slew of local and imported beers.

Hager's Farm Market, 1232 Mohawk Trail, Shelburne, MA 01370; (413) 625-6323; hagersfarmmarket.net; Grocery. This market on the Mohawk Trail is removed from the Hager's five-generation farm in Colrain, but it features a real taste of the Valley. The farmers belong to the Cabot cheese cooperative and sell Cabot cheeses as well as other local cheeses. They feature their own maple products and jams, jellies, pickles, and other products from local farms. Fifty local farms provide a cornucopia of fruits and vegetables in season. The store also serves breakfast and lunch (including a maple hot dog) and turns out a full array of breads, pies, and other baked goods.

Heavenly Chocolates, Thornes Marketplace, 150 Main St., Northampton, MA 01060; (413) 586-0038; heavenly-chocolate.com; Chocolatier. Technically a department of the Cornucopia natural foods and supplements store one floor down, Heavenly Chocolates spread its wings for a stand-alone spot on the Main Street level of Thornes. The shop's own exquisite chocolates are made principally with fresh local ingredients and they are meant to be savored until every last bit of unctuous dark chocolate has dissolved. (They're especially good with a demitasse of espresso.) Local favorites include the honey vanilla sea salt—cream and chocolate ganache with honey and vanilla beans enrobed in dark chocolate—and the peanut butter sizzle, which contains organic peanut butter, caramelized sugar, and a touch of cayenne pepper inside of dark chocolate. The rosemary nib caramel and the lavender sea salt caramel headline the herbal chocolates, while pistachio with rosewater strikes a subtle Indian note.

Herrell's, 8 Old South St., Thornes Marketplace, Northampton, MA 01060; (413) 586-9700; herrells.com; Ice Cream/Yogurt. This Northampton shop is the sole remaining New England outlet of the once-mighty ice cream empire that was proclaimed one of the top three ice cream stores in the country by *USA Today*. In fact, super-premium ice cream pioneer Steve Herrell is generally credited in ice cream circles for inventing the "smoosh-in"—the practice of mashing broken cookies or candy bars into already incredibly rich ice cream. The empire has shrunk but the cravings remain. The line of customers can move slowly as each person selects the desired smoosh-ins and the counter clerk dutifully mixes them in. But it is worth the wait for your own unique ice cream creation.

Hungry Ghost Bread, 62 State St., Northampton, MA 01060; (413) 582-9009; hungryghostbread.com; Bakery. Jonathan Stevens and Cheryl Maffei create organic bread baked in small batches in a wood-fired oven. After only one bite, you will agree that they were robbed when they were only semifinalists for a James Beard pastry chef award in 2011. Hungry Ghost is what happens when Buddhist-hippie breadmaking (remember the *Tassajara Bread Book*?) meets the locavore movement. The breads here are mostly whole grain, and most of the grain is grown and milled in the Pioneer Valley, a lot of it by the L'Etoile family of Four Star Farm in Northfield. Stevens and Maffei use their own sourdough starters to make the bread rise, and the bakery smells like a wonderful mixture of live cultures and fresh bread. The bakery is open long hours every day, but if you crave a particular loaf in their repertoire, it's best to reserve ahead. Neapolitan-style pizza is available for takeout most evenings.

La Fiorentina, 883 Main St., Springfield, MA 01103; (413) 732-3151; 25 Armory St., Northampton, MA 01060; (413) 586-7693; 236 Shaker Rd., East Longmeadow, MA 01028; (413) 526-0905; lafiorentina pastry.com; Bakery Cafe. Established in Springfield in 1947, La

Fiorentina calls itself the "home of the rum cake," but it's even better known among aficionados of sfogliatelle for making some of the best this side of the Atlantic. "We make a couple thousand every week," says Anna Daniele, who runs the bakery with her husband, Leo. It's a laborious process that begins on Tuesday (the dough has to rest overnight between steps) and finally culminates with the custard-filled, clam-shaped pastries going on sale on Friday. By Sunday they're all gone. Indeed, La Fiorentina is the home of Italian pastries of all sorts, including whipped cream cakes, ricotta cakes, and delicate sugar cookies spiked with a little anise seed. It is also one of the valley's premier makers of classic wedding cakes.

Lamson and Goodnow Manufacturing Company, 45 Conway St., Shelburne Falls, MA 01370; (413) 625-0201; lamsonsharp.com; Housewares. Established in 1837, during the early days of the Industrial Revolution, Lamson and Goodnow is the oldest continuous producer of cutlery in the United States. Some of the craftsmen who produce knives for such catalog retailers as Sur La Table, Williams-Sonoma, and Crate & Barrel are descendants of the artisans who worked at the company when it first opened. The factory store just above the falls on the Buckland side of Shelburne Falls has informative displays showing the difference between forged and stamped knives (they make both, but the forged knives last longer, cut better, and cost more). Both types are for sale and are discounted about 25 percent. In addition, the factory store is the only place to buy seconds at a much deeper discount. Lamson and Goodnow also produces barbecue tools, spatulas, spreaders, and other stovetop utensils, some of which are available in both right- and left-handed versions.

McCusker's Market, 3 State St., Shelburne Falls, MA 01370; (413) 625-9411; greenfieldsmarket.com; Grocery. There are those in the Connecticut Valley who hold that Shelburne Falls is as much a state of mind as a real place. The village's only real food store provides an instant scan of that peculiar local psyche. Large bins of culinary herbs and local produce share floor space with patent-medicine herbal remedies. The deli counter has several vegetarian entrees and sandwiches and separates dairy from nondairy sweets. Despite the countercultural hoopla, this is a great place to buy local organic vegetables, apples, cider, cheese, and breads.

Paper City Brewing, 108 Cabot St., Holyoke, MA 01040; (413) 535-1588; papercity.com; Brewery. Owner Jay Hebert, an ardent homebrewer, launched Paper City in 1995, on the fifth floor of an old warehouse building overlooking one of Holyoke's industrial canals. Fittingly enough, the 1996 initial offering from head brewer Rick Quackenbush was named Holyoke Dam Ale. Now with Ben Anhalt heading up the brewing, the company counts its Ireland Parish Golden Ale as the flagship and brews a hop-laden Indian Ale (named in honor of the Indian motorcycles Hebert collects) as well as several seasonal brews. Rollie's Premium Style Root Beer is also made on the premises. Though you can buy the products in most area package and liquor stores, Paper City hosts an open house on Thursday and Friday evenings when you can sample the offerings and check out the collection of memorabilia from vanished breweries of the Connecticut Valley, especially Hampden Brewery, as well as Hebert's vintage motorcycles.

Pekarski's Sausage, 293 Conway Rd., South Deerfield, MA 01373; (413) 665-4537; Butcher. You might sniff out Pekarski's before you see it on the twisting road between South Deerfield and Conway. Last time we were in, the woman at the counter asked, almost rhetorically, "Can you smell it? We're smoking pork loins." They also smoke hocks, spareribs, hams, kielbasa, and bacon on the premises, and they make unsmoked kielbasa, cheese kielbasa, bratwurst, breakfast sausage, Canadian bacon, and Italian sausages that run the gamut from sweet to hot to extra-hot. Despite the vegetarian bent of this end of the Connecticut Valley, Pekarski's is always busy. Some products are also available at area farm stands, grocers, and gourmet shops.

RAO's Coffee Roasting Company, 17 Kellogg Ave., Amherst, MA 01002; (413) 253-9441; raoscoffee.com; Coffee. On a Sunday morning in nice weather, the line at RAO's sometimes extends out the door, as Amherstites descend on their local roaster for tall skinny lattes and big fat pastries to devour at leisure over the *Times*. Actually, RAO's tends to be extremely busy on all days in all seasons. Subscribing to the East Coast philosophy of medium and overall lighter roasts, RAO's offers a full line of world coffees. Its special passion, though, is reserved for Central American and South American beans.

Richardson's Candy Kitchen, 500 Greenfield Rd. (Routes 5 and 10), Deerfield, MA 01342; (413) 772-0443; richardsonscandy .com; Chocolatier. One of the classic small New England candymakers, Richardson's is known for several specialties, including Dixies (turtles entirely enrobed in chocolate), Hedgehogs (similar to turtles but made with crisped rice), and wintergreen mints, offered both as chocolate patties and as dipped creams. Barbara Woodward, who operates Richardson's with her daughter, Kathie Williams, says that when it comes to the pink wintergreen, "People do or don't like it. There's not much middle ground." The shop has a few seasonal specialties as well. During the three weeks of local strawberry season, a farmer custom-picks berries with intact stems for Richardson's. Barbara and Kathie dip the berries first in fondant, then in chocolate. The  strawberries are sold only on the day they are picked, and it's worth making a special trip to the shop during June for one of the most perfect pairings of fruit and chocolate. If you miss the strawberries, you can cool off with a frozen banana dipped in a mixture of dark and milk chocolates. In October, try chocolate-covered caramel apples. And during November and December, Richardson's makes pecan logs—nougat dipped in caramel and rolled in pecans. No chocolate? "No," says Barbara. "It's a relief."

Table & Vine, 1119 Riverdale Rd. (Route 5), West Springfield, MA 01089; (413) 736-4694; tableandvine.com; Wine, Beer & Spirits. Despite the homey name, Table & Vine is a branch of the Big Y grocery chain. But don't let that deter you from checking out one of New England's most extensive displays of wine and spirits—more than 4,000 selections in all. Table & Vine is especially strong on small wineries of northern Italy, southern France, and Spain, where some of the best bargains are currently available. In addition, the shop stocks literally hundreds of cognacs, Armagnacs, single-malt whiskeys, and imported lagers and ales. The store offers frequent tastings and carries an array of gourmet products (including cheeses, pâtés, olives, and terrines) to pair with your wine purchases.

Viva Fresh Pasta Co., 249 Main St., Northampton, MA 01060; (413) 586-5875; vivafreshpasta.com; Grocery. The founders got started making pasta on Martha's Vineyard in 1985 but moved to Northampton a year later, where another partner helped them open a small bistro in downtown NoHo to showcase their pastas and sauces. Retail cases right inside the door offer tortellini, ravioli, lasagna sheets, linguine, and fettuccine (including whole organic spelt). There are plenty of sauces to pair with the pasta, including Alfredo, olive and

herb, pesto, puttanesca, romesco, roasted red pepper, and *xató*, a Spanish-style sauce of toasted almonds, garlic, and olive oil. Of course, if you'd rather taste before you buy, you can sit down to lunch or dinner in the two-floor restaurant or, during warm weather, at the handful of outdoor tables.

West County Cider, 106 Bardswell Ferry Rd., Shelburne, MA 01370; (413) 624-3481; westcountycider.com; Wine, Beer & Spirits. Only the quirks of Massachusetts law make West County a winery, for its real products are a range of small-batch hard ciders crafted from both single varietals and custom blends. The cider-making style continues to evolve at West County, ranging from simple American ciders to fruitier English versions to more refined, elegant styles reminiscent of Normandy and Brittany. Alcohol content tends to range from 6 to 7 percent, and most varieties are naturally sparkling. On Cider Days (see Appendix C), West County opens for tastings.

Wheatberry, 321 Main St., Amherst, MA 01002; (413) 253-1411; wheatberry.org; Bakery Cafe. Amherst has an embarrassment of riches when it comes to bread bakeries, but Wheatberry opened in 2007 because Ben and Adrie Lester's customers at the farmers' market wanted a place to buy their organic breads every day. The couple dropped their wholesale business and opened the bakery cafe, where they serve healthy breakfasts (organic maple millet granola, for example,) and lunchtime soups, sandwiches and fresh-ground grits topped with cheese.

Williamsburg General Store, 12 Main St. (Route 9), Williamsburg, MA 01096; (413) 268-3036; wgstore.com; Grocery. Hardly the unsophisticated, old-fashioned country store it pretends to be, Williamsburg General Store is crammed with crafts, country-decor knickknacks, pottery, and greeting cards. Look past all that to the bulk spices, local honey, and the store's own jellies, preserves, fruit butters, and "good and evil" pickles with garlic. The real draw here is the bakery, where you can purchase roasted garlic, three-cheese, or cheddar breads, or indulge in cinnamon pecan buns, pumpkin cream-cheese pie, or chocolate raspberry cream-cheese coffee cake.

Apex Orchards, Peckville Road, Shelburne, MA 01370; (413) 625-2744; apexorchards.com. The sweeping hilltop view is a bonus when you come here to pick McIntosh, Gala, Paula Red, and other apples, all growing on compact trees. Owner Timothy Smith, one of the area's most active beekeepers, packs his own extraordinarily spicy honey under the Shelburne Honey Company label. You'll find both clear and creamed honey, as well as a particularly well-rounded cider vinegar. Open Aug through Apr.

Atkins Farms Country Market, 1150 West St., Amherst, MA 01002; (413) 253-9528; atkinsfarms.com. Atkins has been farming this acreage near the Belchertown border since 1887 and sells its own apples, peaches, and pears at a supersize farm stand. (You can also pick your own apples and peaches.) You'll need one of the full-size shopping carts to stock up on produce from many other local farms, as well as Atkins' own maple syrup, jellies, fruit butters, preserves, marmalades, applesauce, and mixes (buttermilk and apple cinnamon pancakes, for example, and maple pecan or apple cinnamon scones). The bakery breads include raisin, wheat, garlic, pesto, honey oatmeal, and cheddar cheese, as well as English muffins. They're made with unbleached, unbromated flour—the next best thing to whole grain from a nutritional standpoint. Even harder to resist are the sweets, especially the dense, moist apple cider doughnuts and the apple squares with cream cheese frosting. Atkins' bakers also create wedding cakes with a month's advance notice.

Austin Brothers Valley Farm, 270 West St., Belchertown, MA 01007; (413) 668-6843; austinsfarm.com. The Austins raise their cattle naturally, letting them graze on green pasture much of the year and on the farm's own hay and silage through the winter. The beef are finished on grain for four months to boost marbling and flavor, and then dry-aged for 14 to 21 days after slaughter. The results are both economical—buying direct is actually cheaper than buying a poorer grade at a supermarket—and delicious. Family members sell at some farmers' markets and operate a farm store. Call ahead.

Boisvert Farm and North Hadley Sugar Shack, 181 River Dr. (Route 47), Hadley, MA 01035; (413) 585-8820; northhadley sugarshack.com. Even if your kids don't like vegetables, they will love this busy farm stand. From mid-February through April, the sugar shack serves pancake breakfasts and in mid-May an enhanced petting zoo opens with lots of cute animals and even a baby chick hatchery. When the kids grow tired of the animals, they can try the mini-golf course or other diversions. (The petting zoo area, which has a small admission fee, stays open through late October.) The farm stand, which is open through late December, sells all varieties of local produce as well as the farm's own honey, maple syrup, and mixes for blueberry muffins,

 peach cobbler, peach crisp, apple crisp, carrot cake, and pumpkin bread. In the height of the season, a weekend grill offers hot dogs and hamburgers and maple soft-serve ice cream. For a recipe for **Pork Tenderloin with Maple Glaze,** see p. 298.

Clarkdale Fruit Farms, 303 Upper Rd., West Deerfield, MA 01342; (413) 772-6797; clarkdalefruitfarms.com. Reached off the Route 2 traffic circle in Greenfield, Clarkdale grows 35 apple varieties. The farm stand also sells pears, peaches, and cider, as well as deeply discounted McIntosh drops. Open Aug through Mar. For Clarkdale's recipe for **Mulled Cider,** see p. 309.

Cold Spring Orchard, 391 Sabin St., Belchertown, MA 01007; (413) 323-6647; coldspringorchard.com. This research facility for agricultural scientists at the University of Massachusetts at Amherst grows more than 100 varieties of apples to test new varietals and to find more environmentally friendly ways to grow them. A pioneer in integrated pest management (the use of pest traps and other devices to reduce and better target spraying), Cold Spring Orchard offers pick-your-own opportunities for 18 varieties of apples, which range from such antiques as Baldwin and Golden Russet to standards (McIntosh, Golden Delicious) to new varieties. Among the recently developed apples showing promise for this region are Akane, a cross between Jon-

athan and Worcester Pearmain, and Ginger Gold, a spicy-sweet natural sport that appears to have both Golden Delicious and Pippin in its ancestry. Profits from the farm are plowed back into further research. As you drive down Sabin Street from Route 9, you'll pass a number of orchards that have benefited from the efforts at Cold Spring. Open Aug through Nov.

Davenport Maple Farm, 111 Tower Rd., Shelburne, MA 01370; (413) 625-2866. Dairy farmer and maple producer Norman Davenport and his wife, Lisa, operate a springtime sugarhouse restaurant, serving pancake and waffle breakfasts. They produce maple syrup, spread, candy, and granulated sugar, as well as maple-coated peanuts, cranberries, and soybeans. All the items are available by mail order and in local grocery and gourmet stores. The restaurant is open Sat and Sun from early Mar to early Apr.

Gould's Sugarhouse, 570 Mohawk Trail, Shelburne, MA 01370; (413) 625-6170; goulds-sugarhouse.com. The willful rusticity of Gould's farm store and restaurant makes it a classic bit of Americana. From its prime spot on the Mohawk Trail, Gould's sells pure maple syrup as well as its own dill and bread and butter pickles. During the limited season, the restaurant serves breakfast and lunch. Most diners order pancakes, waffles, or corn fritters with maple syrup, but you can also get a few sandwiches as well as homemade apple pie with cheddar cheese or ice cream. In 2009, the sugarhouse marked its 50th year. Open Mar to Apr and Sept to Oct.

Hamilton Orchards, 25 West St., New Salem, MA 01355; (978) 544-6867; hamiltonorchards.com. The season starts early with strawberries and continues all summer and fall with plums, cherries, peaches, raspberries, pears, apples, pumpkins, and gourds. The farm stand serves breakfast and offers a range of baked goods. Open weekends June through Oct; call for weekday availability.

Nourse Farms, 41 River Rd., Whately, MA 01093; (413) 665-2650 (24-hour berry information line); noursefarms.com. Best known to home gardeners around the Northeast as the premier source for berry plants, this nursery also operates a huge pick-your-own operation across the summer and into the fall. Because it raises plants for the berry industry, Nourse has the longest strawberry season in the state—from early June into August. You can also pick your own raspberries and blueberries. Open June through Sept.

Pine Hill Orchard and Bear Meadow Farm, 248 Greenfield Rd., Colrain, MA 01340; (413) 624-3325. How many ways can you use an apple? This inviting little complex by a small pond might be just the place to find out. Head to the Pine Hill Orchard farm stand for some of its own applesauce. (They also sell peach sauce, local honey, maple syrup, and cheeses.) Products with the Bear Meadow Farm label are made in the old sugarhouse on the property and include cinnamon cider jelly, apple blueberry preserves, and apple butter. While you're making your selections, sample "The Drink," a tasty concoction of apple cider, cider vinegar, grape juice, and honey. And don't forget that on weekends in September and October you can pick your own apples. Any day, you can grab a bag of Red Delicious, Honeycrisp, Spencer, Macoun, Mutzu, or Empire apples at the farm stand. Select a perfect apple and take a big bite—the simplest of apple pleasures.

Red Fire Farm, 7 Carver St., Granby, MA 01033; 504 Turners Falls Rd., Montague, MA 01351; (413) 467-7645; redfirefarm.com. Certified organic since the farm launched in 2001, Red Fire maintains two farm stands at the addresses above and also sells at farmers' markets in Springfield and Boston. In addition to the farm's organic produce, the stands also carry local bread, honey, butter, cheese, maple syrup, pickles, and other foods. The Granby farm is also the site of the annual Red Fire Farm Tomato Festival (see Appendix C). There's usually a cider pressing and potluck dinner at the Granby farm in October. Open May through Oct.

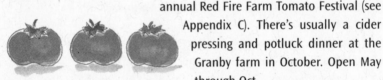

Round Hill Orchard, 1 Douglas Rd. (Route 10), Southampton, MA 01073; (413) 562-4985. Round Hill has blueberries and raspberries when it opens in July, followed quickly by peaches and apples. The farm stand also sells the orchard's own honey, and children can feed the horses and sheep. Open mid-July to mid-Oct.

Smiarowski Farm Stand & Creamy, 320 River Rd., Sunderland, MA 01375; (413) 665-3830; smiarowskifarm.com. This vegetable-oriented farm stand invariably has a wide selection of red, white, and yellow potatoes, as well as several varieties of winter squashes, including buttercup, blue Hubbard, and acorn. Look also for native onions, carrots, lettuce, broccoli, beets, cucumbers, parsnips, and peppers. The adjoining food stand offers Polish specialties, including cabbage pierogi, golumpki (ground beef and rice wrapped in cabbage leaves and fried), and a popular kielbasa sandwich on rye

GRADING MAPLE SYRUP

Many maple producers will let you sample their various grades when you visit their sugar shacks. Standards for maple syrup vary slightly from state to state, but Massachusetts recognizes four grades, which are established on the basis of color and season.

Grade A Light Amber is the most delicate of all the maple syrups. Sometimes called Fancy Grade or, in Canada, No. 1 Extra Light, this grade is pale and mild. Made early in the season when the weather is still cold, Grade A Light Amber is the best for maple candy and maple cream.

Grade A Medium Amber is the most popular table syrup. It is a bit darker and has a more pronounced maple flavor. It is usually produced at midseason when the weather begins to warm.

Grade A Dark Amber, as the name suggests, is even darker and has a robust maple flavor. It is usually produced later in the season as the days get longer and warmer. It is good for sweetening yogurt or oatmeal.

Grade B Syrup is very dark and has a strong maple flavor and a caramel tang. Sometimes called cooking syrup, it is particularly good for baking and for flavoring puddings and custards. Hard-core maple fans sometimes favor Grade B as a table syrup. It is also used as a flavoring agent in syrup blends that combine maple and corn syrups. It is usually made from sap tapped at the end of the season.

bread. The kielbasa can be dressed with sautéed onions and peppers or sauerkraut, or just slathered with horseradish. The "creamy" also sells soft-serve ice cream, but you might prefer to hold out for homemade blueberry crisp with whipped cream. Open May through Oct.

South Face Sugarhouse, 755 Watson–Spruce Corner Rd., Ashfield, MA 01330; (413) 628-3268; southfacefarm.com. A succession of owners have made maple syrup commercially on this farm for more than a century and a half, and some of the massive, gnarled trees might well be the original stock. Grade A and B maple syrup, maple cream, and maple-coated walnuts are available by mail order or through the website. The sugarhouse is open to sell maple products during March and April when a restaurant also offers pancakes, waffles, corn fritters, and french toast to douse with maple syrup.

Upinngill Farm, 411 Main Rd., Gill, MA 01354; (413) 863-2297; upinngil.com. Clifford and Sorrel Hatch operate this dairy and row crop farm with an eye toward healthful living. The milk from their herd of Ayrshire cattle is sold raw at the farm in glass or plastic bottles, and they make five different cheeses that range from a 60-day-old feta to a mild blue to a cheddar-like Ayrshire that can be aged up to two years. The farm sells produce CSA shares and maintains a farm stand. In season, you can pick your own strawberries, raspberries, and grapes.

Farmers' Markets

Amherst Farmers' Market, Spring Street parking lot, Amherst Center. Sat from 7:30 a.m. to 1:30 p.m., late Apr through mid-Nov.

Amherst Wednesday Market, Kendrick Park, North Pleasant Street, Amherst. Wed from 2 to 6 p.m., mid-May to mid-Oct.

Amherst Winter Farmers' Market, Amherst Regional Middle School, Amherst. Sat from 10 a.m. to 2 p.m., Dec through Mar.

Chicopee Farmers' Market, under I-391 overpass, at the "Y"
Willimansett, Chicopee. Wed from 11 a.m. to 3:30 p.m., late June to
early Sept.

Easthampton Farmers' Market, Municipal Building parking
lot, 50 Payson Ave., Easthampton. Fri from 2 to 7 p.m., June through
mid-Oct.

Florence Farmers' Market, Florence Civic Center, Florence.
Wed from 2 to 6 p.m., late Apr through Oct.

Greenfield Farmers' Market, Court Square, Greenfield. Sat
from 8 a.m. to 12:30 p.m., May through Oct.

Holyoke Donahue Elementary School Farmers' Mar-
ket, 210 Whiting Farms Rd., Holyoke. Sat from 10 a.m. to 2 p.m., late
June through Oct.

Holyoke Farmers' Market, High Street between Suffolk
Street and City Hall, Holyoke. Thurs from 11:30 a.m. to 3:30 p.m.,
May through Oct.

Holyoke Open Square Farmers' Market, 4
Open Square Way, Holyoke. Sat from 9 a.m. to 1 p.m.,
early May through Oct.

Holyoke Peoples Bank Farmers' Market,
333 Whitney Ave., Holyoke. Fri from 10 a.m. to 3 p.m.,
May through Oct.

Northampton Farmers' Market, Gothic Street,
Northampton. Sat from 7 a.m. to 1 p.m., May to early
Nov.

Northampton/Thornes Marketplace Farmers Market, behind Thornes Marketplace, off South Street, Northampton. Tues from 1:30 to 6:30 p.m., May to mid-Nov.

Northampton Winter Farmers' Market, Thornes Marketplace basement, 150 Main St., Northampton. Sat from 9 a.m. to 2 p.m., mid-Nov to mid-Apr.

Orange Farmers' Market, Butterfield Park, East River Street, Orange. Thurs from 3 to 6 p.m., late May to mid-Oct.

Springfield Farmers' Market at Forest Park, Cyr Arena parking lot, Springfield. Tues from 12:30 to 6 p.m., May through Oct.

Springfield Mason Square Farmers' Market, Mason Square Neighborhood Health Center, Springfield. Fri from 10 a.m. to 2 p.m., July through Oct.

Springfield Winter Farmers' Market, Forest Park, Trafton Road entrance to former monkey house, Springfield. Second and fourth Sat 10 a.m. to 2 p.m., Nov through Apr.

Turners Falls Farmers' Market, Great Falls Discovery Center, 2nd Street and Avenue A, Turners Falls. Wed from 2 to 6 p.m., May through Oct.

Central Massachusetts

Highway builders of the 20th century took a dim view of central Massachusetts, assuming that travelers would like to get through it as quickly as possible. As a result, the flavor of the region remains mostly intangible until you get off the main roads and onto the byways. Turn off and drive just out of earshot of the highway, however, and you will encounter another world. Even New England's vaunted fall foliage can barely compare with apple blossom time along the Nashoba and Nashua River valleys, when a sudden breeze can create a snowstorm of pink and white petals. A seminal figure in the settling of the West, John Chapman was born in this orchard country, in Leominster, in 1774. In 1797 he started moving west with his Bible and his apple seedlings, always one step ahead of the waves of settlement. Johnny Appleseed (as he became known) may have left, but the apples persist. Not all of the region is so bucolic. A string of industrial cities lines Route 2 west of the orchards, and Worcester itself introduces a gentle, low-rise, urban sprawl into the center of central Massachusetts. These locales harbor food lovers' destinations every bit as endangered as the family farm: the classic roadside diners from the 1930s into the 1950s. In an age of corporate fast food, the diners seem almost surreal—havens of home-slung hash, eggs over easy, and "wouldja like a warm-up on that, hon?"

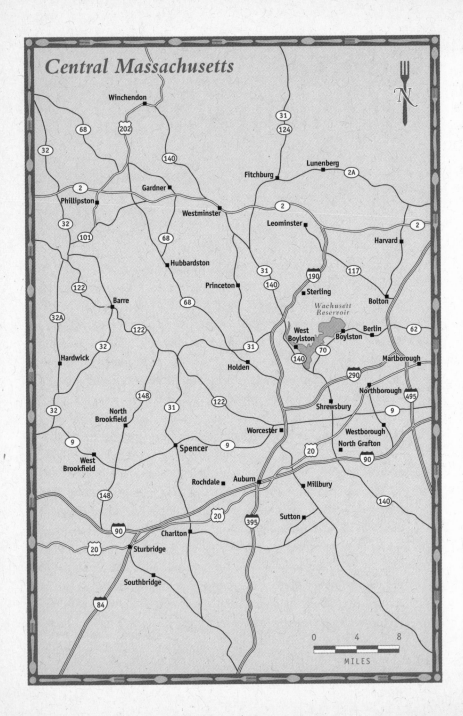

Central Massachusetts

N

Winchendon

68
202

32

140

Gardner

Phillipston

2

32

101

68

Hubbardston

122

Barre

32A

122

32

Hardwick

148

32

North
Brookfield

31

9

West
Brookfield

148

Westminster

Fitchburg

Lunenberg

2A

2

Leominster

2

Harvard

31

140

Princeton

117

190

Sterling

Wachusett
Reservoir

West
Boylston

Boylston

Berlin

62

31

140

70

Marlborough

Holden

290

122

Northborough

495

Shrewsbury

9

Westborough

9

North Grafton

90

Spencer

9

Worcester

20

Rochdale

Auburn

Millbury

140

20

395

Sutton

Charlton

90

20

Sturbridge

Southbridge

84

0   4   8

MILES

West of Worcester, the landscape opens up into the rolling high country of the Worcester Hills. Many of the state's dairy cattle roam these upland meadows, and you will even find tracts nibbled by sheep and dairy goats. Some of these backcountry farms can be tricky to find, but once you've navigated the back roads, you'll be rewarded with treats such as truly fresh milk, farmstead cheese, and homemade dairy ice cream. Turn southward from Worcester and the microclimate changes to produce moist, warm summers that support some of the state's most productive vegetable and berry farmers. We have highlighted some of the larger operations, but from the first asparagus of May to the last gourds and pumpkins of November you can drive through the agricultural countryside and find dozens of makeshift farm stands—often a card table and an honor-system coffee can for payment. Look, too, for the "Buy Local" sticker or sign at stores or even plastered on intersection telephone poles and marked with an arrow. They'll lead you to the best and freshest produce, meat, poultry, and dairy products.

Foodie Faves

Armsby Abbey, 144 Main St., Worcester, MA 01608; (508) 795-1012; armsbyabbey.com; Casual American; $–$$. Celebrated as being in the vanguard of American beer bars, Armsby Abbey is also a serious gastropub with a staunch commitment to local food. The farmstead cheese plates are outstanding showcases of great (mostly) New England cheeses, while the "slates" are a fresh take on bar fare that range from charcuterie prepared on site to an assortment of housemade pickles. Moroccan spices come in by way of *ras el hanout* rillons using Adams Farms heritage pork belly cooked in duck fat, while local farms supply the veggies for some truly exuberant salads. Pizzas and sandwiches all have suggested beer pairings.

Blue Moon Diner, 102 Main St., Gardner, MA 01440; 978-632-4333; bluemoondinergardnerma.com; Casual American; $. In 2000, former waitress Jamie Floyd traded her pencil and pad for a grill cook's spatula and apron when she bought the Blue Moon (Worcester #815) and set about getting it listed on the National Register of Historic Places. Fifties memorabilia abounds and bygone stars lend their names to the menu. The Big Bopper breakfast, for example, includes eggs, toast, home fries, and a choice of homemade roast beef or corned beef hash. The Elvis burger is dressed with peanut butter and bananas. The addition in the back of the Blue Moon has a patina of age, but hardcore diner fans favor the 14 stools and five booths of the original dining car. Is it better to be an owner than a waitress? "The headaches are better," Floyd says with a smile.

Brew City Grill and Brew House, 104 Shrewsbury St., Worcester, MA 01604; (508) 752-3862; brew-city.com; Brewery; $. The tap system at Brew City is awe-inspiring, allowing the establishment to offer 40 draft beers at any one time. (Another  115 or so are available in bottles or cans.) Brew City goes equally over the top with the burger section of its menu. Choose to build your own burger and you select among American Kobe, Angus, or Piemontese beef, or farm-raised buffalo. The menu suggests that there are 38 trillion variations, once you factor in the toppings. We didn't check their math, but it's simpler to stick to the line of signature burgers. The Crunch Time, which tops an Angus burger with beer-based barbecue sauce, crisp ridged potato chips, and pepper jack cheese, is so sloppy and fun that it has a juvenile charm. The Piemonte, on the other hand, is a model of sophistication with its milder and sweeter Piemontese beef, fresh mozzarella, sliced tomatoes, and a slather of basil pesto on a ciabatta roll.

Charlie's Diner Bar & Grill, 5 Meadow Rd., Spencer, MA 01562; (508) 885-4033; charliesdiner.com; Casual American; $–$$. The heart and soul of Charlie's is Worcester Lunch Car #816, with a dozen stools and four booths, and that's where you head for breakfast and lunch. Come evening, though, and you'll likely be dining in the attached bar and grill with modern booths, a big flat-screen tuned to sports, and a somewhat fancier menu served most nights until late. There's a real old-fashioned grit about Charlie's—something a nostalgia factory could never generate. They cook a couple of giant turkeys every day, and leftovers from the weekly corned beef special keep the kitchen in hash for the rest of the week. The morning cook bakes fresh muffins daily and makes his own biscuits for shortcake.

Coney Island Lunch, 158 Southbridge St., Worcester, MA 01608; (508) 753-4362; coneyislandlunch.com; Casual American; $. No visitor to Worcester should be allowed to leave the city without making a pilgrimage to this neon-bedecked palace where the lowly dog is elevated to an icon of pop culture. The place still serves the best hot dog in town at a bargain price. Grab a tray and get in line—it shuffles through quickly. The house classic Coney Island is a hot dog with yellow mustard, chopped onions, and chile sauce.

El Basha, 424 Belmont St., Worcester, MA 01604; (508) 797-0884; 256 Park Ave., Worcester, MA 01609; (508) 795-0222; 2 Connector Rd., Westborough, MA 01581; (508) 366-2455; elbasha restaurant.com; Middle Eastern; $$. The original El Basha has become a fixture in Worcester. Stuffed grape leaves are the signature dish, but if you have a hankering for smoky eggplant, tabouli, and a pervasive taste of green olives, this popular Lebanese family restaurant is the spot for you in central Massachusetts. The newer El Basha West (on Park Avenue) and the Westborough outpost offer the same menu. Diners unfamiliar with real Middle Eastern cooking are invariably surprised by the subtlety of the seasoning and preparation.

J's at Nashoba Valley Winery, 100 Wattaquadock Hill Rd., Bolton, MA 01740; (978) 779-9816; nashobawinery.com; New American; $$$. Executive Chef Keith Desjardin displays finesse and panache in this restaurant associated with the pioneering fruit winery (see p. 76). The New American menu, which changes seasonally and showcases the fruits, vegetables, herbs, and flowers grown on the grounds, is frankly much more sophisticated than the relatively straightforward fruit wines made next door. Start with duck confit ravioli, for example, and move on to citrus-herb-crusted swordfish with sweet pea risotto. Luncheon fare is more simple but equally tasty. During warm weather, box lunches are even available so that visitors can dine on the winery porch or at picnic tables on the grounds.

Moran Square Diner, 6 Myrtle Ave., Fitchburg, MA 01420; (978) 343-9549; Casual American; $. Owner Chris Giannetti can point out some rare vintage touches at his compact yellow-and-red diner, like the discreet brass and enamel plate on one door that identifies it as #765 (which means it was the 565th Worcester diner built, since numbering began at 200). It was delivered to Fitchburg in 1940, and Giannetti has owned it since the nineties. He and his brother sanded and stained the oak panels to restore the interior wooden trim. Giannetti handles the usual breakfast dishes, burgers, and sandwiches, but family members make the puddings, cobblers, and cakes. Closed Sat.

Salem Cross Inn, Route 9, West Brookfield, MA 01585; (508) 867-2345; salemcrossinn.com; Traditional American; $$–$$$$. A family restaurant since 1961, the Salem Cross occupies a restored 1705 home, filled with an extensive collection of colonial- and federal-period antiques. The restaurant always has a fairly traditional American-Continental menu, but the "fireplace feasts" offered select nights from late November through April are even more fun (reservations essential). These 18th-century-style meals are prepared on the open hearth of the fieldstone fireplace, with prime rib turned over the cherry-log fire on a circa-1700 roasting jack and apple pie baked in the 1699 beehive oven.

Smokestack Urban Barbecue, 139 Green St., Worcester, MA 01604; (508) 363-1111; bbqstack.com; Barbecue; $–$$. Barbecue isn't just for bubbas anymore. Kudos to owner Richard Romaine for continually upgrading the smokers and the standards at Smokestack, which since its move to Green Street has become a force to reckon with. Almost everything is cooked low and slow in a custom-built smoker outside the restaurant, which means that when the smoked wings or smoked brisket are gone for the day, they're done until tomorrow. The barbecue portion of the menu, in fact, is limited to brisket, pulled pork, pork spareribs, and chicken. That said,  you can eat N'Orleans-style po' boys (shrimp or catfish), fried chicken with mac and cheese and collards, or even (for hardcore Southerners) chicken-fried steak. Best bet among the sides is probably the cheesy grits.

Sonoma, 206 Worcester Rd., Princeton, MA 01541; (978) 464-5775; sonoma-princeton.com; New American; $$–$$$. Chef-Owner Bill Brady is in his glory when the summer harvest starts to peak and he can serve local field greens, tomatoes, corn, and other garden vegetables alongside local lobster and goat cheese. Brady's culinary inspirations come from every corner of the globe—witness Korean barbecued short ribs next to French duck cassoulet—but his wines come mostly from California.

CLASSIC WORCESTER DINERS

Over the half-century between 1907 and 1957, the Worcester Lunch Car and Carriage Manufacturing Company helped create one of the most enduring icons of the American roadside—the diner. Known affectionately as Worcester Lunch, the company transformed the humble horse-drawn lunch wagons invented in Providence, Rhode Island, into compact metal diners with galley kitchens, long counters lined with stools, and a wall of small booths.

Over the years, the company built 651 diners, and many of them are still found along the streets and highways of central Massachusetts. Worcester Lunch was slow to adopt the streamlined, chromed look that the other two major diner builders employed after World War II. As a result, Worcester diners have a distinctive look of period graphics on porcelain-enamel exteriors. Many have real wood trim and wooden booths inside.

Twigs Cafe, Tower Hill Botanic Garden, 11 French Dr., Boylston, MA 01505; (508) 869-6111, ext. 147; towerhillbg.org; Casual American; $. The home of the Worcester County Horticultural Society occupies a hilltop with sweeping views down to the Wachusett Reservoir and acres of beautiful flower and vegetable gardens. But the hungry traveler has two other good reasons to visit: the small demonstration orchard of more than 30 heirloom apple trees (scions are sometimes sold to home orchardists in the spring) and Twigs, where Chef Tom Simons celebrates fresh fruits and vegetables in the new lunch menus he creates every week.

Vienna Restaurant & Historic Inn, 14 South St., South-bridge, MA 01550; (508) 764-0700; thevienna.com; Continental; $$$. With a name like "Vienna," you shouldn't be surprised to find a menu stuffed with schnitzel, wursts, stroganoff, and sauerbraten—not

Three lovingly maintained Worcester diners still operate in their home city, serving such diner classics as meat loaf, burgers, grilled cheese sandwiches, and eggs any style at all hours. The **Miss Worcester Diner** (300 Southbridge St., Worcester, MA 01608; 508-753-5600) is yellow with blue trim and classic lettering. The **Boulevard Diner** (155 Shrewsbury St., Worcester, MA 01604; 508-791-4535), built in 1936, is registered as a National Historic Landmark. With its bold illuminated clock and extensive neon, it is guarded around the clock by surveillance cameras. Essentially across the street, the **Parkway Diner** (148 Shrewsbury St., Worcester, MA 01604; 508-753-9968) is covered with pebbled cement that obscures its 1934 exterior. Inside, however, it retains the original features, including a second counter and row of stools in lieu of the usual booths. The Parkway is also known locally for its red-sauce Italian specials. All three serve breakfast and lunch daily and are sometimes open around the clock (or nearly) on the weekends.

to mention an abundance of sauerkraut and dumpling dishes. It's a *gemütlich* haven of *Mittel Europa* in central Massachusetts, complete with Hungarian goulash soup, that staple of every restaurant from the Dolomites north to the Baltic. Viennese desserts, of course, conclude the meal.

Worcester Art Museum Cafe, 55 Salisbury St., Worcester, MA 01609; (508) 799-4406, ext. 3068; worcesterart.org; Casual American; $. Easily the favorite venue for ladies who lunch, this dining room next to the Salisbury Street lobby also has seasonal seating in the outdoor courtyard. The menu stretches to make artistic connections, but the grilled cheese sandwich (the Grandma Moses) does use real Vermont cheddar along with slices of Granny Smith apple, caramelized onion, and fig spread between slices of whole wheat bread. There's a more successful art connection (referencing the museum's great Roman mosaic floor) with the Mosaic Madness salad, which is essentially a big plate of Mediterranean mezzes, including hummus, stuffed grape leaves, marinated artichoke hearts, roasted red peppers, cucumber slices, Kalamata olives, and pita bread. Consider starting a meal with the cafe's signature pear and wild mushroom soup finished with a dollop of Gorgonzola cheese.

Specialty Stores, Markets & Producers

Country Gourmet, 547 Summer St., Barre, MA 01005; (978) 355-6999 or (888) 355-6999; thecountrygourmet.net; Specialty Shop. Owner Sally Harrington (sometimes confused with her coffee-grinding trademark mouse, Java Belle) believes that every cook deserves the best. Her small shop virtually overflows with such sought-after tools as Chicago Metallic professional baking tins, Henckels knives, and Scanpan Titanium pots and pans. Harrington stocks coffee, tea, olive oil, and vinegar, as well as more than 100 bulk herbs and spices. Customers are welcome to purchase small amounts, a real advantage when you are trying something unfamiliar or just need a pinch of a specialty herb for a particular recipe. Country Gourmet also has an extensive line of kitchen and table linens. "You have to have a great-looking table to show off good food," says Harrington.

The Crown Bakery & Cafe, 133 Gold Star Blvd., Worcester, MA 01606; (508) 852-0746; thecrownbakery.com; Bakery. In the early 1960s, Ake Lundstrom recruited a batch of bakers from his native Sweden and opened this wonderful Scandinavian-style bakery that's served Worcester ever since. Celebrated around the region for its wedding cakes, Crown also makes a range of pastries based on yeasted sweet doughs and generous use of almonds, butter, and marzipan. Son

Jon Lundstrom now runs the operation. There's a small deli with a few tables to enjoy sandwiches or a coffee and a Danish, but the bakery takeout dominates.

Crystal Brook Farm, 192 Tuttle Rd., Sterling, MA 01564; (978) 422-6646; crystalbrookfarm.com; Cheese. According to Eric Starbard, his grandfather bought this farm in the heart of dairy country in 1920 and "milked cows all his life. I milked cows for 20 years before I switched to goats." In 1998, Eric and wife Ann bought their first herd of goats and within a few years, the cows were gone. Ann often handles the twice-daily milking of the 55 or so goats that provide milk for Crystal Brook's cheesemaking operation. Goats too young to milk have the run of pens behind the barn, while the milkers move freely between the hay feed in the barn and the open green pasture—always under the watchful eye of a gigantic livestock guard dog (nearly the size of a small black bear, but extremely affectionate). Eric makes cheese  every other day, producing about 13,000 pounds of soft goat cheeses—chèvre—per year. Logs are sold both plain and flavored from the refrigerator in the tiny cheese shop. There are also goat cheeses marinated in olive oil and herbs. Goats are bouncy, joyous creatures, and the memory of seeing the sprightly milkers makes the cheese taste even better when you get it home.

Eaton Farm Confectioners, 30 Burbank Rd., Sutton, MA 01590; (508) 865-5235; eatonfarmcandies.com; Chocolatier. Some of Lynwood Eaton's candy recipes date back to the 19th century, but this small shop on a backcountry farmstead (Burbank Road is off of Sibley Road) is best known for its thoroughly modern "ultimate candy sensation." In the mid-1990s, one of Eaton's employees invented the Peanut Butter Lust Bar, a concoction of peanut butter, crisped rice, marshmallows, cashews, and chocolate chips surrounded with milk chocolate. The San Diego Zoo can't keep them on the shelves, but you can stock up through mail order or by visiting the shop. (If you visit, you will probably be offered a sample.)

Ed Hyder's Mediterranean Marketplace, 408 Pleasant St., Worcester, MA 01609; (508) 755-0258; edhyders.com; Grocery. There's good reason that Ed Hyder's own name is part of his shop's title. He's the kind of hands-on proprietor who's enthusiastic about his products and always pleased to help his customers. The wide-ranging selection of imported cheeses and to-die-for Greek olives is reason enough to visit, and you'll probably exit laden with specialty meats, exotic nuts and oils, premium tea, and some of the obscure Middle Eastern spices (zaatar, anyone?) that you must have but can't find at Stop & Shop. (Hyder estimates that he carries more than 2,000 items.) Best of all, the prices are set for everyday, not special occasion, shoppers.

Hardwick Vineyard & Winery, 3305 Greenwich Rd., Hardwick, MA 01037; (413) 967-7763; hardwickwinery.com; Wine, Beer & Spirits. Current owners cleared 150 acres of the 1795 farm established by Giles E. Warner to plant vineyards and build a barn-like winery and tasting facility. Ten acres are planted in French-American hybrid varietals, and all the grapes are laboriously handpicked. Hardwick makes six wines in all. The Giles E. Warner, a dry wine fashioned from Seyval grapes, is the closest to a classic European wine. Sweeter wines made from Catawba, the foundation grape of America's 19th-century wine industry, are popular, but the bestseller is a blend of grape wine with cranberries from a nearby dry bog. Called Massetts Cranberry, its sweet-tart profile complements Thanksgiving dinner well. Open Mar through Dec.

Hebert Candies, the Candy Mansion, 575 Hartford Turn-pike, Shrewsbury, MA 01545; (508) 842-5583; hebertcandies.com; Chocolatier. One of the giants among regional candymakers, Hebert makes thousands of bars of chocolate every day, along with all sorts of filled and dipped candies, including cognac, apricot brandy, peach brandy, Irish cream, and rum cordials. The company was launched in 1917 when Frederick Hebert paid $11 for a copper kettle, knife, thermometer, table, marble slab, and stove. For 30 years he developed and made candies that were sold throughout central Massachusetts in small neighborhood stores. In 1946 he bought a Tudor-style stone mansion in Shrewsbury and launched what the company calls America's first roadside candy store. Frederick Hebert is credited with perfecting white chocolate in the United States after having tasted it in Europe. The company claims the Geneva as its signature sweet. You can watch through a glass window as workers make the bite-size pieces of white, mocha, and dark chocolate, each with or without a toasted almond. You can also find the Hebert family candies at **Colonial Candies,** 47 Sugar Rd. (exit 27 off I-495), Bolton, MA 01740 (978-779-6586).

Madrid European Bakery & Patisserie, 1019 Boston Post Rd., Marlborough, MA 01752; (508) 485-8844; madridbakery.com; Bakery. Baker Sergio Mendoza knows Spanish pastry—after all, he was born in Madrid and started baking in his parents' bakery at the age of nine. The specialties of Madrid include delicate little éclairs and cream puffs, European cream cakes, butter cookies, and the flaky butterfly-shaped pastries called palmiers. On the weekends Mendoza also makes croissants. But he is justly celebrated for his Spanish *tartas*—cakes made mostly with nut flours rather than wheat flour in the batter. The most famous is the *tarta de Santiago,* a dense cake made with ground almonds, butter, sugar, and citrus rind. By all accounts, the cake has Sephardic Jewish origins. Mendoza also makes other nut-flour cakes, including one with ground hazelnuts and small morsels of chocolate.

Brew It Yourself

There's a Scrub-a-Dub across Route 9 from their location, but the only suds that interest the folks at **Deja Brew** in Shrewsbury come from pouring a bottle of home brew into a beer mug. The first brew-on-premises operation in Massachusetts, Deja Brew lets aspiring homebrewers (and home winemakers) practice their craft in a retail environment. They provide the recipes, ingredients, brewing kettles, storage areas, and bottling equipment. Even better, they clean up the mess. This means your cellar or garage need not smell like a brewery—unless the bottles explode after you get them home because you ignored the brewer's advice and added too much sugar before capping them. Deja Brew has prepackaged more than 60 beer recipes and more than a dozen wine recipes for use on the premises. Each beer batch makes six dozen 22-ounce bottles. Wine runs produce almost 5 gallons.

If you get hooked, you'll find that homebrewers tend to be an enthusiastic bunch, and brewer/vintner Bruce Lucier is no exception. He established **West Boylston Homebrew Emporium**, a

Nashoba Valley Winery, 100 Wattaquadock Hill Rd., Bolton, MA 01740; (978) 779-5521; nashobawinery.com; Wine, Beer & Spirits. Nashoba Valley Winery is as much a destination as a winery. Acres and acres of fruit trees surround the property, and the grounds are deliberately set up to encourage picnicking. Or picking, for that matter—pick-your-own is available for raspberries, peaches, blackberries, plums, and apples. If you don't pick them, they'll likely end up in the wines. NVW was a regional pioneer in developing fine fruit wines and has the blue ribbons to prove it. Apple wines (from a sparkling brut and several dry varietals to the semisweet Maiden's Blush) remain the core of the offerings. Other wines incorporate blueberries, cherries, plums, and peaches. In recent years, the winery has also begun making a few grape wines: Chardonnay, Vidal Blanc, Riesling, and Gewürztraminer.

store that provides everything for making beer at home—including all sorts of grains, spices, gadgets, and brewing chemicals you didn't think you needed but absolutely cannot live without. Novices will appreciate the canned and boxed kits, while experienced (or, as they prefer to style themselves, "visionary") homebrewers can mix and match yeasts, dry malts, crystal malts, malt extracts, and different styles of hops and hop extracts. The shop also carries winemaking supplies, including a wide range of concentrated grape juices for no-hassle vinting. If you want to introduce your kids to classic soda flavors, you can purchase the ingredients for sarsaparilla, ginger beer, and birch beer, as well as orange soda, passion fruit, and cream soda.

Deja Brew, 510B Boston Turnpike Rd. (Route 9), Shrewsbury, MA 01545; (508) 842-8991; deja-brew.com.

West Boylston Homebrew Emporium, Causeway Crossing Mall, 45 Sterling St. (Route 12), West Boylston, MA 01583; (508) 835-3374; wbhomebrew.com.

Owner Richard Pelletier also crafts a single-malt whiskey called Stimulus. Open year-round for tastings and sales. Tours are available on weekends.

Obadiah McIntyre Farm Winery, at Charlton Orchards, 44 Old Worcester Rd. (Route 20), Charlton, MA 01507; (508) 248-7820; charltonorchard.com; Wine, Beer & Spirits. Owner Nate Benjamin Jr.'s Charlton Orchards produces wonderful apples, peaches, pears, strawberries, and blueberries, and the farm store, which is open all year, has quite a local following for its apple pies and ciders. But Benjamin began planting *vinifera* and French-American hybrid wine grapes in the 1990s, and in 2002 opened Obadiah McIntyre Farm Winery, named for the man who received the farm as a land grant in 1733. Benjamin makes fruit wines from apples, strawberries, raspberries, peaches, blackberries, plums, and cherries. He's also vinting wines from Riesling, Chardonnay, Zinfandel, Vidal, and Chenin Blanc grapes and makes hard cider and hard cider blends, including Razzy Apple, which mixes cider with red raspberries. Open weekends May through Dec.

Pecorino, a Country Cheese Shop, 135 Westboro Rd., North Grafton, MA 01536; (508) 839-9200; pecorinografton.com; Cheese. Simone Linsin is an evangelist of artisanal and farmstead cheeses, and the cases in her shop in rural North Grafton are filled with little treasures from New England and far beyond, including a raft of Italian sheep's milk cheeses. (Pecorino is the Italian designation for sheep cheeses.) Located in a former pizzeria, Pecorino also carries an extensive line of condiments, jams, jellies, honey, vinegar, and oils as well as a small selection of French, Italian, and Californian wines.

Pioneer Brewing Company, 195 Arnold Rd., Fiskdale (Sturbridge), MA 01566; (508) 347-7500; pioneerbrewingcompany.com; Brewery. Based on the old song, and a rate of 7.5 bottles of beer per minute, Pioneer estimates that it is located 450 bottles of beer on the wall from Boston, 1,350 bottles of beer on the wall from New York, and 338 bottles of beer on the wall from Hartford, Connecticut. Who said brewers took themselves seriously? The brewery occupies a 12,000-square-foot former barn at **Hyland Orchard** (see p. 86). Its flagship beer is the Pioneer Pale Ale, a medium-bodied brew with a rich copper color.

The Pioneer Industrial Pale Ale carries a sharper hops flavor and more alcohol. Pioneer has developed a full line of a half-dozen year-round ales, four seasonals, and some special high-alcohol Manifest Destiny ales. The taproom offers live music (no cover) on Saturday and Sunday, and is open mid-afternoon to early evening daily except Monday.

Priscilla Hand Made Candies, 4 Main St., Gardner, MA 01440; (978) 632-7148; priscillacandy.com; Chocolatier. Located in the heart of Gardner, Priscilla was founded in 1936 and is now in the hands of the third generation of candymakers. The shop makes all sorts of milk and dark chocolates with nuts, chewy centers, and soft centers, but it is best known for its unique French Roll. "We are the only ones who make it," say the counter clerks. If you weren't from Gardner, you wouldn't know what it was." For the record, the French Roll has a chocolate center that has been flattened, dipped in milk chocolate, and rolled in crushed cashews.

Publick House Bake Shoppe, 277 Main St. (Route 131), Sturbridge, MA 01566; (508) 347-3313; publickhouse.com; Bakery. As the quaint spellings suggest, the Bake Shoppe at this 18th-century inn is a logical place to find such recherché treats as molasses-ginger hermit cookies and a Joe Frogger, a large molasses cookie that holds its freshness so well that fishermen used to take them to sea. The shop also sells some of the inn's own brand of Indian pudding, various relishes, strawberry jam, apple butter, and a whole range of mustards and ice cream toppings.

Robinson Farm, 42 Jackson Rd., Hardwick, MA 01037; (413) 477-6988; robinsonfarm.org; Cheese. Ray and Pam Robinson grow organic vegetables and sell grass-fed beef and raw milk from the 40-cow herd. In 2006, they began to consider cheesemaking as a way to expand the thin margins of traditional dairy farming. "I've always been fond of Swiss cheese," says Ray, "and once we had the name 'Robinson Family Swiss,' we were on our way." Punning name aside, Ray notes that "there are a lot of good farmstead cheddars. We needed to do something different." They took classes and began trial efforts. "We practiced in the kitchen," says Pam. "Then we graduated to the laundry room, and then to the milk room." The raw milk is piped warm from the milking parlor to the Dutch cheese vat and ultimately is pressed into round forms that yield 22-pound wheels. Aging varies from three to nine months, depending on the variety. In all, the Robinsons produce about 15,000 pounds a year. In addition to the Swiss-style cheese, they also make Tekenink Tomme (a rustic, sharp Alpine style), the complex Prescott (a nutty Comté style), A Barndance (a buttery homage to French Abondance), and Hardwick Stone (an American brick style).

Rose 32 Bread, 412 Main St. (Route 32), Gilbertville (Hardwick), MA 01031; (413) 477-9930; rose32bread.com; Bakery Cafe. Owners Glenn and Cindy Mitchell used to run a bakery empire of 250 stores based in San Francisco. When they sold the business and moved to Hardwick, they just couldn't keep their hands out of the flour bins, so they launched Rose 32 Bread. All the breads are prepared in small batches and baked in a wood-fired oven. The choices vary by day, but ciabatta, baguettes, and some sort of sandwich loaf are always among them. There are also to-die-for morning pastries, cakes, tarts, and cookies. Egg-based breakfasts are great, but since we don't live near enough, we're usually there for lunchtime sandwiches instead. You've never really had tuna salad until you've tasted it on a fresh croissant, or egg salad until you've had it with cornichons and bacon bits on sourdough bread. Diners can take a seat at the big communal table in the middle of the room and join the ongoing conversation with regulars.

Smith's Country Cheese, 20 Otter River Rd., Winchendon, MA 01475; (978) 939-5738; smithscountrycheese.com; Cheese. Founder Dave Smith was a pioneer in Massachusetts farmstead cheese when he began making Gouda-style wheels from the milk of his Holstein herd in 1985. Now the company is one of the best established in the

Commonwealth, and its farmstead Gouda, cheddar, and Havarti-style cheeses are sold in grocery stores, natural food shops, and most of the state's wineries. If you visit, you might see the cheese being made. (Call ahead for times.) Even if you miss the live operation, a video at the entry details the process. This factory store sells the whole line of cheeses, including plain, aged, and smoked Gouda, and the relatively new and well-received chipotle-rubbed Gouda. Bargain hunters favor the bags of Gouda trimmings, which are perfect for making fondue. The store also offers one-stop country gift shopping, with decorative items as well as food products from other farms.

St. Joseph's Abbey, 167 N. Spencer Rd. (Route 31), North Spencer, MA 01562; (508) 885-8720; spencerabbey.org; Specialty Shop. The monks of the Cistercian Order of the Strict Observance, founded by reformist Benedictine monks in 1098, follow an austere life of prayer, contemplation, and manual labor. Hospitality has always been a special work of monks, who have a long tradition of preserving foods to offer their guests. The fruit and wine jellies, jams, and marmalades made by the Spencer monks since the 1960s are part of that tradition. The monks produce more than 30 varieties and sell them at supermarkets and stores in New England.  But experiencing the silent beauty of the monastery gives each jar a little more meaning. A gift shop located at the foot of the abbey's driveway is open daily; afternoon only on Sunday. Look for some of the more unusual items, such as ginger preserve, kadota fig preserve, and sherry wine jelly.

Wachusett Brewing Company, 175 State Rd. East (Route 2A), Westminster, MA 01473; (978) 874-9965; Brewery Store, 175A State Rd. East, Westminster, MA 01473; (978) 874-0455; wachusett brew.com; Brewery. Three friends who confess to developing a significant "appreciation" for beer as students at Worcester Polytechnic

Institute opened Wachusett in 1994. Year-round products include a pale ale (Country Ale), a wheat ale with blueberries, Nut Brown Ale, an IPA, and Black Shack Porter. The company also brews a summer wheat ale with a hint of lemon, Winter Ale (a Scottish-style amber), and Quinn's Irish (an Irish-style pale ale available around St. Patrick's Day). Tours are offered Mon through Sat and the store is open Wed through Sat.

Wegman's, 9102 Shops Way, Northborough, MA 01532; (508) 936-1945; wegmans.com; Grocery. Shoppers can be excused if they are under the impression that this 140,000-square-foot emporium is a full-fledged shopping center rather than just a supermarket. There's a 250-seat cafe to sit down and enjoy the fresh pastries and lattes from the coffee shop, the sandwiches on freshly baked rolls from the sub shop, or the pies from the pizza shop. The produce shelves are filled with exotica (dragonfruit, anyone?), and the cheese shop stocks more than 300 varieties. The Wegman's chain is based in Rochester, NY, and the Northborough store is the first Massachusetts foray. It feels like shopping the world.

Westfield Farm, 28 Worcester Rd., Hubbardston, MA 01452; (978) 928-5110; chevre.com; Cheese. Bob and Debbie Stetson produce about 1,500 pounds of cheese per week. Most are made with goat's milk, including a Plain Capri (simple chèvre) and flavored logs of herb, herb garlic, pepper, chive, and hickory smoked. One of their most striking products is a log with a blue edible rind formed by Roquefort mold during the aging process. The Stetsons seem to have a particularly fine touch with aged blue cheeses, also producing a Hubbardston Blue cow's milk cheese. They also transform cow's milk into a creamy Camembert. When you drive up to the small, self-serve store, don't be surprised that the operation seems shockingly small to produce cheeses with such sophistication and big flavors. For the Stetsons' recipe for **Pasta with Tomato Sauce, Broccoli, and Goat Cheese,** see p. 294.

Berberian's Farm, 68 Otis St., Northborough, MA 01532; (508) 393-8079. You'll drive past fields and fields of vegetables when you turn off Route 20 toward the farm—a spread that gives credence to Berberian's claim to have the greatest variety of homegrown produce in New England. Should it be late summer, you'll smell the onions before you even open the car door. At the height of the season, boxes and flats are full of the farm's own scallions, arugula, dandelion greens, mint, dill, rhubarb, parsley, cilantro, basil, celery, Romano beans, yellow beans, green beans, carrots, beets, Chinese cabbage, lettuces (iceberg, salad bowl, red leaf, Simpson, buttercrunch, Boston, romaine), escarole, squash (acorn, blue Hubbard, buttercup, butternut, Cousa, summer, zucchini), cabbage, cauliflower, potatoes (red, white, Yukon gold), peppers (red, green, sweet Italian, sweet Hungarian, sweet banana, hot Hungarian, jalapeño, hot cherry, Thai dragon, hot finger), Butter and Sugar corn, cucumbers, tomatoes (plum, beefsteak, cherry, grape), cucumbers, pickling cukes, Armenian cucumbers, and eggplant. As if its own production were not enough, Berberian also sells locally grown nectarines, peaches, blueberries, and raspberries, as well as locally packed turkey and chicken potpies. Open Apr through Nov.

Berlin Orchards, Route 62 and Lower Sawyer Hill Road, Berlin, MA 01503; (978) 838-2400; berlinorchards.com. The orchard, situated in rolling hill country, occupies the former Chedco Farm, where the foundation herd of America's Guernsey cattle was raised in the early 20th century. In the fall, visitors can take a hay wagon ride to the orchards, where about a dozen varieties of apples are waiting to be picked, and then make a stop at the pumpkin patch.

Bolton Orchards, 125 Still River Rd., Bolton, MA 01740; (978) 779-2733; boltonorchards.com. One of the very large suppliers of apples to the Boston market, Bolton Orchards has 250 acres in active production, growing 25 different apple varieties, 15 types of peaches, and five types each of nectarines and plums. Long fields also grow tomatoes, squash, and pumpkins. Bolton presses a blended cider through the fall season and, from mid-October until almost Christmas, also produces a sweet, light yellow cider pressed from Golden Russet apples. Far from being a mere farm stand, the store can serve as one-stop shopping: it carries a full line of dry goods; a wide variety of canned goods, jellies, jams, and preserves; and all manner of pickled items in canning jars, including hot asparagus bullets, pickled beets, dilled pickles, pickled garlic, and spicy dilled beans. This is also a fabulous spot to stop for baked goods and snacks while touring the area's orchards, as Bolton has its own bakery (top item: apple pies) and sells a variety of breads, cookies, and cakes from other small bakers in the region. Open year-round.

Brookfield Orchards, 12 Lincoln Rd., North Brookfield, MA 01525; (508) 867-6858; brookfieldorchardsonline.com. The country store at Brookfield Orchards is famous (at least locally) for its hot apple dumplings and ice cream served in the snack bar. The bakers also make apple pies and coffee cakes and a range of homey cookies. In September and October, when the pick-your-own portion of the apple harvest season is in full swing, the snack bar also offers hot dogs, hamburgers, chili, and macaroni and cheese. The country store sells the farm's apples and cider and the whole gamut of country store fare, including penny candy, jams, honey, collectibles, and crafts. Open year-round.

Carlson Orchards, 115 Oak Hill Rd., Harvard, MA 01451; (978) 456-3916; carlsonorchards.com. Possibly the largest cider producer in the state, Carlson is a no-nonsense working farm and orchard— no petting zoo, no hay rides, just fruit and vegetables. Pick-your-own blueberries are available around mid-July; six varieties of peaches and five varieties of nectarines from early August into September. Carlson grows about 15 varieties of apples to pick in September and October. These include Gingergold, Royal Gala, Empire, Cameo, Macoun, Cortland, Red Delicious, McIntosh, and the popular Honeycrisp, a golden eating apple. Not everything is pick-your-own: All the fruits are available by the pound in the rudimentary shop, which also sells the orchard's applesauce, apple juice, apple cider vinegar, mulling spices, jams, jellies, and preserves. The store is open all year, but payment is by the honor system from Jan to mid-July.

Carter & Stevens Farm Store, 500 West St. (Route 122), Barre, MA 01005; (978) 355-4940; carterandstevensfarm.com. Leaving the kids home when you visit this farm store is a form of cruel and unusual punishment. Principally a dairy farm that packages its own milk in glass bottles, Carter & Stevens also has a free farm animal petting zoo, makes and sells ice cream from its milk, and operates an outdoor open-fire barbecue restaurant in the summer. The store carries some of the farm's own vegetables and produce from other central Massachusetts farms, as well as local cheeses. The farm also produces honey and maple syrup, both for sale at the store. Open Apr through Oct.

Clearview Farm, 4 Kendall Hill Rd., Sterling, MA 01564; (978) 422-0442; clearviewfarmstand.com. This venerable hilltop farm was first planted more than two centuries ago and has been in Diane Melone's family since 1906—a "long line of Yankees," she jokes. In fact, if encouraged, she'll admit to being a descendant of Mary E. Sawyer, the author (so people in Sterling claim) of the nursery rhyme "Mary Had a Little Lamb." Diane and her husband, Rick, grow a wide variety of vegetables ("Rick mulls over the seed catalogs over the winter looking for new things to try," Diane says), and offer pick-your-own peaches, blueberries, pumpkins, raspberries, and more than 20 varieties of apples. For those who want to try their hands at pressing cider, the Melones set up a hand press on the lawn. That's about as fresh as it can get. Open mid-Aug through late Nov.

Coopers Hilltop Dairy, 515 Henshaw St., Rochdale, MA 01542; (508) 892-3720; coopershilltopfarm.com. This picturesque dairy operation at the edge of the village of Rochdale milks its own herd and processes and bottles the milk and cream. The dairy shop sells whole, skim, and low-fat milk as well as heavy and light cream. At Easter and Christmas, you'll also find eggnog. Coopers sells ice cream, but does not make it on the premises.

Dick's Market Garden, 647 Northfield Rd., Lunenburg, MA 01462; (978) 582-4896. Probably best known to Boston and Cambridge shoppers as "that farm with the incredible vegetables" at many of the farmers' markets, Dick's also has a stand at the farm. Greenhouses on the property (Dick's also sells garden and landscape plants in the spring) let the Violette family extend the season in the fall with such spring-like delicacies as tender lettuce and pea tendrils. Open Apr through late Nov.

Hyland Orchard, 199 Arnold Rd., Sturbridge, MA 01566; (508) 347-7500; hylandorchard.com. Offering wagon rides and hayrides and music festivals, Hyland Orchard also has pick-your-own apples and pumpkins in September and October and peaches in August. The tap room for **Pioneer Brewing** (see p. 78) is also on the property, and the farm shop has cider and maple syrup made on the premises, ice cream, and jellies, jams, honey, and baked goods.

Pearson's Elmhurst Dairy Farm, 342 W. Main St., Millbury, MA 01527; (508) 865-2158. Don't expect the Pearsons to answer the phone at this dairy farm stand, as they are usually tending to chores, milking the herd of 60 cows, churning ice cream, or weeding and picking the vegetable patch. Pearson's not only processes its own milk; the family also delivers to homes in the immediate area. The little shop has fresh milk and cream as well as 26 flavors of ice cream and, during the summer, vegetables from the fields. In the spring, Bob Pearson taps maple trees around West Millbury and makes syrup, which is generally sold out by late April. The farm stand is open year-round.

Red Apple Farm, 455 Highland Ave., Phillipston, MA 01331; (978) 249-6763; redapplefarm.com. In addition to a farm stand crammed with goodies—cider doughnuts, fudge, maple candy and sugar—Red Apple operates one of the most extensive pick-your-own operations in the middle of the state. The season begins with both wild and cultivated blueberries in mid-July (hint: the wild are more expensive and more work to pick—and worth every bit of extra effort). It's the only spot we know that has dig-your-own potatoes. Peaches, pears, and raspberries round out the fruits. The farm stand, open from mid-July through December, also carries a lot of jams, jellies, relishes, pickles, and salsas. The bestseller of the bunch, though, is the Vidalia onion salad dressing.

Sholan Farms, 1125 Pleasant St., Leominster, MA 01453; (978) 840-3276; sholanfarms .com. The last apple orchard in Leominster, birthplace of John Chapman (aka Johnny Appleseed), Sholan Farms was purchased by the city in 1999 to prevent conversion of the farmland into a subdivision of 150 single-family homes. Conservation-minded volunteers have been reclaiming and restoring the orchard and working to renovate the barn. More than two dozen varieties are available for picking—Vista Bella, Jersey Mac, Gingergold, Paula Red, McIntosh, Cortland, Empire, Golden Delicious, Macoun, and Red Delicious—from Aug through Oct.

Stillman Dairy Farm, 991 **Lancaster Ave., Lunenburg, MA 01462; (978) 582-5533; stillmandairy.com.** Envy the lucky folks of north-central Massachusetts who can actually get milk from the Stillman herd of Jerseys delivered to their doorsteps in glass bottles! Stop by the farm store (it opens at 5 a.m. weekdays and 7 a.m. weekends) for milk in glass or plastic containers, as well as fresh baked goods made with the dairy's own milk, cream, and butter.

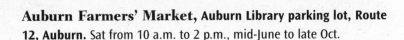

Farmers' Markets

Auburn Farmers' Market, Auburn Library parking lot, Route **12, Auburn.** Sat from 10 a.m. to 2 p.m., mid-June to late Oct.

Barre Farmers' Market, Barre Common, Barre. Sat from 9 a.m. to 12:30 p.m., May through Oct.

Fitchburg Burbank Campus Farmers' Market, Health Alliance Hospital, 275 Nichols Rd., Fitchburg. Mon and Wed from 10 a.m. to 4 p.m., July through Oct.

Fitchburg Farmers' Market, Wallace Civic Center parking lot, John Fitch Highway, Fitchburg. Fri from 8:45 a.m. to noon, July through Oct.

Fitchburg Farmers' Market at Riverfront Park, 40 Commercial St., Fitchburg. Thurs from 3 to 7 p.m., July through Sept.

Fitchburg Winter Farmers' Market, Fitchburg Art Museum, **25 Merriam Parkway, Fitchburg.** First Thurs from 4 to 7 p.m., Nov through June.

Gardner Farmers' Market, Monument Square (Park Street side), Gardner. Thurs from 8:30 a.m. to 1 p.m., May through Oct.

Gardner/Heywood Hospital Farmers' Market, 242 Green St., Gardner. Wed from noon to 4 p.m., mid-July through Oct.

Holden Farmers' Market, Damon House parking lot, Holden center. Tues from 3 to 6:30 p.m., May through Oct.

Sturbridge Farmers' Market, Town Common, Sturbridge. Sun from noon to 4 p.m., late May through early Oct.

Worcester Main South Farmers' Market, YMCA upper parking lot, 104 Murray Ave., Worcester. Sat from 10 a.m. to 2 p.m., mid-June through Oct.

Worcester Westside Farmers' Market, 306 Chandler St., Worcester. Mon, Wed, and Fri from 9:30 a.m. to 2 p.m., mid-June through Oct.

Worcester Winter Farmers' Market, 9 Mann St., Worcester. Sun from 11 a.m. to 3 p.m., Nov through May.

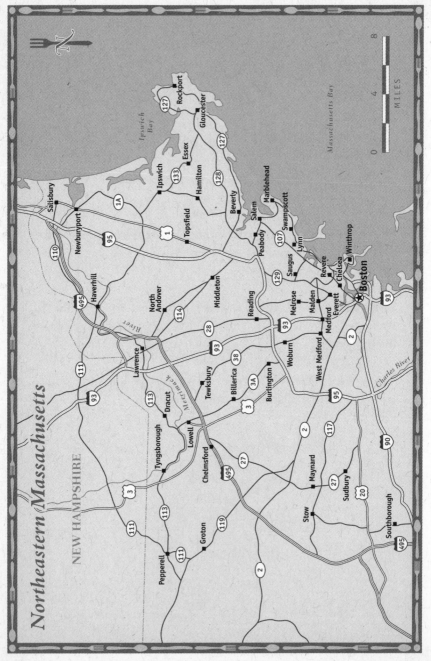

Northeastern Massachusetts

Northeastern Massachusetts

The Gloucester fisherman is as iconic a figure in American myth as the lumberjacks of Minnesota and the cowboys of the Southwest. He is forever fixed in his yellow raingear, gritting his teeth in the face of a storm and hauling his lines to feed a hungry nation. With declining fish stocks and other economic opportunities available, the number of Gloucester fishermen has dwindled, but representatives of this venerable breed still stride the docks of Cape Ann, and the shore towns north of Boston retain a fishing identity.

"North Shore fish" used to mean cod, but these days it's more likely to refer to clams or lobsters. The sandy flats and marshy inlets north of rocky Cape Ann remain some of the world's most pristine and productive shellfishing beds, and the restaurants of northeastern Massachusetts revel in the bounty of the nearby sea and the orchards and fields of the Merrimack Valley. Even in this age of agricultural conglomeration, family farms persist in the rural areas north and west of Boston. Pushed out of their own local markets by nationwide distributors, they thrive by supplying restaurants and selling directly to consumers at farm stands and, increasingly, at weekly farmers' markets. When driving back roads in the summer, keep your eyes peeled for small roadside stands operated by dairy farmers who make their own ice cream.

As you get closer to metropolitan Boston, where old fishing and farming towns have matured into commuter suburbs, you'll also find a proliferation of fine bakeries, gourmet shops, and restaurants. And in communities like Chelsea, Everett, and Malden, you'll find substantial immigrant populations that have brought their own cuisines intact from the old country.

Foodie Faves

Bistro 5, 5 Playstead Rd., West Medford, MA 02155; (781) 395-7464; bistro5.com; Italian; $$$. Medford may have a significant Italian-American population, but Chef-Owner Vittorio Ettore has no truck with the mamma's meatballs tradition. He serves a sleek, modern Northern Italian menu that draws as much from Piemonte and Friuli as from Tuscany. He makes his own *trofie* pasta (little ropes) that he serves with braised boar, cranberries, and broccoli rabe, and unapologetically offers seared rabbit with squash spaetzle, candied bacon, brie, and sage-almond pesto. During the full flush of white truffle season (usually the last two weeks of November), he offers a white truffle tasting menu that could include sea scallops and mushrooms, pheasant with kale, and a chestnut bisque. Diners who want to overdrink will be pleased that the restaurant is adjacent to the West Medford commuter rail stop.

Blackstrap BBQ, 47A Woodside Ave., Winthrop, MA 02152; (617) 207-1783; blackstrapbbq.com; Barbecue; $. It would be easy to dismiss a barbecue joint in Winthrop—unless you happen to know its pedigree. Quick history lesson: Kent Jacobs introduced real Southern barbecue to Boston with his rolling grill on Blue Hill Avenue in Dorchester in the 1970s. Chris Schlesinger so loved it that he brought Jacobs into **East Coast Grill** (see p. 137) in Cambridge as pitmaster to show how it was done. The folks who launched Blackstrap got their start at East Coast Grill. It's a little like the papal succession, keeping the one true faith of Slow and Low. The dry rub pork ribs, the pulled pork or burnt end brisket sandwich, and the corn and andouille fritters are reason enough to fire up the GPS and make your way to Winthrop. For the ultimate mashup of meat and smoke, go for The Hog. That's a bacon-wrapped kielbasa that's been smoked and then fried to crisp the bacon and served on a bun. Just to push it over the top, you can order it with melted cheese and some of Grammy Kath's Rip Your Lips Off Chili (which isn't as hot as it sounds). That makes for some serious south in your mouth.

Bobby's Burger Palace, Burlington Mall, 75 Middlesex Tpke., Burlington, MA 01803; (781) 425-3652; bobbysburgerpalace.com; Casual American; $. TV celebrity chef Bobby Flay gets props for capitalizing on his name without sticking it to the consumer. It's nice to find a mall restaurant—it's tucked between Legal Sea Foods and a Rainforest Cafe—with simple, good food at prices even a  family can love. As the name suggests, this is a burger joint where the combo of added toppings is meant to suggest some part of the country. The Santa Fe burger, for example, has cheese sauce, pickled jalapeño peppers, and pieces of blue corn tortillas. The LA burger has watercress, avocado relish, and thick tomato slices. Any burger can be "crunchified" for free by adding potato chips atop the patty.

Brine, 25 State St., Newburyport, MA 01950; (978) 358-8479; brine oyster.com; Seafood/Steakhouse; $$–$$$$. With its Carrara marble and chrome bar and an emphasis on *crudo* (Italian sashimi) and chops, Brine is perhaps the hippest place to eat in Newburyport. The single-page "Sea and Land" menu balances fish (raw tuna with fried olives, lardo, a crouton, and a pickled hot pepper, for example) with a short list of prime meats, including a rib eye with a potato croquette. Lots of very Italian small dishes offer some real taste sensations—like the gnocchi in a smoked bacon broth with early spring peas, pig's ears, and shaved Tuscan sheep's cheese. And then there are the oysters—all sorts of them, mostly to be devoured on the half shell. The wine list is studded with fish-friendly whites and some hairy-chested California Cabs among the reds. The bottled craft brews are just as carefully chosen.

Cape Ann Brewing Company, 11 Rogers St., Gloucester, MA 01930; (978) 282-7399; capeannbrewing.com; Brewery; $. The year-round stalwarts at Cape Ann are an American amber ale with a hoppy finish, a light and mellow Kolsch ale, and a well-balanced IPA. Several seasonal beers round out the tap rotation. They're all called "Fisherman's" in deference to Gloucester's history, and the pub menu includes baked haddock, a Portuguese fisherman's stew, and that new pub cliché, the fish taco with salsa and guacamole. Free tours of the brewing facility are available for the asking, and the pub hosts live music, trivia games, and other pastimes to hold your attention between sips.

Ceia Kitchen + Bar, 38 State St., Newburyport, MA 01950; (978) 358-8112; ceiakitchenbar.com; Portuguese; $$–$$$. When Ceia moved into its current digs in a three-story brownstone, it gained a second bar and—most important—more seating for what has become Newburyport's favorite casual fine-dining spot. It's still low-lit and romantic, though, making it the perfect date restaurant with a grown-up menu. New England seafood speaks with Portuguese and Spanish accents here in dishes like the hearty appetizer of grilled North Atlantic octopus with linguiça and potatoes fried in duck fat, or lobster with fava beans, mushrooms, parsnips, and smoked pork belly. Charcuterie ranges all over southern Europe from pistachio mortadella (Italy) to dry-aged chorizo and *jamón ibérico* (Spain) to *rosette de Lyon* (France). Half a dozen artisanal cheeses are available by the small plate, as are some nibbles like lardo with smoked pecans and truffle honey. The wine list parallels the food, with crisp whites and soft and rounded reds. Going on the Mediterranean diet for your heart? You could eat here every night.

Duckworth's Bistrot, 197 E. Main St., Gloucester, MA 01930; (978) 282-4426; duckworthsbistrot.com; New American/Vegetarian; $$$. A young Ken Duckworth was the final chef at the famed Maison Robert in Boston, and when that temple of French haute cuisine closed in 2004, the people of Gloucester were the beneficiaries. His French style has been thoroughly naturalized as Duckworth makes great use of North Shore shellfish and the Gloucester catch, as well as produce from Merrimack Valley farms. We also love Duckworth's approach to moderation: Almost every dish (including a killer seafood stew any other restaurant would call bouillabaisse) is available in half or full portions, and the eclectic wine list includes many choices by the glass and by the half bottle. Even better, the menu gives vegetarians at least three options.

Enzo Restaurant & Bar, 50 Water St., Ste. 304, Newburyport, MA 01950; (978) 462-1801; enzo-restaurant.com; Italian; $$–$$$. We're suckers for the food of Italy's northernmost regions, and Enzo delivers some classics rarely seen elsewhere. They salt and cure their own hake to make crisp little fritters served with garlic and pickled chile pepper mayo, for example, and prepare a pan-roasted pressed chicken (chicken under a brick) that comes with sautéed turnips. For dessert, they offer "One Perfect Cheese," which happens to be a Pingree Hill Tomme from Valley View Farm in Topsfield that they drizzle with local honey and sprinkle with sugar-toasted walnuts. The wine list stays north as well, with robust reds from Tuscany and Piemonte and crisp whites from Piemonte and Friuli.

Four Sisters Owl Diner, 244 Appleton St., Lowell, MA 01842; 978-453-8321; owldiner.com; Casual American; $. Martha Kazanjian was seven years old when her family bought the Owl in 1982, "but I tell people I was born in a booth," she says. Kazanjian seems to know most of the clientele by their first names, from the families who pile into the booths on weekends, especially after church, to the police and politicos who stop by for coffee on weekday mornings. No one leaves hungry. Monday to Friday, construction workers come in for breakfast so they can skip lunch. Plate specials include diner classics like American chop suey or baked haddock. Breakfast and lunch only.

Franklin Cape Ann, 118 Main St., Gloucester, MA 01930; (978) 283-7888; franklincafe.com; New American; $$. With its late dinner hours (until midnight on weekends), comfort food menu, and extensive beer list, this sister of the Boston branches of **Franklin Cafe** (see p. 140) is the new favorite of Gloucester beer drinkers who also happen to enjoy good food. Bar-snacking small plates like smoky skillet-roasted mussels, braised short ribs with polenta, and fried lobster dumplings make it feasible to have a tapas-style meal, or you can eat more conventionally with bigger plates like sunflower-crusted catfish with pico de gallo or a grilled hanger *steak-frites* with habañero butter.

Gibbet Hill Grill, 61 Lowell Rd., Groton, MA 01450; (978) 448-2900; gibbethillgrill.com; Traditional American; $$–$$$$. Farm to fork is no exaggeration at this unpretentious rural steak house in a hundred-year-old post-and-beam barn. Although it sits at the edge of Groton village, the restaurant actually has a small produce farm on the property, and while the beef cattle visible in the surrounding pastures aren't exactly those on the plates, the Black Angus steaks are simply perfect. At the same time, diners with smaller appetites and lesser means can enjoy the beef as a *steak-frites* or the Gibbet Hill meat loaf. The restaurant's setting is such a bucolic idyll that it's frequently used for weddings, but when there are no nuptials it can be casual enough that bicyclists touring the country roads often fill the grill on weekend afternoons.

The Herb Lyceum at Gilson's Farm, 368 Main St., (Route 119), Groton, MA 01450; (978) 448-6499; gilsons lyceum.com; New American; $$$$. Tending herbs on a historic farm is certainly a reflective way of life, and since David Gilson established the Herb Lyceum in 1989, he's been the philosophical sage behind the Friday and Saturday night dinners. Diners are encouraged to come early for the six-course prix fixe so that they can wander about the place, inspecting the gardens and sipping wine on the terrace. As Gilson tells diners, the Slow Food philosophy prevails here. The dishes typically feature produce and herbs from the farm, but only one menu is offered per month. So if everyone in your party isn't on board with roast leg of lamb, then you might want to wait until the main course is chicken ballotine with brown butter risotto. Vegetable CSA shares are also available at the farm.

Ithaki, 25 Hammatt St., Ipswich, MA 01938; (978) 356-0099; ithakicuisine.com; Greek; $$–$$$. The first hint at Ithaki's cuisine is provided by the exterior: four Corinthian columns supporting an angled pediment in imitation of the Parthenon. The Greek and Mediterranean cooking is far more up to date, and the stylish interior is purely contemporary. Ithaki is famous for its delectable version of moussaka: layers of potato and eggplant covered in béchamel and topped with shaved Romano cheese.

J. T. Farnham's, 88 Eastern Ave., Essex, MA 01929; (978) 768-6643; Seafood; $$. This "in the rough" clam shack has picnic tables on a salt marsh. Locals debate whether the **Clam Box** (see p. 100),

Farnham's, or **Woodman's** (see p. 106) is best, with 10th-generation Yankees usually favoring Farnham's for a lighter batter and creamier cole slaw.

Kelly's Roast Beef, 410 Revere Beach Blvd., Revere, MA 02151; (781) 284-9129; kellysroastbeef.com; Casual American; $. This year-round kiosk has been a Revere Beach fixture since the days when only sailors and tough guys sported tattoos. The ostensible specialty is the sliced roast beef sandwich, but the perfectly fried seafood is an even better choice. Order fish-and-chips or a fried shrimp basket, wander across the road to the beach to sit on the seawall, and munch away as the waves roll in and the jetliners swoop down to land at nearby Logan Airport. Just beware of the very aggressive seagulls who will do their best to claim their share of your meal.

L'Andana, 86 Cambridge St., Burlington, MA 01803; (781) 270-0100; landanagrill.com; Italian; $$$–$$$$. Chef-Restaurateur Jamie Mammano says he modeled this restaurant on a trattoria in the Tuscan countryside, though this location in the tangle of interstate highways, Route 3 spurs, and back ways to the Burlington Mall is not exactly a picturesque hillside dotted with olive trees. That said, Mammano really does know Tuscan food and his iteration of it at this big-occasion subur-ban restaurant leans strongly on the wood grill and dry-aged American beef. (Veal chops, salmon, and swordfish are also available grilled.) Pastas are available as smaller *primi* plates or larger *secondi*. Even they tend to be big and hearty, though there is a nice delicacy to the tortel-lini stuffed with crabmeat and served with a puree of sweet peas and  a Parmesan cream. The dessert menu throws aside all Tuscan restraint. Our favorite might be the *ciambella* of apple cider doughnut rounds with crème anglaise and homemade cider glaze. The Tuscan, Abruzzese, and Piemontese reds on the wine list are great food wines at fair prices.

Lanna Thai Diner, 901 Main St., Woburn, MA 01801; (781) 932-0394; lannathaidiner.com; Thai; $. All diners serve comfort food, but this 1952 stainless steel and enamel beauty does it with a twist. Only open for lunch and dinner, the diner is dedicated to Thai street food. So instead of burgers and fries or eggs and hash, the kitchen whips up generous plates of pad thai and tamarind duck. Instead of banana cream pie, dessert might be deep-fried bananas wrapped in egg-roll skin or a choice of ginger or green tea ice cream. Lanna Thai is one of the rare Thai restaurants that specify the heat levels of its dishes and proudly announces, "We do not use MSG."

Lobster Pool, 329 Granite St. (Route 127), Rockport, MA 01966; (978) 546-7808; lobsterpoolrestaurant.com; Seafood; $–$$. This unpretentious beachside seafood shack (delicious chowders, big portions of grilled fish, sweet steamed clams) also has one of the best locations on Cape Ann. Time your visit to sit out on the back deck and watch the sun set over Folly Cove. Open Apr through Nov.

Longfellow's Wayside Inn, 72 Wayside Inn Rd., Sudbury, MA 01776; (978) 443-1776 or (800) 339-1776; wayside.org; Traditional American; $$–$$$. This country inn has been taking in and feeding travelers since 1716, though it finally became famous when Henry Wadsworth Longfellow used it as a setting for his 1863 book, *Tales from a Wayside Inn.* The setting couldn't be more colonial, although the cozy Tap Room with its wood-burning fireplace is actually a 1929 addition, built by Henry Ford back when he was thinking of making the place a base for his American history village. In cool weather, the Tap Room is a favorite for cozy dining. Diners migrate to an outdoor patio in summer. While some of the menu has a more modern flair, several dishes are Wayside Inn traditions, including the crumb-topped lobster pie with béchamel sauce. The pastry cook works wonders with flour and meal ground at the mill along a stream on the property, producing airy

Steak and Clam Road Feasts

Northeastern Massachusetts has some of the state's strangest restaurant architecture and signage. The strangest of all must be the **Hilltop Steak House** in Saugus, founded by Frank Giuffrida, a butcher from Lawrence, in 1961. The 68-foot-tall neon cactus sign is visible from miles away, and the herd of fiberglass steers out front leaves no question that this place is about meat, plain and simple. Hilltop is as legendary for its long waits (reservations for parties of eight or more only) as for the 18-ounce bone-in sirloin. The restaurant also has an on-premises butcher shop, should you still be hungry.

Somewhat more subtle, **Clam Box of Ipswich** was built in 1938 by Dick Greenleaf to resemble the open-flapped pasteboard box in which fried clams are served. Some aficionados of North Shore bivalves rank the Clam Box above **Woodman's** (see p. 106), citing superior breading (pastry flour followed by cornmeal) and the unique blend of meat and vegetable fats in which they're fried. Enjoy the dining room or the outdoor picnic tables. Open June through Sept; call for spring and fall hours.

Hilltop Steak House, 855 Broadway (Route 1), Saugus, MA 01906; (781) 233-7700; hilltopsteakhouse.com.

Clam Box of Ipswich, 246 High St. (Route 1A), Ipswich, MA 01938; (978) 356-9707; ipswichma.com/clambox.

breads and corn muffins, delicate pie crust, and silky Indian pudding. The flour and meal are also available in the gift shop.

The Market Restaurant, 33 River Rd., Gloucester, MA 01930; (978) 282-0700; themarketrestaurant.com; New American; $$–$$$. Chefs Nico Monday and Amelia O'Reilly met when both worked for Alice Waters at Chez Panisse in California. The Market is where they spend their summers (late May through Sept) spreading the Waters' fresh-market gospel on Lobster Cove in Annisquam. The dockside digs might look like a clam shack, but the cooking is pure New American joy, drawing principally on the local catch and the bounty of nearby fields. The menu is usually about nine items long and changes almost completely every day.

Mark's Deli, 2 Railroad Sq., Haverhill, MA 01832; (978) 374-9402; Casual American; $. We consider this neighborhood diner one of the unsung treasures of Haverhill. With just 12 stools, four booths, and two tables, seating can be tight, but everyone is so friendly at this Greek-American diner that you'll soon be chums with staff and customers alike. It's open daily for breakfast and lunch, but only for breakfast on Sunday.

Nancy's Airfield Cafe, 302 Boxboro Rd., Stow, MA 01775; (978) 897-3934; nancysairfieldcafe.com; Casual American; $–$$. On HungryTravelers.com, we do a series of popular posts loosely titled "What to eat at the airport in ____." If you find yourself at the Minuteman Air Field in Stow, there's really only one choice, but it's a great one. Nancy McPherson serves a menu that she calls "autobiographical" because it reflects her taste memories from years spent abroad. For example, while her BBQ burger is a pretty good sweet and smoky piece of charbroiled Angus, the lamb burger with *berbere* spices and a salad of chopped cucumber with strained yogurt is pure Middle Eastern. She serves breakfast and lunch Wednesday through Sunday and a fancier dinner menu on Friday and Saturday night. As international as McPherson's tastes might be, her loyalties are to producers close to home. Most vegetables and cheeses, a lot of meats and dairy products, and even some of the wine and hard cider are local. And with big plate-glass windows overlooking the airstrip, the entertainment is free.

Organic Garden Cafe, 294 Cabot St., Beverly, MA 01915; (978) 922-0004; organicgardencafe.com; Vegetarian; $–$$. This Beverly outpost has weathered many a food fad since it opened in 1999 as a vegetarian organic restaurant that specializes in raw food as well as vegan and gluten-free cuisine. Most "cooking" is done in dehydrators, but some very inventive dishes result—nut butter ravioli in shells of red beet with a cashew Alfredo sauce, for example. All meals come with a healthy side of nutritional philosophy.

Red Rock Bistro, 141 Humphrey St., Swampscott, MA 01907; (781) 595-1414; redrockbistro.com; New American; $$–$$$. Almost every table at Red Rock has a water view, and in warm weather, there's the option of dining on the two outdoor patios with waves crashing below. In any season, try to time dinner for a great sunset view of the Boston skyline. The menu is primarily seafood (with steak, coq au vin, and pork ribs for non-fish eaters), with simple dishes such as grilled swordfish with mashed chickpeas and a salad of roasted red peppers with feta cheese. During the summer, simple fish shack fare (fried clams, lobster rolls) is also available at a take-out window on the sidewalk. A range of choices from challah french toast to *salade niçoise* or shrimp flatbread pizza make Sunday brunch very popular.

Salem Beer Works, 278 Derby St., Salem, MA 01970; (978) 745-2337; beerworks.net; Brewery; $$. One of the state's pioneer brewpubs, Salem Beer Works sits on the waterfront like a pirate at the mouth of a harbor, beguiling passersby with the wafting aromas of freshly brewed ales and hot charcuterie. Big TV screens highlight sporting events, and soaring ceilings give the room a warehouse-like feel, so it doesn't seem crowded, even when every seat is taken. Best food bets are the barbecue plates; best beers, the simple ales. Beer purists might look askance, but the menu even offers a "Beer Float" for dessert. Pick your beer and a scoop of ice cream to top it off.

Salt Kitchen & Rum Bar, 1 Market St., Ipswich, MA 01938; (978) 356-0002; saltkitchenandrumbar.com; New American; $–$$. Working closely with Privateer Rum Distillers, also in Ipswich, Salt is the Essex County answer to a gastropub—except that the drinking emphasis is on New England's historically favorite spirit, rum. Lots of little plates are available for snacking. They range from cheddar polenta with Cajun spiced shrimp (a variant on shrimp and grits) to lobster poutine to duck ravioli with hoisin sauce for dipping. There's a certain cheekiness to the kitchen. The "fish selection" on the menu is honestly described as "whatever we feel like cooking." Sandwiches include the requisite beef and tuna burgers but also stretch to include a lobster Reuben. Someone should have thought of that long ago. Maybe the Privateer Cask was the inspiration.

Scratch Kitchen, 245 Derby St., Salem, MA 01970; (978) 741-2442; scratchkitchensalem.com; Casual American; $. This sandwich shop with a local bent and an extensive wine list is just what the doctor ordered for Salem. The Carolina-style pulled pork and dry-rubbed smoked brisket are both superior to other barbecue in town, and while the BLT probably can't live up to the Phantom Gourmet's billing as "best ever," it's pretty good if you like artisanal bacon with hard rind left on. Burgers are exquisite, especially with house-made onion jam, and the wines are available by the glass or bottle. Bacon powder on the french fries turns them into a delicious food group all their own.

There's also a lot of beer, some on draft, almost all of it micro- or nano-brewed—except for the retro versions of Narragansett.

Stonehedge Inn, 160 Pawtucket Blvd., Tyngsboro, MA 01879; (978) 649-4400; stonehedgeinnandspa.com; New American; $$$$. The heart of the Stonehedge Inn's country getaway is the gourmet experience of Left Bank restaurant and the world-class 100,000-plus-bottle Stonehedge cellars. Proprietor Levent Bozkurt has been buying case upon case of great wines for many years, laying them aside until they're ready to drink. This is one of the rare places in New England where you can taste verticals of famous Bordeaux and Burgundies. Stonehedge also offers frequent wine dinners, pairing the courses with the wines of one company. The winemaker or estate owner is usually on hand to discuss the wines. Left Bank serves a seasonal cuisine driven largely by what's available from nearby fishermen and farmers. For a lighter repast, book a table for weekend afternoon tea with a full complement of dainty sandwiches, sweet scones, tea cookies, and other pastries or enjoy small plates in the lounge.

Tomasso Trattoria, 154 Turnpike Rd., Southborough, MA 01772; (508) 481-8484; tomassotrattoria.com; Italian; $$. An authentically Italian (not Italian-American) casual restaurant, Tomasso uses local produce, fish, and meat along with Italian technique, cheese, and wine to create a thoroughgoing Italy-in-America experience. His tiny artichokes fried in olive oil or his citrus-marinated olives are perfect antipasti, and his pastas confound a lot of diners used to American conventions. For example, he doesn't serve ravioli—he serves a single raviolo filled with black truffle mascarpone and egg yolk. The grilled *secondi* cover all the bases (beef, pork, chicken, flounder, and a member of the bass family) in preparations that vary with the season. The restaurant has as good an Italian wine list as you'll find in Massachusetts and holds a number of educational wine events to acquaint customers with the possibilities.

Turner's Seafood Grill & Market, 506 Main St., Melrose, MA 02176; (781) 662-0700; turners-seafood.com; Seafood; $$. You have to love a seafood house where the first thing you see when you walk in the door is a vast cooler where the fish of the day sprawl on a bed of crushed ice and lobsters swim in the adjacent bubbling tank of seawater. Not to be confused with the Westin Copley Place fish restaurant of a similar name, this Melrose spot strikes just about the perfect match of casual, tavern-like atmosphere with spectacular fish and simple but often inventive preparations. When the eyes are clear and the scales are clamped down tight on the flesh, fish needs little more than a good sear over a hot fire. But the chefs here can do more. Orange ginger salmon is a good variation on an old baked salmon favorite, for example, while tossing the calamari with hot cherry peppers gives those little squid a delicious piquancy. Every Sunday afternoon the restaurant offers a bargain fixed-price three-course menu. The kids' menu even includes fish sticks. The same folks own a seafood distribution operation on the Gloucester waterfront and sell retail fish at **Gloucester Seafood Market,** 4 Smith St., Gloucester, MA 01930; (978) 281-7172. For Turner's Seafood Grill's recipe for **Classic New England Oyster Stew,** see p. 286.

The Willow Rest, 1 Holly St., Gloucester, MA 01930; (978) 283-2417; willowrest.com; Casual American; $. This breakfast and lunch spot in Annisquam/Riverdale is a favorite with neighborhood artists for the ridiculously affordable frittata of the day and the juicy burgers served on a St. Joseph's roll. During the busy summer season, owner Melissa Donati stocks fresh produce and cheese and makes lunch and dinner entrees, which are also available to go.

Woodman's of Essex, 121 Main St. (Route 133), Essex, MA 01929; (978) 768-6057; woodmans.com; **Seafood; $–$$.** "'Twas a brave man who first did eat an oyster," quipped author Jonathan Swift, but that pioneer couldn't hold a candle to Lawrence "Chubby" Woodman, who seems to have been the first to bread and fry a clam. He did so in 1914, and his once-tiny seafood shack has prospered and grown into the iconic Woodman's of Essex, where the family continues the tradition. The "in-the-rough" seafood restaurant is less rough than others, offering spacious and sunny dining rooms as well as picnic tables and a large parking lot (an important feature in parking-starved Essex, one of the great historic shipbuilding towns of the North Shore). Woodman's also ships live lobsters and clams.

Specialty Stores, Markets & Producers

A & J King Artisan Bakers, 48 Central St., Salem, MA 01970; (978) 744-4881; ajkingbakery.com; **Bakery.** Andy and Jackie King have a thing about the crackle of the salted crust of a baguette, the elastic crumb of ciabatta, and the perfect flake of a great croissant. So do we. In addition to a wide range of mouthwatering breads, they also make delicious little tarts and sticky buns, and offer deli sandwiches at midday. The chocolate cinnamon tarts, often offered in the fall, rely on the dark goodness of Somerville's **Taza** chocolate (see p. 179).

Alfalfa Farm Winery, 267 Rowley Bridge Rd., Topsfield, MA 01983; (978) 774-0014; alfalfafarmwinery.com; **Wine, Beer & Spirits.** This farmstead winery makes fruit wines and some grape wines from French-American hybrid grapes grown on their own property, as well as wines from European wine grapes grown elsewhere in Essex County. The winery is popular for social events, and is open for tastings on Sunday afternoons in the summer and weekend after-noons in the fall.

Annarosa's Bakery, 175 Elm St. (Route 110), Salisbury, MA 01952; (978) 499-8839; annarosas.com; Bakery. When you hand-fashion 350 or more loaves a day, it's okay to take a three-day hiatus every week. For Jane Kenny and Bill Malatesta, the baker-owners of Annarosa's, Sunday through Tuesday are their days of rest. But then Bill is already baking at 3 a.m. for the  rest of the week, with a special emphasis on perfect French baguettes with a crisp crust, open crumb, and tantalizing fresh-bread aroma. The other "daily bread" at Annarosa's is the rustic Italian cousin, ciabatta. They also bake an organic seeded baguette on Wednesday, an organic six-grain bread on Thursday, and an heirloom whole-wheat bread on Saturday. Kenny and Malatesta warn against storing their breads in the refrigerator as the chilling accelerates the process of going stale.

Chococoa Cafe, 50 Water St., Newburyport, MA 01950; (978) 499-8889; chococoabaking.com; Bakery. Co-owners Alan Mons and Julie Ganong are always making whoopie—specializing in a refined version of that childish treat that they sell big time for showers and weddings. The Whoopie, as they dub their creation, is also central to this cafe in The Tannery building, but you can also purchase a number of other baked treats and some pretty good espresso.

Cote's Market, 175 Salem St., Lowell, MA 01854; (978) 458-4635; Grocery. Ti-Jean of Jack Kerouac's novels and memoirs probably shopped at Cote's Market—certainly most of the French Canadians of Lowell have since it was established in 1917. In addition to standard groceries, the market offers a tremendous array of prepared French-Canadian comfort foods—everything from "Chinese pie" (*pâté chinois,*

LEARN TO COOK

Whether you are looking to sharpen your techniques or expand your culinary horizons by tackling a new cuisine, you'll find that great equipment helps to make great cooks.

Culinary Underground School for Home Cooks, 21 Turnpike Rd. (Route 9), Southborough, MA 01772; (508) 904-6589; culinaryunderground.com. Founder Lori Leinbach may have moved her cooking school out of her home and into a well-equipped commercial kitchen with Wolf and Subzero appliances, but she is still committed to nurturing the time-honored tradition of home cooking. We are sure many North Shore families are grateful for her efforts. Many of the classes offered by Leinbach and her staff are suitable for beginners, while others branch out from basic techniques to explore international cuisines or the subtleties of baking.

Eurostoves, Commodore Plaza, 45 Enon St., Beverly, MA 01915; (877) 232-0007; eurostoves.com. This top-of-the-line retailer does indeed carry European stoves such as AGA from England or Bertazzoni and Verona from Italy along with small appliances and kitchenware. They also offer an ambitious schedule of cooking classes in their Culinary Centre. Master a new cuisine or two and you'll feel worthy of a $4,000 stove.

or shepherd's pie) to a *tourtière* (ground pork pie) to whoopie pies and *fêves au lard,* or baked beans. The beans made Cote's famous. They age their white pea beans for a year so they cook up with a tooth, and they sell about 300 pounds a week. They're available "with" or "without." That's with a nice big chunk of salt pork, or not. The market also offers hamburger ground to order.

Danish Pastry House, 330 Boston Ave., Medford, MA 02155; (781) 396-8999; danishpastryhouse.com; Bakery Cafe. The students, faculty, and staff at Tufts University are a lucky bunch. This cheery bakery cafe is near the campus and has all manner of great choices for breakfast, lunch, and sweet snacks. You haven't tasted authentic Danish pastry until you've had a Kringle—the perfect combination of buttery pastry, marzipan, and almonds. Lunch options include salads, panini sandwiches, and crepes, such as the "Perfect Lunch" of Black Forest ham, cheese, and basil pesto. For an afternoon pickup, the "floderbolle," an almond cookie filled with Italian meringue and then dipped in chocolate, is perfect with tea or coffee. For the Watertown baking facility, see p. 204.

Dante Confections, 199 Boston Rd., Billerica, MA 01821; (800) 933-2683; danteconfections.com; Chocolatier. Piano maker turned chocolatier Santi Falcone is such a perfectionist that it takes months of experimentation before he introduces a new truffle flavor. Fortunately, he's been at it awhile, so he has 26 flavors for you to enjoy as you wait for the next great inspiration. Falcone hasn't forgotten his Sicilian origins: He makes an amaretto truffle and another flavored with limoncello. Falcone also has his own version of a classic turtle that he calls Caramel Chocolate Nut Oysters.

Fisherman's Fleet, 689 Salem St., Malden, MA 02108; (781) 322-5200; fishermansfleet.com; Fishmonger. This retail fish market is just the tip of the iceberg for this fourth-generation family-owned company that packs and ships top seafood around the country. Walk in the door and you're hit with the fresh, clean smell of the sea and confronted with tanks of swimming lobsters segregated by size. The Graffeos started shipping fish to friends in Florida in 1996, and the direct-sale business has exploded since, with good-value clambakes and lobster bakes that include everything but the pot. The shop is often ice-cold—all the better to keep the fish fresh. We particularly like being able to point to a slab of tuna or a side of swordfish and explain just how thick we'd like the steaks cut.

H Mart, 3 Old Concord Rd., Burlington, MA 01803; (781) 221-4570; hmart.com; Grocery. This first Massachusetts outpost of H Mart, the New Jersey–based chain of Korean supermarkets, is heaven for Korean cooks. Dozens of *banchan*—dishes of seasoned vegetables, seaweed, wild herbs, and tiny fish—are sold to save home cooks from the intensive labor necessary to produce the bowls themselves. The store carries at least 20 varieties of kimchi—and special kimchi refrigerators for making and storing the fermented cabbage at home. The seafood section includes crock after crock of salt-preserved fish items like pollock roe while tofu fans can pick and choose their favorite brands in every degree of firmness. Tastings are offered on weekends and if shopping makes you really hungry, there's a food court serving a range of Korean dishes.

Harbor Sweets, 85 Leavitt St., Salem, MA 01970; (978) 745-7648; harborsweets.com; Chocolatier. In 1973 Ben Strochecker decided he wanted to create the best piece of candy in the world. What he ended up with was the Sweet Sloop, a sailboat-shaped piece of almond butter-crunch covered in white chocolate and dipped in dark chocolate and crushed pecans. Although Harbor Sweets now produces a broad line of premium chocolates, the sailboats still lead the company's regatta. Strochecker now spends his time on the tennis court while former part-time candy dipper Phyllis LeBlanc has risen through the ranks to become CEO and owner. Harbor Sweets chocolates are also found in hundreds of gourmet and gift shops across the country. Call for hours for factory tours.

Harrows Chicken Pies, 126 Main St., Reading, MA 01867; (781) 944-0410; 352 Broadway, Saugus, MA 01906; (781) 231-7410; 275 Mystic Ave., Medford, MA 02155; (781) 306-0410; 345 Main St., Tewksbury, MA 01876; (978) 858-0411; chickenpie.com; Specialty Shop. This mini-chain of chicken pie operations started in Reading in the 1930s and though it's expanded over the years, there's no mystery to the product. The pies consist of slow-cooked white meat chicken and gravy made daily from scratch, all encased in flaky pastry. The cooks also make the pastry daily along with sides of mashed potatoes and squash. Pies are available with just chicken or with chicken mixed with potatoes and carrots. Call ahead and you can even pick it up warm!

Haverhill Beef Co., 117 Merrimack St., Haverhill, MA 01830; (978) 374-4795; haverhillbeef.com; Butcher. Old-fashioned full-service butchers and meat markets like Haverhill Beef are a vanishing breed. Established in 1952, the staff can advise you on how to handle each cut and what to buy for a specific recipe. Want to make a traditional osso buco? Come here for the veal shanks. Want to roast a saddle of lamb? No problem—just call a day in advance. The staff make a lot of ready-to-cook foods as well, including meatballs, stuffed pork chops, stuffed mushrooms, and seafood chowder. For Haverhill Beef's recipe for **Braciola,** see p. 299.

Il Pastificio, 328 Broadway, Everett, MA 02149; (617) 387-3630; Specialty Shop. This small shop has more varieties of fresh pasta than we've ever seen before, and shopping here is like getting a crash course in the do's and don'ts of southern Italian cooking. Select a pasta and staff will advise on which homemade sauce makes the best match. A fine capellini, for example, requires a light marinara sauce that keeps the pasta loose and easy to turn. *Bombolotti,* a chunky tube with a star-shaped interior, can hold up to hearty Bolognese sauces (with or without mushrooms). Sicilian-style twisted *cannolicchio* has enough grooves to hold rich sauces such as pesto or Alfredo. Once you've got the pasta and sauce, you can round out the meal with homemade spumoni ice cream and a selection of Italian cookies for dessert.

Ipswich Shellfish Fish Market, 8 Hayward St., Ipswich, MA 01938; (978) 356-6941; ipswichfishmarket.com; Fishmonger. Ipswich Shellfish is a giant wholesale distributor of fresh fish and shellfish, and this modern market adjacent to the warehouses and shipping terminal puts owner Chrissi Pappas's personal stamp on the operation. In addition to a full line of the freshest catch (and all the shellfish you can imagine), the shop also offers prepared seafood entrees such as lobster pie, chowders, and stuffed fish. The shelves, refrigerator cases, and freezers are filled with imported cheeses, smoked fish, oils, vinegars, mustards, breads, pastas, sauces, and condiments. Frozen ravioli are filled with shrimp, lobster, or duck and brie. You can also arrange to have lobster and Ipswich clams shipped anywhere in the country. For Chrissi Pappas's recipe for **Rice, Lobster, and Cucumber Salad,** see p. 291.

Kane's Donuts, 120 Lincoln Ave., Saugus, MA 01906; (781) 233-8499; kanesdonuts.com; Bakery. Insomniac doughnut junkies can get a fix at Kane's from 3:30 a.m. every day. Established in 1955, this internationally acclaimed small-town bakery makes plain, chocolate coconut, honey-dip, and a myriad of other doughnuts so large that you'd need a bowl of coffee to dunk them. The classic cake-style plain doughnuts—the gold standard among doughnut aficionados—have a delicate crumb, a light texture, and just the slightest hint of nutmeg. Watch for the pink neon sign—it really pops in the hours before sunrise.

Karl's Sausage Kitchen & European Market, 1 Bourbon St., Peabody, MA 01960; (978) 854-6650; karlssausage.com; Grocery. Forget the old line about not wanting to see sausage being made. The process at Karl's is so clean and delectable that you need never wonder about sausage again. Most of the house specialties are German and other central European classics—knackwurst, weisswurst, beerwurst, liverwurst. . . . The deli sells the whole range of sausages as well as a good array of cheeses and allied European foodstuffs, like pickles and mustards. The cafe is open for breakfast, lunch, and early dinner serving pastries and pretzels, sausages, potato pancakes, and (naturally) beer.

Katz Bagel Bakery, 139 Park St., Chelsea, MA 02150; (617) 884-9738; Bakery.  The Katz (pronounced *kates*) family has been making and selling bagels from this location since 1940, when Chelsea was a city of Jewish immigrants and supported a dozen synagogues. Although now more than half Hispanic, Chelsea still has pockets of European Jewish immigrants, and Richard Katz carries on his Russian immigrant father's line of work for an increasingly diverse clientele. His old-fashioned New York–style bagels are smaller than the homogenized and Americanized versions prepared by the fast-food giants, and far tastier. They're crunchy on the outside, soft on the inside, and they come in garlic, raisin, plain, egg, pumpernickel, sissel, and onion. The bakery also sells "teething bagels"—a dozen small bagels on a string to help babies through the pain of teething.

Mozzarella House, 355 Broadway, Everett, MA 02149; (617) 387-6810; mozzarellahouse.com; Cheese. Located in a clapboard building at the edge of a parking lot, the Mozzarella House can be hard to find. But it's worth the search to buy the soft young cheeses—mozzarella, burrata, ricotta, and "fresh cheese" similar to farmer cheese that is especially popular at Easter. The facility also makes the firmer scamorza, aged for three to four months. Much of the output of this small operation goes to restaurants and grocery stores, but you get it cheapest and freshest from the source.

Mrs. Nelson's Candy House, 292 Chelmsford St., Chelmsford, MA 01824; (978) 256-4061; Chocolatier. An entire display case facing the entrance at this old-fashioned candy shop at the edge of a strip mall is filled with milk, dark, and white chocolate barks variously combined with pecans, cashews, almonds, nut crunch, and thin slabs of peanut butter or mocha candy. Barks are a specialty of Mrs. Nelson's, though this venerable candymaker also handcrafts fine dipped chocolates and slabs of rich fudge. With advance notice, you can have boxes  of chocolates customized with your initials. Mrs. Nelson may have retired in the 1980s, but the classic candies continue.

Mystic Brewery, 174 Williams St., Chelsea, MA 02150; (617) 800-9023; mystic-brewery.com; Brewery. We've always thought that the transubstantiation of malted grain into beer was a pretty mystical event, and we're glad to see that the folks at Mystic Brewery are happy to play along, even if the establishment is named for the river rather than the brewer's spiritual aspirations. Mystic specializes in various twists on a saison beer. Although saisons are typically light and low in alcohol, Mystic's Belgian-style saisons inevitably top 7% ABV. The Mystic Saison is their take on a Belgian farmhouse ale, and it's made with a wine yeast. Think of it as a beer-drinker's answer to California

Chardonnay. Mystic Descendant is the other extreme—also fermented with a wine yeast to something like a cross between a dry Irish stout and a hefty English porter. The dark malts and touch of molasses give it a rich cherrywood flavor that complements red meats. Think of it as an alternative to a glass of Merlot. The tasting room gives out free 2-ounce samples and sells growlers (and refills). The brewery is open Thurs and Fri from 3 to 7 p.m. and Sat noon to 4 p.m. Tours are given on Sat.

Night Shift Brewing, 3 Charlton St., #9, Everett, MA 02149; (617) 294-4233; nightshiftbrewing.com; Brewery. Set in the industrial hinterlands off Route 99 a few miles north of Sullivan Square, Night Shift is a nanobrewery that represents the dreams come true of a trio of home brewers. True to its name, the little taproom at the brewery is open weeknight evenings as well as Saturday afternoons. Visitors can get free samples of whichever beers are on draft, as well as full drafts. Bottles and growlers to go are also available. The brewers decided that it wasn't worth going into business unless they were doing something distinctive, so their two year-round standards are unusual. Trifecta is a Belgian pale ale of gentle malts, zingy hops, and vanilla beans brewed with three different Trappist yeasts. The resulting ale has a bold head and a clear, clean, but full-bodied taste. The Viva Habanera is a very different beer—a rye ale smoothed with agave nectar and given a mouth-filling heat with habañero peppers. The brewery also does a series of seasonal Berlin sour ales; the Somer Weiss (in honor of Somerville) has tangy lemongrass and ginger in the mix.

Peabody Bread Co., 168 Main St., Peabody, MA 01960; (978) 854-5280; peabodybread.com; Bakery Cafe. Daniela Deoliveira opened her modest bakery cafe to offer the taste of home to the North Shore's Brazilian immigrants, but it has become a showcase of Brazilian sweet and savory pastry for all of her neighbors. The fried soft pastry known as a *pastel* comes with a choice of cheese, chicken, or beef fillings, while diners with bigger appetites might prefer the *empadão*, which the bakery describes as a Brazilian chicken pie. Everything is available to go, but there are also a few seats to enjoy breakfast or lunch—complete with a steaming cup of Brazilian coffee.

Prides Crossing Confections, 590 Hale St., Prides Crossing (Beverly), MA 01965; (978) 927-2185; pridescrossingconfections .com; Chocolatier. The green miniature chalet-style building at the commuter rail stop might look like a train station, but it's the home of Christopher Flynn's candy-making operation. While Flynn makes outstanding clusters, barks, and soft-center chocolates, he's best known for his creamy caramels, either coated with chocolate or as the body of his nut-studded, chocolate-coated turtles.

Roy Moore Lobster Company, 39 Bearskin Neck, Rockport, MA 01966; (978) 546-6696; Fishmonger. You can buy live clams, crab, and lobsters here, but most people come to eat them on the premises, preferably out back on the deck, looking across to Motif No. 1. This may be the most authentic bit of old Bearskin Neck left in a district where tourism has otherwise overwhelmed the original reasons to visit. BYOB. Open late March through Oct.

Ryan & Wood Distilleries, 15 Great Republic Dr., Gloucester, MA 01930; (978) 281-2282; ryanandwood.com; Wine, Beer & Spirits. This small-batch artisanal distillery calls itself "The Spirit of Cape Ann." Using just a 600-liter copper alembic still, Ryan & Wood crafts two clear spirits—a spicy Knockabout Gin named for the fishing schooners without a bowsprit and Beauport Vodka—as well as a pair of brown spirits. Folly Cove Rum is fermented from the traditional molasses and aged in charred white oak barrels, as is the Rye Whiskey fermented on the grains. Distillery tours are offered twice daily Mon through Sat.

Shubie's Liquor & Marketplace, 16 Atlantic Ave., Marble-head, MA 01945; (781) 631-0149; shubies.com; Wine, Beer & Spirits.
Shubie's modestly advertises itself as carrying the "best in specialty foods, cheeses, wines, and spirits," and it's the truth. What's even better is that they believe in letting customers taste before they buy, and there's usually an array of cheeses, salsas, crackers, and dips to whet your appetite. Still hungry? The FoodBar offers hot and cold sandwiches to take away or eat in the shop. The selection of wines from California, Australia, New Zealand, and Europe emphasizes small producers who supply quality for the dollar. The range of culinary oils and vinegars is broad, and the cheese case, while relatively small, includes a number of fine chèvres, some outstanding Dutch cheeses, and a few French options. Shubie's excels at prepared foods to reheat at home: maple–Dijon mustard grilled chicken, roasted vegetables, four-cheese lasagna, and rosemary beef stew.

Tito's Bakery, 333 Broadway, Chelsea, MA 02150; (617) 884-3313; Bakery. The Hispanic markets of eastern Massachusetts get many of their pastries from Tito's, but the sweets are sweetest at the source. Turnovers (empanadas) are filled with a range of luscious concoctions, from pineapple, guava, and apple to cheese and raspberry. The caramel-filled turnover—nuked for 10 seconds—is a hot taste of heaven. In addition to coffee and chocolate, you can get cool and creamy milk shakes with papaya, pineapple, or guanabana. Tito's style is more Argentine than Mexican, so there's also a thick flan and a scrumptious bread pudding.

Tuck's Candies, 15 Main St., Rockport, MA 01966; (978) 546-6352; tuckscandy.com; Chocolatier. Walter F. Tuck began making candies in Rockport in 1929 and established such a high standard that he became a Massachusetts confectionery hero—one of the true pioneers. Bob and Dan Tuck (second and third generation, respectively) continue the tradition. The chocolate-covered buttercrunch was Tuck's calling

The Saintly Sandwich

The bread makes the sandwich, proclaims the sign in the front window of Virgilio's Italian Bakery & Groceria, established in 1939 by Joseph Virgilio Sr. Fittingly, the bread in question is the St. Joseph roll, a pillowy white bread with a slight crunch to the crust, originally made on the saint's feast day. Now the rolls are baked daily in the shop's original round shape or as the submarine roll that is filled with Italian cold cuts, provolone cheese, lettuce, tomato, pickles, oil, and oregano to create Virgilio's signature St. Joseph Roll Sandwich. Joseph Virgilio invented the sandwich for the fishermen who would hang around the shop and his family continues the tradition, which is a good thing—aficionados say the sandwich can't be duplicated.

Virgilio's Italian Bakery & Groceria, 29 Main St., Gloucester, MA 01930; (978) 283-5295.

card for many years, but Tuck's has kept up with changing tastes: Some of the most popular candies now are the chocolate-covered pretzels, caramel nut patties, and fudge.

Turtle Alley Chocolates, 42 Rogers St., Gloucester, MA 01930; (978) 281-4000; 177 Essex St., Salem, MA 01970; (978) 740-0660; turtlealley.com; Chocolatier. The aroma of chocolate smacks you in the face as you walk in the door of the tiny Gloucester shop where the staff mixes fudge and hand-dips chocolates behind the counter. When owner Hallie Baker was growing up in Gloucester, she had a pet turtle—now she makes a whole menagerie of the sweet critters in milk, dark, and white chocolate with pecans, macadamias, almonds, and (her favorite) cashews. (She says the cashews look most like flippers.) The shop also produces truffles, brittles, and barks. Try the tulip—a Brazil nut wrapped in caramel, sprinkled with chocolate shots, and dipped in milk or dark chocolate.

Ye Olde Pepper Candy Company, 122 Derby St., Salem, MA 01970; (978) 745-2744; 59 Main St., North Andover, MA 01845; (978) 689-3636; peppercandy.net; Chocolatier. In business since 1806, this is possibly the oldest candy company in the country. The house specialty is the Gibralter, available in lemon or peppermint. The candy, which consists of sugar and oil, is hard when first made but mellows to the texture of an after-dinner mint and supposedly never spoils (a jar of Gibralters on the counter dates from 1830). The company claims the Gibralter is the first candy made commercially in the United States. Ye Olde Pepper also pioneered the Black Jack molasses stick candy, another American first. But they've kept up with the times, and you'll find a full assortment of hard candies and chocolates at this landmark store.

Farm Stands & PYOs

Apple Street Farm, 35 Apple St., Essex, MA 01929; (978) 890-7082; applestreetfarm.com. Chef Frank McClelland tends the gardens of this two-century-old former horse farm primarily to keep his Boston fine-dining restaurant **L'Espalier** (see p. 145) in all manner of fresh produce. But there's more growing here than even the patrons can consume, so Apple Street Farm offers produce and flower CSA shares as well as poultry CSA shares. There's a small farm stand open weekends late June to mid-October. Each month during the summer, McClelland offers outdoor four-course dinners with wine pairing at the farm. Details are announced on the website.

Autumn Hills Orchard, 495 Chicopee Row, Groton, MA 01450; (978) 448-8388; autumnhillsorchard.com. The vistas at Autumn Hills are some of the most jaw-dropping of any of the orchards in this region. 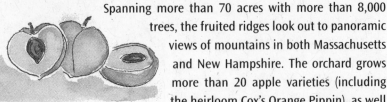 Spanning more than 70 acres with more than 8,000 trees, the fruited ridges look out to panoramic views of mountains in both Massachusetts and New Hampshire. The orchard grows more than 20 apple varieties (including the heirloom Cox's Orange Pippin), as well as peaches, pears, fall-bearing raspberries, and Italian prune plums that are favored for jam-making. All fruits are available pre-picked or as pick-your-own, beginning in late July.

Green Meadows Farm, 656 Asbury St., Hamilton, MA 01982; 978-468-3720; gmfarm.com. With 10 acres under vegetable cultivation and another three in berries, this organic farm produces a bumper crop of North Shore produce from early-season (fall-sown!) spinach to frost-kissed brussels sprouts around Christmas. Green Meadows offers CSA shares for produce and flowers, as well as meat shares for beef raised at another nearby farm or for their own chicken and pork. Surplus of everything is sold through the farm stand, which is open April through December. The farm also offers outdoor farm to table dinners monthly during the summer. Check website for dates and details.

Kimball Fruit Farm, 184 Hollis St., Pepperell, MA 01463; (978) 433-9751; kimballfruitfarm.com. From the time the Cambridge farmers' market opens in May until the middle of July, we wait with barely restrained anticipation for the first tiny but explosively delicious peaches from Kimball. They mark the beginning of an 8- or 9-week season of peach after peach, as we glut ourselves on stone fruit the way some people devour corn and tomatoes. Of course, Kimball also has great corn, great tomatoes, bushy fresh herbs, and some of the best, most vigorous leaf lettuces we've ever seen. And when peach season is done, there are still the apples (including hard-to-get Russets), which we keep buying until they're gone. Kimball sells extensively at farmers' markets around eastern Massachusetts, but it's worth a drive to the farm itself, located west of Lowell on the New Hampshire border. The farm stand is open June through Thanksgiving with pick-your-own strawberries, raspberries, apples, and pumpkins.

Marini Farm, 259 Linebrook Rd., Ipswich, MA 01938: (978) 356-0430; marinifarm.com. The farm stand is open June through October for vegetable sales, although you may see a table with early greens and asparagus in May. The CSA program is usually subscribed far in advance, since Marini has a reputation for extraordinary produce. The farm's 12 acres of strawberries open for pick-your-own around the second week of June.

Richardson's Farm, 156 S. Main St., Middleton, MA 01949; (978) 774-5450; richardsonsicecream.com. You can get freshly bottled milk at this charming dairy farm, but the main reason folks stop by is to indulge in the super-premium ice cream (more than 50 flavors) or the more virtuous 95 percent fat-free frozen yogurt (11 flavors). There are a lot of candy-bar or cookie combo flavors, but it's hard to beat simple vanilla, chocolate, or (for the adventurous) ginger. The farm has cows, sheep, chickens, and ducks to amuse the little ones, while teens might want to wander next door to the miniature courses of Golf Country.

Russell Orchards, 143 Argilla Rd., Ipswich, MA 01938; (978) 356-5366; russellorchardsma.com. Located on the road to Crane Reservation (and the famous bird-watching strand of Crane Beach), Russell Orchards is as much an agritourism destination as a farm, offering hayrides, barn tours, and group picnics. About 120 acres are under cultivation, and Russell has pick-your-own strawberries, raspberries, cherries, blueberries, and apples. The gift shop even sports its own bakery. The busy farm winery produces an extensive line of hard ciders and perries as well as a long list of fruit wines. We know no other commercial winery in New England that makes dandelion wine—an old-fashioned favorite that turns a summer yard blight into a winter delight. Other unusual fruit wines include elderberry and jostaberry, a cross between a gooseberry and a black currant. Open May through Nov.

Shaw Farm Dairy, 204 New Boston Rd., Dracut, MA 01826; (978) 957-0031; shawfarm.com. Founded in 1908, Shaw Farm is the last independent farm dairy in the greater Lowell area. It bottles fresh milk in glass quarts as well as plastic pints and makes its own ice cream; its products are widely available in northeastern Massachusetts at farm stands and some grocery stores. An expanded farm store at the dairy enables folks to pick up baked goods, meat, and cheese as well as milk products, including Shaw's New England Organic Creamery organic line. Ice cream remains a big seller—not surprising given that more than 60 flavors are available.

Smolak Farms, 315 S. Bradford St., North Andover, MA 01845; 978-682-6332; smolakfarms.com. Folks come from far and wide to the farm stand here just for Smolak Farms cider doughnuts, though the bakery also makes cookies, scones, and pies. The 300-acre farm grows all the usual crops and offers PYO strawberries, raspberries, sweet and tart cherries, currants, gooseberries, tomatoes, peaches, apples, pumpkins, and winter squashes. Open June through Oct, and then Dec for Christmas trees.

Farmers' Markets

Chelsea Farmers' Market, City Hall parking lot, 500 Broadway, Chelsea. Sat from 10 a.m. to 1 p.m., mid-July to Oct.

Haverhill Farmers' Market, 40 Bailey Blvd., Haverhill. Sat from 9 a.m. to 1 p.m., late-June to mid-Oct.

Ipswich Farmers' Market, Ebsco parking lot, Estes Street, Ipswich. Sat from 9 a.m. to 1 p.m., mid-July to mid-Oct.

Lawrence Farmers' Market, Appleton Way, Lawrence. Wed from 9 a.m. to 2 p.m., mid-July through Oct.

Lawrence Farmers' Market, 165 Park St., Lawrence. Sat from 9 a.m. to 3 p.m., July through Oct.

Lowell Farmers' Market, City Hall Plaza, Arcand Drive, Lowell. Fri from 2 to 7 p.m., July to mid-Oct.

Lynn Farmers' Market, intersection of Washington and Exchange Streets, Lynn. Thurs from 11 a.m. to 3 p.m., July through Oct.

Marblehead Farmers' Market, Middle School, Vine Street, Marblehead. Sat from 9 a.m. to noon, mid-June to mid-Nov.

Maynard Farmers' Market, Clock Tower Place, Mill Pond parking lot, Maynard. Sat from 9 a.m. to 1 p.m., late June to early Oct.

Melrose/Sally Frank's Farmers' Market, Bowden Park, Melrose. Thurs from 1 to 7 p.m., mid-June through Oct.

Topsfield Farmers' Market, Topsfield Fair Grounds, Route 1, Topsfield. Sat from 8 a.m. to noon, early July to late Sept.

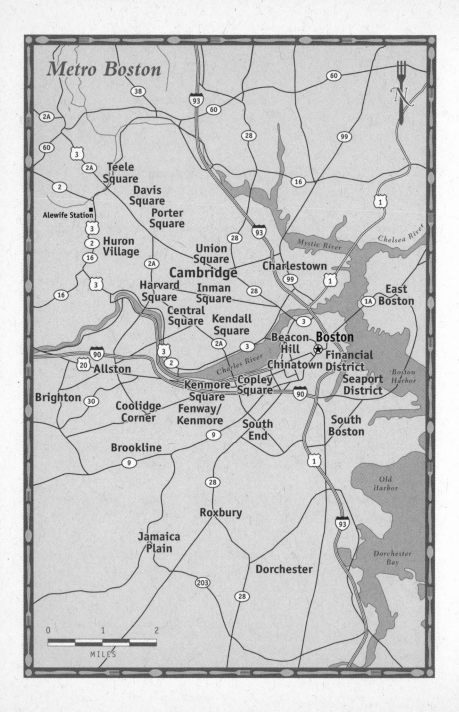

Metro Boston

It is no fluke that most of the Massachusetts restaurants with national or international reputations are found in metropolitan Boston. The city has thousands of places to eat—and several hundred where you can dine. While our *Food Lovers' Guide to Boston* goes into much greater depth, this chapter hits the historic restaurants, the kitchens of leading chefs, and a handful of special places that reflect their neighborhoods and hint at the city's cultural diversity. It covers the neighborhoods of Boston and the adjoining communities of Brookline, Cambridge, and Somerville. For ease of navigation, we've added neighborhoods and MBTA stops.

The dining scene—who's cooking where, what's the hot new dish, who has the best bartender—is constant grist for local press, Internet enthusiast sites, and casual conversation. Metro Boston also has an exciting mix of ethnic cultures and cuisines—from Spanish tapas to Vietnamese sandwiches to Salvadoran seafood to Polish pierogi. Several popular restaurants also serve food from the American South. In Boston, the venerable American myth of the melting pot yields to the modern paradigm of the multiethnic stew.

Although Greater Boston raises very little of its own food, it's an amazing place to shop—whether you're dickering over flats of fresh fruit with Haymarket vendors at the end of the day or wandering wide-eyed down the aisles of Kam Man Market in Dorchester, struck dumb by the unending choices. Fresh produce flows into the farmers' markets, fresh fish into the fishmongers. With the finest foods coming to Boston from all over the state—indeed, from all corners of the earth—the taste of the city is truly world class.

Foodie Faves

Antico Forno, 93 Salem St., North End, Boston, MA 02113; (617) 723-6733; anticofornoboston.com; Italian; $$; T: Haymarket. A neighborhood favorite since 1996, Antico Forno was among the first North End restaurants to cook most menu items in a wood-fired brick oven. From the stuffed eggplant on the antipasti menu to the baked pastas of the *primi* to the oven-roasted chicken and the wood-grilled swordfish of the *secondi,* there's no escaping the kiss of smoke and fire. Since the restaurant starts serving dinner in the late afternoon, many North Enders pop in for an early supper of one of the ample pizzas with a glass of house wine. Our favorite features homemade sausage and mozzarella, broccoli rabe, and cherry tomatoes.

Aquitaine, 569 Tremont St., South End, Boston, MA 02118; (617) 424-8577; aquitaineboston.com; French; $$$; T: Back Bay Station. Parisian bistro classics such as onion soup with sherry, chicken liver mousse terrine with mustard and cornichons, lemon sole meunière, and *filet au poivre* with cream and green peppercorns constitute comfort food in the South End. Aquitaine also offers daily *plats du jour* that can range from barbecue braised brisket to pan-roasted trout with almond puree, green beans, and figs. The *pommes frites* come with a delicious basil-garlic aioli—a French-Italian mixed marriage of pesto and mayonnaise. The wine list represents most of the regions of France and some of the bigger names in California.

Artú Rosticceria & Trattoria, 6 Prince St., North End, Boston, MA 02113; (617) 742-4336; T: Haymarket; 82 Charles St.,

Beacon Hill, Boston, MA 02114; (617) 227-9023; T: Charles Street; artuboston.com; Italian; $$. Artú's roasted meats set it apart, and the best—and least expensive—way to try them is to order a panini sandwich at lunch time. Choices from the rotisserie include chicken with tomato and basil; beef with lettuce, tomato, and cheese; and either leg of lamb or pork with marinated eggplant. That eggplant is also part of a delicious vegetable antipasto plate that makes a perfect accompaniment to the sandwiches or to a side dish of homemade meatballs with tomato sauce. A more traditional trattoria menu prevails at dinner, with pastas such as linguine with squid and mussels in tomato sauce and meat dishes including sweet Italian sausage with peppers and potatoes and veal stuffed with prosciutto, provolone, and mushrooms.

Ashmont Grill, 555 Talbot Ave., Dorchester, Boston, MA 02122; (617) 825-4300; ashmontgrill.com; New American; $$; T: Ashmont. A longtime Dorchester resident, restaurateur Chris Douglass was finally persuaded by his friends and neighbors to open this sassy, chic, and affordable restaurant in 2005. It's been mobbed ever since, and for good reason. Every Thursday is buck-a-shuck night for oysters, and Monday evening is "give-back" night, when part of the sales support a neighborhood charity. Bargains and bonhomie abound every night, with tasty starters like wood-grilled lamb sliders on focaccia with cucumber raita and crispy onion strings, and American bistro entrees like a roasted half chicken or oven-roasted flounder in a parsley-garlic sauce. The succinct wine list is packed with value-priced fun wines as unpretentious and delicious as the food. For a recipe for **Honey and Thyme Roasted Pears**, see p. 302.

Atasca Restaurant, 50 Hampshire St., Kendall Square, Cambridge, MA 02139; (617) 621-6991; atasca.com; Portuguese; $$;

T: Kendall Square. Located where Portuguese East Cambridge meets polyglot Kendall Square, Atasca specializes in elegant Portuguese food. There's a distinctly Azorean cast to the cuisine—such as the chicken breast sauteed with São Jorge cheese, linguiça, and white wine—but mainland classics are also a good bet. The *cataplana*, for example, is actually steamed in the copper vessel that gives the combo of clams, mussels, shrimp, onions, red peppers, prosciutto, and linguiça its name. True to its Portuguese roots, Atasca serves at least three *bacalhau* (salt cod) dishes every evening.

B&G Oysters, 550 Tremont St., South End, Boston, MA 02116; (617) 423-0550; bandgoysters.com; Seafood; $$$; T: Back Bay Station. This modern take on the classic oyster bar is a great place to hang in the South End. Hunker down around the marble bar surrounding the open kitchen in the winter; eat on the back patio in the summer. You can always count on a selection of a dozen different oysters drawn from America's three coasts, local classics like lobster and clam rolls, and a menu of Mediterranean seafood dishes such as pollock (aka "blue cod") with saffron-braised beans. The restaurant also offers its seafood shack items (like the BLT with lobster) for takeout.

Barking Crab, 88 Sleeper St., Waterfront, Boston, MA 02210; (617) 426-2722; barkingcrab.com; Seafood; $$; T: Court House (Silver Line). Nowhere in Boston will you get closer to the shoreline fish shack experience than at the Barking Crab, perched on the edge of Fort Point Channel. In fact, if you have a boat in Boston Harbor, you can tie up at the floating dock and walk up the ramp to dinner. Prices vary widely through the year with availability, but you can always count on local clams, oysters, mussels, and stuffed quahogs. It's unfortunate but true that many tourists gravitate to the formerly frozen Alaskan crab legs over the smaller and sweeter local Atlantic crabs, but the Barking Crab tries to have both, along with lots of lobster. In the summer, we like eating at the picnic tables in the open air, ordering the grilled catch of the day and a bucket of longnecks. It may not be Cape Cod, but it's a good facsimile.

Beacon Hill Bistro, 25 Charles St., Beacon Hill, Boston, MA 02114; (617) 723-1133; beaconhillhotel.com/bistro; French; $$$; T: Charles Street. This bistro in the Beacon Hill Hotel serves three meals a day, but it's no mere hotel restaurant. Breakfast service is aimed mainly at hotel guests, and the lunch menu is replete with American favorites like a grilled sirloin burger or a chicken club sandwich. At night, though, the kitchen swaps baseball hat for beret with dishes like roasted cod with a potato-apple mille-feuille, roasted monkfish with steamed mussels and hen of the woods mushrooms, or cassoulet with pork sausage and confit duck leg. House-made charcuterie and fresh oysters are available nightly as starters.

Blue, Inc., 131 Broad St., Financial District, Boston, MA 02110; (617) 261-5353; blueincboston.com; New American; $$–$$$; T: Aquarium. Chef Jason Santos (of the blue hair) loves to play with the tools of so-called molecular gastronomy, delighting in serving a liquid nitrogen salsa that smolders on the plate or an orange gel that turns into noodles when it hits hot broth. Probably the best way to ease into the cuisine is to drink at the bar and order from the "bucket list" that includes treats like rosemary and sea salt kettle corn, pretzel roll pizza, fresh cinnamon doughnuts, a liquid nitrogen milk shake, or truffle and Gouda tater tots. Think of the food as the kind of bistro fare you'd expect in the staff kitchen at Cirque du Soleil. So the braised Berkshire pork belly comes with crunchy barbecue grits and a poached pear and Gorgonzola salad. The signature duck confit is glazed with honey and hoisin sauce and served with a dish composed of sticky rice, mango, cashews, and coconut milk.

Boston Beer Works, 61 Brookline Ave., Fenway, Boston, MA 02215; (617) 536-2337; T: Kenmore Square; also 112 Canal St., Downtown, Boston, MA 02114; (617) 896-2337; T: North Station; beerworks.net; Brewery; $–$$. These cavernous brewpubs produce small batches of many beer types, ranging from IPAs to fruit-flavored wheat beers to heavy porters. They also have pretty good restaurants, with an emphasis on pastas, barbecue, salads, and a very hearty mixed-grill plate that will feed one linebacker or an entire table of sports fans. Unlike many brewpubs, these are as popular with women as with men.

Bricco, 241 Hanover St., North End, Boston, MA 02113; (617) 248-6800; bricco.com; Italian; $$$; T: Haymarket. In the summer, when the windows are thrown open and the party nearly spills onto the sidewalk, Bricco feels like it stepped from an Italian movie. One of the higher-end restaurants operated by Frank DePasquale, Bricco shows its owner's penchant for uncovering the best specialty ingredients. Let everyone else serve *prosciutto di Parma* on their antipasti menus—Bricco has the more delicate and nuanced *prosciutto di San Daniele.* Pastas at Bricco are truly something special, from the ravioli made around the corner at **DePasquale's Homemade Pasta Shoppe** (see p. 168) to the "Big Night" *timpano,* which is a drum-shaped pasta filled with meatballs and a slow-braised meat *ragù.* Oven-finished meat and fish dishes (grilled bone-in swordfish, oven-braised sea bass, veal osso buco with saffron risotto) tend to be large, but there's no harm in ordering a pasta each and splitting a *secondo.*

Butcher Shop, 552 Tremont St., South End, Boston, MA 02118; (617) 423-4800; thebutchershopboston.com; Mediterranean; $$; T: Back Bay Station. Rustic French and Italian cuisine—especially charcuterie—dominates the menu at this wine bar and full-service butcher shop modeled by Barbara Lynch on the *boucheries* of France. That means lots of nibbles, with appetizer and entree plates about the same size. Expect seasonal salads like roasted beets with chèvre in winter or sliced tomatoes with fresh mozzarella in summer, along with pastas tossed with meat sauces, and whole sausages that can range from a house hot dog to a *merguez* (lamb) sausage with preserved anchovies. Sommelier Cat Silirie pulls out the stops for reds here, the way she does with whites at nearby **B&G Oysters** (see p. 128).

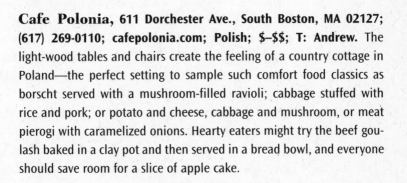

Cafe Polonia, 611 Dorchester Ave., South Boston, MA 02127; (617) 269-0110; cafepolonia.com; Polish; $–$$; T: Andrew. The light-wood tables and chairs create the feeling of a country cottage in Poland—the perfect setting to sample such comfort food classics as borscht served with a mushroom-filled ravioli; cabbage stuffed with rice and pork; or potato and cheese, cabbage and mushroom, or meat pierogi with caramelized onions. Hearty eaters might try the beef goulash baked in a clay pot and then served in a bread bowl, and everyone should save room for a slice of apple cake.

Cambridge Brewing Company, 1 Kendall Square, #100, Cambridge, MA 02139; (617) 494-1994; cambrew.com; Brewery; $–$$; T: Kendall Square. Established in 1989, CBC is the area's longest-operating brewery restaurant. Brewmaster Will Meyers is known for both his skill at executing classic and traditional beers and his enthusiasm for more adventurous suds like his Blunderbuss Barleywine, aged in port and sherry barrels, his medieval-style heather-infused Scottish ale, and a pert peculiarity called Sgt. Pepper—which is brewed with three malts, two kinds of hops, and four kinds of peppercorns. While many of the brews are now available in 22-ounce bottles, the best place to drink them is fresh at the brewery, either inside the refurbished mill building or out on the brick patio in the heart of the former industrial square. Meyers is known for making food-friendly beer, and Executive Chef David Drew makes equally beer-friendly food.

Catalyst, 300 Technology Sq., Kendall Square, Cambridge, MA 02139; (617) 576-3000; catalystrestaurant.com; New American; $$$; T: Kendall Square. Chef-Owner William Kovels handles fine dining with a relaxed atmosphere. Lunch really hops, with service so well planned that you can enjoy a leisurely sit-down meal and still get back to work in an hour. In the evening, though, you might prefer to linger, if only because the food is so good. Kovels understands that the point of an appetizer is to awaken your hunger, not to show off what can be done in a small plate. So the house-pickled vegetables are just right—tart, slightly crisp, brightly colored. A lobster strudel might have a small pool of bisque, but the dressing on the accompanying greens immediately cleanses the palate. That's all the better to get you ready for well-rounded and satisfying main dishes like the roasted "blue cod" (pollock) served with a chowder of mussels, bacon, and herbs, or the cider-glazed pork chop with mustard spaetzle.

Charlie's Sandwich Shoppe, 429 Columbus Ave., South End, Boston, MA 02116; (617) 536-7669; Casual American, $; T: Back Bay Station. Minutes after you're seated at Charlie's you will be chatting with the person on the next stool at the long counter or with your fellow diners at one of the communal tables. "We have a lot of regulars who sit at the same table every day," says Marie Fuller, daughter of Christi Manjourides, who started working at Charlie's when it opened in 1927. "In 1946 he bought half ownership for $1,000," says Fuller. She and three siblings now preside over this quintessential neighborhood breakfast and lunch joint. Breakfast, including turkey hash with eggs, blueberry griddle cakes, and omelets with home fries, is served all day. But you might opt instead for a chicken club or meat loaf sandwich, plate of franks and beans, or fish-and-chips for lunch. In 2005 the James Beard Foundation recognized Charlie's as one of its America's Classics eateries.

Chez Henri, 1 Shepard St., Harvard Square, Cambridge, MA 02138; (617) 354-8980; chezhenri.com; French; $$$; T: Harvard Square. Chef Paul O'Connell had never been to Cuba when he started serving empanadas and Cubano sandwiches at his bistro's tiny front bar. Then people started coming just for the Cuban snacks and he had to expand the bar. Over time, Latin accents have crept into the French dishes of the main dining room and O'Connell now bills Chez Henri as "a modern French bistro with a Cuban twist." His Criollo Bouillabaisse injects Latin spices into a saffron fish soup full of New England shellfish and served with a chipotle-garlic rouille. Just when you think that the chef has waded a little deep into the Caribbean, he comes back with a strict French dish like *blanquette de lapin*—pasta tossed with white-wine-braised rabbit, cream, and Provençal herbs.

Clio, 370 Commonwealth Ave., Back Bay, Boston, MA 02215; (617) 536-7200; cliorestaurant.com; French/New American; $$$$; T: Hynes. When Ken Oringer opened Clio in 1997, it was a rather formal restaurant designed to upgrade the dining scene at the recently overhauled Eliot Hotel. Clio earned Oringer the James Beard Best Chef Northeast award, an appearance on *Iron Chef,* and a bevy of investors delighted to back some of his other ventures. Clio remains Oringer's platform for invention, from his signature tomato-water nonalcoholic "martini" that captures the essence of tomato flavor, to escargots cooked with butter, ginger, and lemongrass and paired with stewed oxtail with chocolate and cocoa nibs. Clio can become precious, but it is one of a handful of Boston establishments offering all the subtleties of food and service one expects from a world-class restaurant.

Craigie on Main, 853 Main St., Central Square, Cambridge, MA 02139; (617) 497-5511; craigieonmain.com; New American; $$$; T: Central Square. Chef Tony Maws trained in Burgundy and has essentially reinvented the Lyon *bouchon* for American food. Roasted meats figure heavily on his menu of big, bold dishes. Many Cambridge foodies graze at the bar, loading up on fried pig tails (the favorite bar snack), roasted bone marrow (they split the bone for you), and a pricey burger that could be the best beef you've ever eaten. And those are just the snacks. Dinner ramps up the scale of the food. Most diners opt for the three-course prix fixe, but you can order a la carte for nearly the same price. (All dishes in a given course are priced the same.) Maws is famous for using all the pig but the squeal. You might find a salad of pig's ears paired with beets or an entree of roasted swordfish wrapped with house-cured pig's cheek (*guanciale*) and served with pine nuts and golden raisins in a robust Sicilian style. A stunning house specialty is the confit and roasted suckling pig head for two, which is accompanied by Peking pancakes, spicy pumpkin chile paste, *boudin noir,* and hoisin sauce. Charcuterie is part of the restaurant's signature, and it's all done on site.

Daily Catch, 323 Hanover St., North End, Boston, MA 02113; (617) 523-8567; T: Haymarket; 2 Northern Ave., Waterfront, Boston, MA 02210; (617) 772-4400; T: Court House (Silver Line); 441 Harvard St., Brookline, MA 02446; (617) 734-2700; T: Coolidge Corner; thedailycatch.com; Seafood/Italian; $. The Hanover Street location of the Daily Catch opened in 1973 and it's had a line out the door every night since, partly because the food is so good and partly because it is no-nonsense cheap. Locals call the place the Calamari Cafe, as it was the first place in the North

End to popularize squid for the tourists. On any given night the menu might feature fried calamari, calamari meatballs, calamari salad, and calamari with pasta and sauce. Most of the other proteins are

shellfish—clams, mussels, scallops, and shrimp—though monkfish, haddock, scrod, and lobster put in frequent appearances. The menu is scrawled daily on a chalkboard, and you may be seated with strangers. Beer and wine are available. The Brookline and Seaport versions are bigger, and the Seaport location has nice harborside outdoor seating in warm weather. North End location cash only.

Darryl's Corner Bar & Kitchen, 604 Columbus Ave., Roxbury, Boston, MA 02118; (617) 536-1100; darrylscornerbarboston .com; Southern; $$; T: Massachusetts Avenue. Darryl Settles has been bringing folks together for decades now, and the latest iteration of his restaurant/bar/music venue at the intersection of Roxbury and the South End preserves many of his beloved menu standards (the "glo-rifried chicken" and what might be Boston's best jambalaya) and pairs the grub with live music, often from jazz students who attend Berklee College of Music, just down the street. It's one of the rare lounges that actually welcomes children and it even has a small menu of kiddie food (chicken strips and fries, mac and cheese). Settles refers to the place as having "soul, spice, and all that jazz," and that pretty much sums it up. On Sunday, Darryl's offers a jazz buffet brunch laden with soul food like collard greens, candied yams, and (of course) grits.

Doyle's Cafe, 3484 Washington St., Jamaica Plain, MA 02130; (617) 524-2345; doylescafeboston.com; Traditional American; $–$$; T: Green Street/Forest Hills. Founded in 1882, just eight years after Boston annexed Jamaica Plain, Doyle's is possibly the most Irish-American of Irish bars and restaurants in the city. It was long the unofficial headquarters of the Hibernian contingent of the Massachusetts Democratic Party, and the sort of place to celebrate the election and reelection of Irish-American mayors. Doyle's appears often in films and TV shows as representative of blue-collar Boston, and tourists often stop by to see "real" Boston Irish characters. The collection of more than two dozen beers on tap makes it a mecca for beer drinkers as well, and the proximity to the **Boston Beer Company**'s headquarters (see p. 162) means that Doyle's often serves experimental batches of Sam Adams. Doyle's also serves a large menu of simple American fare, ranging from barbecued steak tips to broiled rainbow trout to a German sausage plate or spaghetti and meatballs.

Dumpling Cafe, 695-697 Washington St., Chinatown, Boston, MA 02111; (617) 338-8858; dumplingcafe.com; Chinese; $; T: Chinatown. The namesake dumplings are made fresh every day by one chef, who fills the beautiful little pockets with vegetables, beef and cabbage, pork and leek, seafood, or chicken. For a light, healthy meal and pretty 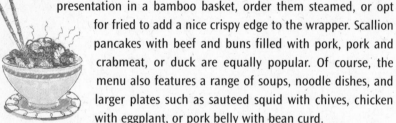 presentation in a bamboo basket, order them steamed, or opt for fried to add a nice crispy edge to the wrapper. Scallion pancakes with beef and buns filled with pork, pork and crabmeat, or duck are equally popular. Of course, the menu also features a range of soups, noodle dishes, and larger plates such as sauteed squid with chives, chicken with eggplant, or pork belly with bean curd.

Durgin-Park, 340 Faneuil Hall Marketplace, Downtown, Boston, MA 02109; (617) 227-2038; durgin-park.com; Traditional American; $–$$; T: Haymarket. Boston's quintessential Yankee dining room was famously established "before you were born," in the 1820s to feed the workers at Quincy Market. With its red-and-white checked tablecloths and long communal tables, it's still the place to go for lively conversation and such time-honored food standbys as roast prime rib, Yankee pot roast, baked scrod, Boston baked beans, and baked Indian pudding. Diners are sometimes disappointed that the waitresses, while brisk and efficient, seem to lack the legendary surliness. "I've been here 20 years," Laura Seluta told us when we last visited, "and we have our moments." Durgin-Park is recognized by the James Beard Foundation as one of its America's Classics eateries.

East by Northeast, 1128 Cambridge St., Inman Square, Cambridge, MA 02139; (617) 876-0286; exnecambridge.com; Chinese; $. Phillip Tang makes magic cooking Chinese food with New England ingredients, bringing together his French training, years in fancy Boston restaurants, and his experience with his family's Washington, DC–area dim sum palaces. The roots of Tang's dishes are either northern Chinese (roasted meats, hot spices, steamed breads) or Taiwanese (pork bun cooking), but the execution is all his own. He is likely to add duck confit and pickled mustard greens to congee (perhaps echoing Shanghai's French concession) or cross cultures with smoked cod and pork wontons in a hot and sour broth (a bit of the Portuguese influence on Macao). All dishes are small plates meant for sharing—if you can bring yourself not to lick up every morsel.

East Coast Grill, 1271 Cambridge St., Inman Square, Cambridge, MA 02139; (617) 491-6568; eastcoastgrill.net; New American; $$. East Coast Grill pioneered casual fine dining in Metro Boston with an emphasis on open wood grill dishes. Fish specials abound (mahimahi with a hot pepper rub, for example) and the shredded pork platter sets the bar in these parts for Carolina pulled pork. A grilled veggie plate is always available for the non-meat eater in the party. The Sunday brunch scene here is one of the busiest in Boston—and there are no reservations.

East Ocean City, 25–29 Beach St., Chinatown, Boston, MA 02111; (617) 542-2504; eastoceancity.com; Chinese/Seafood/Vegetarian; $; T: Chinatown. Six hundred pounds of fresh fish arrive daily at this Cantonese-style seafood emporium. A lot of that is trucked in from New York, but the squid mostly hails from the Rhode Island port of Point Judith, and you can't beat the lightly breaded salt-and-pepper squid. Many Chinese diners like to order live fish from the tanks near the entrance—don't hesitate to follow suit if you see glass shrimp swimming around. If you wait, they will almost certainly be gone. There are some meat and vegetarian dishes available for non-fish eaters, but the kitchen's heart lies with the ocean.

Elephant Walk, 900 Beacon St., Boston, MA (617) 247-1500; T: St. Mary's Street; 2067 Massachusetts Ave., Cambridge, MA 02140; (617) 492-6900; T: Porter Square; elephantwalk.com; Cambodian/ French/Vegetarian; $$. French Indochina may have been an imperialist debacle, but it yielded some of the world's great fusion cuisines. Elephant Walk serves upscale Cambodian food, including the signature *amok*. This spicy dish suspends fresh crab, shellfish, and catfish fillets in a coconut-milk custard laced with aromatic Khmer spices. Yet the same menu also contains a Parisian-style *steak-frites* with Roquefort sauce. A third branch is in Waltham (see p. 192.)

El Oriental de Cuba, 416 Centre St., Jamaica Plain, MA 02130; (617) 524-6464; elorientaldecuba.com; Cuban; $–$$; T: Jackson Square. While the majority of Jamaica Plain's Hispanic population hails either from Central America or the Dominican Republic, there remains a strong Cuban presence from the migrations of the 1960s. They all come here for braised beef tongue, *bistec a caballo* (grilled skirt steak with a fried egg on top), and *ropa vieja de res,* the Cuban national dish of shredded flank steak in tomato sauce. By necessity, the kitchen compromises tradition in favor of freshness, so a dish usually associated with grouper becomes haddock in coconut sauce. It's a huge plate served with rice, beans, and a choice of fried ripe or green plantain.

EVOO Restaurant, 350 3rd St., Kendall Square, Cambridge, MA 02142; (617) 661-3866; evoorestaurant.com; New American; $$$–$$$$; T: Kendall Square. Peter and Colleen McCarthy began listing their suppliers on the menu long before "locavore" became a dining mantra. Dishes play with expectation. The "surf and turf" might well be braised veal and cornmeal-crusted fried catfish, and the vegetarian special could easily be a sweet potato *tamal* filled with braised onion, raisins, and roasted sweet red pepper. In the fall and winter, Peter offers an outstanding lobster-parsnip bisque with leeks, hedgehog mushrooms, and tarragon butter as a starter. Meals are priced as a three-course prix fixe (with a modest additional charge for wine pairing) with choice of each course, although courses are technically available a la carte. Lunch has many of the dinner dishes (which change constantly), along with good sandwiches like the ABC (apple, bacon, and cheddar).

Figs, 67 Main St., Charlestown, Boston, MA 02129; (617) 242-2229; T: Community College; 42 Charles St., Beacon Hill, Boston, MA 02114; (617) 742-3447; T: Charles Street; toddenglish.com; Italian; $$. The Charlestown branch holds down the spot where the Todd English saga began, while the Charles Street branch is convenient for tourists and those who work or shop on Beacon Hill. Both showcase what English does best—delicious thin-crust free-form pizzas and simple baked pastas. One of the founding dishes was the fig and prosciutto pizza and it remains a favorite: a crisp rosemary-flecked crust, fig and balsamic jam, prosciutto, and crumbles of Gorgonzola cheese. The mountain of food in the chicken parmigiana (crisp chicken cutlet, heap of baked rigatoni, smothering quantities of mozzarella cheese) ensures that you'll have plenty to reheat for tomorrow's lunch.

The Fireplace, 1634 Beacon St., Brookline, MA 02446; (617) 975-1900; fireplacerest.com; New American; $$$; T: Washington Square. The dinner menu here reads like an issue of *Food & Wine* magazine, and when the plates come out, they look like they were styled there too. The emphasis on fresh produce (local when possible) and the extensive use of a wood grill and rotisserie to prepare meat and

MOVABLE FEAST

Boston may have gotten off to a slow start with licensing food trucks, but 56 trucks plied the Hub's streets in 2013, and the trend is definitely on the upswing. Food trucks serve everything from organic vegan dishes to Southern barbecue to lobster, cupcakes, and supersized hot dogs. As the Boston food truck scene has flourished, the trucks have also hit the streets of Cambridge, Somerville, Brookline, and the suburbs. Food trucks often converge on certain areas to take advantage of concentrations of customers. Prime cluster spots include the Rose Fitzgerald Greenway and Dewey Square, City Hall Plaza, the Christian Science Plaza, the corner of Kilby and Milk Streets in the Financial District, and Fort Point Channel Park. On Sunday, several trucks show up at SOWA Open Market at 500 Harrison Ave. in the South End.

fish dishes make The Fireplace an exemplar of contemporary American bistro style. Most meats and fish are simply roasted and served with side dishes and limited sauces. The actual fireplace faces the bar and provides flickering warmth and a certain woodsmoke scent, at least in the winter. When the weather turns warm, diners can also sit at outdoor tables.

Franklin Cafe, 278 Shawmut Ave., South End, Boston, MA 02118; (617) 350-0010; T: Back Bay Station; Franklin Southie, 152 Dorchester St., South Boston; Boston, MA 02127; (617) 269-1003; T: Broadway; franklincafe.com; New American; $$. Ask almost anyone in the Boston restaurant business where they go out to eat and the answer will be the Shawmut Avenue branch of Franklin Cafe. They serve dinner until 1:30 a.m., so staff from other restaurants can eat after their shifts. And the food is so reasonably priced that it doesn't break the bank. Some of the early classics of New American cooking remain on the menu here, like the salad of baby greens, roasted walnuts, figs, and blue cheese, or the homemade roasted pumpkin ravioli with sage-brown butter. Add a few French classics like *steak-frites* and a reasonable, less-rich version of coq au vin, and there's no reason to ever go hungry again. Even vegetarians can eat well on vegetable casseroles or potato gnocchi. The South Boston branch replicates the South End menu and feel—except that it has Pabst Blue Ribbon on tap instead of Narragansett.

Hamersley's Bistro, 553 Tremont St., South End, Boston, MA 02118; (617) 423-2700; hamersleysbistro.com; French/New American; $$$$; T: Back Bay Station. It is only a slight exaggeration to say that Gordon Hamersley's restaurant launched the renaissance of the South End when it opened in 1987. Reservations at Hamersley's remain some of the most sought-after in the city. Two of the restaurant's signature dishes are the roasted garlic and lemon chicken and the souffléed lemon custard. In fact, if you can't get a table seat, we recommend settling for a bar stool and ordering those two homey favorites for a meal you won't soon forget. On the way out, pick up a copy of Gordon Hamersley's cookbook, *Bistro Cooking at Home.*

Harvest, 44 Brattle St., Harvard Square, Cambridge, MA 02138; (617) 868-2255; harvestcambridge.com; New American; $$$; T: Harvard Square. A culinary landmark since 1975, Harvest was a pioneer in market cuisine. Under Chef Mary Dumont, it serves contemporary farm-to-table dishes in a comfortable but classy setting. To taste the seafood of the Northeast, order the "Grand Banks" sampler from the raw bar. It includes local oysters (Island Creek, Duxbury), jonah crab claws, and local fish ceviche along with Gulf shrimp. Seared Atlantic halibut with a saffron broth and a squid-ink-Pernod sauce is a perennial favorite. Bar snacks include a mini Maine lobster roll—the perfect bite to accompany a cold beer in the outdoor summer courtyard bar.

The Haven, 2 Perkins St., Jamaica Plain, MA 02130; (617) 524-2836; thehavenjp.com; Scottish; $$; T: Jackson Square. Scottish food has grit and character, and this pub does it really well. You don't have to be a fan of haggis—which is made weekly here and, as the staff will remind you, is just another form of charcuterie—to enjoy the sausages made in-house. Everything except the sandwich breads are made from scratch, including the delicious oat cakes served with butter before the meal. A delicate flaky pastry makes the "bridies" (a turnover that brides traditionally serve to guests at the wedding) a sensational snack or starter. Yet the single most popular item on the lunch, dinner, and bar menus is the Scotch egg—a deep-fried, sausage-wrapped, hard-boiled egg cut in half and served with mustard.

Henrietta's Table, Charles Hotel, 1 Bennett St., Harvard Square, Cambridge, MA 02138; (617) 661-5005; henriettastable.com; New American; $$; T: Harvard Square. Chef Peter Davis adopted a farm-to-fork philosophy decades before it became a fad. Sunday brunch is a groaning board all-you-can-eat buffet that includes a stupendous raw bar of Wellfleet oysters and jumbo shrimp. Yet the evening meal is called "supper," rather than dinner—an indicator of lower prices and smaller portions. The New American cooking owes a lot to traditional American fare, so Yankee pot roast, baked scrod, and rotisserie chicken share the menu with more unusual offerings such as pulled lamb shank and farro. For Peter Davis's version of a **New England Lobster Bake,** see p. 296.

Hungry Mother, 233 Cardinal Medeiros Ave., Kendall Square, Cambridge, MA 02141; (617) 499-0090; hungrymothercambridge .com; Southern; $$; T: Kendall Square. Chef Barry Maiden hails from Virginia, so there is a Tidewater gentility that tempers the Southern flavors of his cooking. Perhaps the best marriage of classical French technique with down-home ingredients is the crispy cylinder of head cheese accompanied by a succotash of hominy and pinto beans, pureed celeriac, and homemade pickled vegetables. Maiden bakes a different pie daily for dessert, offering it plated at the restaurant or packaged to take home for later.

Istanbul'lu, 237 Holland St., Teele Square, Somerville, MA 02144; (617) 440-7387; istanbul-lu.com; Turkish; $–$$; T: Davis Square. This friendly little storefront restaurant serves Chef Huseyin Akgun's Turkish home cooking. Eggplant in his signature light tomato sauce shouldn't be missed. Tops among the starters is the red lentil soup with mint. One of the more unusual (and delicious) plates is *istim kebab,* a baked casserole of steamed lamb shank cooked with vegetables, wrapped with sliced eggplant and topped with sliced tomatoes and peppers.

Jasper White's Summer Shack, 149 Alewife Brook Parkway, Alewife, Cambridge, MA 02140; (617) 520-9500; T: Alewife; 50 Dalton St., Back Bay, Boston, MA 02115; (617) 867-9955; T: Hynes; summer shackrestaurant.com; Seafood; $$. The original Cambridge location of seafood master Jasper White's casual Summer Shack restaurants seems about the size of an airplane hangar. On top of traditional treatments like steamed clams with drawn butter or plain steamed whole lobster, he offers surprises like lobster pot stickers with ginger; a pumpkin, corn, and lobster bisque; and a killer "shack bouillabaisse" that contains lobster, mussels, littleneck clams, fish, and squid in a saffron-tomato-fennel broth. It's served with jasmine rice and red pepper aioli. Back Bay has the same menu in a smaller space.

KO Prime, 90 Tremont St., Downtown, Boston, MA 02108; (617) 772-0202; koprimeboston.com; Steakhouse; $$$–$$$$; T: Park Street. This glamorous dining room in the Nine Zero Hotel remains true to steakhouse tradition by fairly oozing prestige and power, but the menu is full of the invention and imagination for which Chef Ken Oringer is known. The appetizer menu offers escargot as a fricassee with tiny carrots, mushrooms, and salsify. The beef tartare is Kobe beef accompanied by roasted jalapeño aioli and a deep-fried duck egg in place of the conventional raw chicken egg. Oringer and company grow the salad greens on the restaurant's rooftop, and get most of the other veggies (in season) from small farms near Boston. The whole range of steaks is available, but so is a more reasonable Kobe burger with *foie gras,* crisply fried skate, and even a bouillabaisse. Some of the steakhouse classics survive intact (how do you improve on Oysters Rockefeller?), while others are brilliantly reinvented, like the corned beef tongue hash with a poached duck egg.

Koreana, 158 Prospect St., Central Square, Cambridge, MA 02139; (617) 576-8661; koreanaboston.com; Korean; $$; T: Central Square. Korean diners from around Greater Boston converge on this neighborhood spot with no parking. Tabletop barbecue is the main lure. The most popular order is *yuksu bolgoki,* which includes thinly sliced rib eye beef and enoki mushrooms and clear noodles in a soy and sesame broth. (One order serves two.) Many diners opt for the vegetable barbecue of a couple of kinds of mushrooms, red and green peppers, eggplant, and zucchini—all of which you grill to taste. In lieu of grilled food, you can opt for a hot pot like the *kimchi chigae,* a stew of kimchi, pork, tofu, scallions, and sliced rice cake.

Legal Harborside, 270 Northern Ave., Waterfront, Boston, MA 02210; (617) 477-2900; legalseafoods.com; Seafood; $–$$$$: T: World Trade Center (Silver Line). The new flagship complex of the Legal Sea Foods group returns to its roots with an old-fashioned fish market, an oyster bar, and a casual restaurant with the option of takeout on the first floor; a fine-dining venue on the second level; and a rocking bar with seafood bar bites on the top level. Each overlooks Boston Harbor. The fine dining includes unusual dishes like sautéed abalone served with lemon risotto and brussels sprouts seasoned with *guanciale*. Caviar service is available, and even the seared foie gras starter is unexpectedly served with a chocolate brioche, cherries, and candied ginger. Other branches of Legal Sea Foods dot the city.

L'Espalier, 774 Boylston St., Back Bay, Boston, MA 02199; (617) 262-3023; lespalier.com; French/New American; $$$$; T: Copley. When Frank McClelland moved from L'Espalier's original townhouse into the Mandarin Oriental, the restaurant gained a much larger (and exposed) kitchen, more seating, and the option of lunch as well as dinner. The restaurant team, led by McClelland in the kitchen and Louis Risoli in the dining room, is always in pursuit of perfection, and some of the most inspired (and complex) dishes we've tasted in the US have been at L'Espalier. You can also opt for "bites" in the Salon. These range from servings of caviar, oysters, or farmstead cheeses, to small plates that hint at the brilliance of the dining room menus: roasted *foie gras* with cèpes and a black trumpet mushroom cake, perhaps, or slow-cooked gray sole with Moroccan orange peel puree, pickled fennel, and olive oil. Desserts by pastry chef Jiho Kim are similarly complex little masterpieces.

Local 149, 149 P St., South Boston, MA 02127; (617) 269-0900; local149.com; New American/Vegetarian; $$; T: Broadway. Taking the space of an ancient shot-and-a-beer Irish-American bar, this contemporary pub represents the new Southie. It bustles with a youthful crowd all afternoon and evening, and features a slew of local beers on tap, a taut wine list, and a kitchen that keeps regulars both well fed and amused. Who else does a starter of crispy "fried baloney" or puts buttermilk-batter-fried lobster with a caramel and cheese sauce on the specials menu? Mac and cheese and sweet potato fries are always available for snacking, while big eaters can always order the double-cut pork chop with creamy cabbage.

Lucca, 226 Hanover St., North End, Boston, MA 02113; (617) 742-9200; luccaboston.com; Italian; $$$; T: Haymarket. The North End was crying out for alternatives to pasta houses when Lucca opened several years ago serving a fish- and meat-centric Northern Italian menu. That's not to say there aren't pasta dishes on the menu, but they are not the typical first-course plates. You might find rabbit ravioli with sautéed baby vegetables and a red wine demi-glace, for example, or homemade linguine tossed with cockles, Manila clams, pancetta, and baby tomatoes. Appetizer courses tend toward oven dishes, like the rustic duck tart with caramelized onions, goat cheese, and spinach, or a lasagna of layered potatoes, wild mushrooms, spinach, and balsamic glaze. Lucca's catch of the day specials are always a solid choice. If your heart is set on "red gravy," look elsewhere.

Mare Oyster Bar, 135 Richmond St., North End, Boston, MA 02113; (617) 723-MARE; mareoysterbar.com; Italian/Seafood; $$$; T: Haymarket. With broad plate-glass windows and big mirrors on the wall, Mare (pronounced the Italian way as *MAH-ray*) looks a bit like a Modernist aquarium, but given the dedication to pristine seafood, that's appropriate. In slow seasons there are just a half-dozen oysters from East Coast farms; when business picks up, another half-dozen oysters from the West Coast or Europe join the mix at the shucking station. Oysters are just the beginning at Mare, where Greg Jordan presides over a kitchen that turns out two of the region's great lobster rolls: hot with herbed butter and scallions, or cold with lemon mayonnaise made in-house. Both are served on fresh brioche buns. Truffle crusted grilled tuna—always served rare—is another striking treat, as is Jordan's Italian seafood soup of a half lobster, scallops, mussels, cockles, and clams in a light tomato broth.

Maurizio's, 364 Hanover St., North End, Boston, MA 02113; (617) 367-1123; mauriziosboston.com; Italian; $$; T: Haymarket. Maurizio Loddo was one of the neighborhood's first chefs to break away from Italian-American cooking by concentrating on the light, seafood-oriented cuisine of Sardinia. This is a place to taste some truly distinctive regional Italian dishes, like the antipasto of *mazzamurru,* a Sardinian peasant bowl of toasted bread, chicken broth, and tomato sauce topped with a poached egg and tangy grated sheep's milk cheese and then baked. The fish dishes, however, are where the kitchen really shines. Loddo always manages to get some of the best fish available. His Sardinian-style sole is not to be missed. You might not think of red wine with fish, but Loddo always carries a couple of ruby-red Sardinian reds based on the Monica grape (which typically has pleasant, bright cherry flavors followed by hints of soft chocolate) that pair very well with assertive fish.

Menton, 354 Congress St., Waterfront, Boston, MA 02210; (617) 737-0099; mentonboston.com; New American; $$$$; T: South Station. Barbara Lynch does luxury fine dining at its best at this Fort Point Channel outpost named for a town on the border of the French and Italian Rivieras. The menu formats are limited to a four-course prix fixe or a seven-course tasting menu, with or without wine pairings, and the attention to tiny details justifies the prices. Named a Relais & Châteaux Grand Chef in 2012 (the only woman Grand Chef in North America), Lynch creates dishes with complex layers of flavor. For example, she serves langoustines wrapped in *kataifi* (like shredded phyllo dough) with fresh local Greek yogurt from **Sophia's Greek Pantry** (see p. 213), honey, and a homemade French-Indian curry powder. Her *foie gras* terrine is served with chewy, partially dehydrated segments of grape-fruit and pomelo with warm brioche and a pine-nut brittle. Texture and balance are important in every dish, but that doesn't stop her from presenting bold plates like roast lamb with olives and black garlic.

Miami Restaurant, 381 Centre St., Jamaica Plain, MA 02130; (617) 522-4644; Caribbean; $; T: Jackson Square. Part of the stretch of Centre Street that might be called the Costa de J-P, Miami dukes it out with **El Oriental de Cuba** (see p. 138) over which place serves the better Cubano sandwich and which attracts the most Spanish-speaking professional baseball players. We give a slight edge for the sandwich to El Oriental de Cuba, but Miami's is probably more authentic, from what we've been told by people who grew up eating the real thing. We do know that you get a heap of food when you order a plate here, including mounds of *maduros* and *yuca*. The *carne guisada con papas* (beef stew with potatoes) might eclipse *ropa vieja* as the best Caribbean treatment of beef.

Moksa, 450 Massachusetts Ave., Central Square, Cambridge, MA 02139; (617) 661-4900; moksarestaurant.com; Asian; $; T: Central Square. Chef Patricia Yeo calls Moksa a pan-Asian *izakaya,* a style of Japanese drinking establishment that serves food to go with the booze. Yeo has become famous in New York and Boston for reinventing Asian street food, and she continues that trend at Moksa with dishes like Viet-namese rice paper rolls stuffed with spice-spiked tuna, or Indian roti filled with ingredients as disparate as *paneer* and avocado, lamb breast and crisp anchovies, or lobster and mango. Most dishes are available until midnight.

Mr. Bartley's Gourmet Burgers, 1246 Massachusetts Ave., Harvard Square, Cambridge, MA 02138; (617) 354-6559; mrbartley .com; Casual American; $; T: Harvard Square. New-wave burger joints are popping up all over Metro Boston, yet with all their pretenses, they have yet to measure up to the original gold standard. Under slightly different names, the Bartley family has been making great burgers here since 1960. The formula is simple: grind the beef daily and use 7 ounces per patty. Bartley's has celebrity, political, and punning names for its various combos. The Tom Brady (with cheddar, guacamole, lettuce, tomato, onions, and fries) has the notation "ladies, make a pass at this." The Jersey Shore is denoted as "over the top," which it is with bacon, cheese, grilled mushrooms, and onions, accompanied by onion rings. These are meaty beasts—fistfuls of beef on big buns.

No. 9 Park, 9 Park St., Beacon Hill, Boston, MA 02108; (617) 742-9991; no9park.com; New American; $$$$; T: Park Street. This first restaurant by Barbara Lynch has evolved over the years from a classy spot where high-rollers and lawmakers ate lunch to an elegant dinner-only fine-dining restaurant in the shadow of the State House. The dining room menu is available as a three-course prix fixe or a la carte, or diners have the option of a seven-course chef's tasting menu. This food is simpler and less baroque than Lynch's dishes at **Menton** (see p. 147). Flavors are clean and bold: bacon-wrapped monkfish served with Himalayan red rice, sweet potato, and black trumpet mushrooms, for example.

O Ya, 9 East St., Leather District, Boston, MA 02111; (617) 654-9900; oyarestaurantboston.com; Japanese; $$$$; T: South Station. There are no bargains at O Ya—in fact, the typical meal here is probably the most expensive in Boston. But the exquisitely elegant 37-seat restaurant is a rarity here, offering sure-handed innovation of traditional Japanese dishes. Six chefs are constantly at work producing perfect little morsels for the bite-sized portions. Half the menu is sushi and sashimi, the other half pork, chicken, beef, and vegetarian. One national reviewer cited O Ya for the best *omakase* (tasting) menu in the

US. If you're an aficionado, let head chef Tim Cushman treat you to the meal of a lifetime.

Oak Long Bar + Kitchen, Fairmont Copley Plaza Hotel, 138 St. James Ave., Back Bay, Boston, MA 02116; (617) 585-7222; oak longbarkitchen.com; Traditional American; $$$–$$$$. Much of the decor dates from the Edwardian era, when the hotel was built, but the 2012 remake of the Copley Plaza's main restaurant and lounge put the emphasis on lounge and turned the menu toward the lighter side. You can still get a pricey steak with the Oak's legendary house steak sauce, but now it's a rib eye *steak-frites* with fries cooked in duck fat. Flatbreads are available all day, and they're really stand-ins for pizza. Should you wish a nibble with a single-malt Scotch, you can always order the potted *foie gras* Sauternes mousse with a little oat bran granola and cherry jam, or lamb sliders with a salad of thinly sliced cucumber.

Olé Mexican Grill, 11 Springfield St., Inman Square, Cambridge, MA 02139; (617) 492-4495; olerestaurantgroup.com; Mexican; $$. Chef-Restaurateur Erwin Ramos might be Filipino by birth, but he has a Mexican soul. The menu offers main dish plates but most of the best flavors are available in small dishes—a great way for everyone at the table to taste the *cuitlacoche* crepes, the street-vendor-style grilled corn with chile and lime, the sauteed scallops with roasted garlic, and the chicken *tamal* topped with *mole negro* dark chile-pepper sauce. To see what you've missed at conventional "Mexican" restaurants, order the enchilada plate. You can get it filled with grilled diced chicken, braised pork, or mixed vegetables. It's served with rice and black beans (very Yucatecan), and a choice of *ranchera, mole negro,* or *salsa verde.*

Oleana, 134 Hampshire St., Central Square, Cambridge, MA 02139; (617) 661-0505; oleanarestaurant.com; Mediterranean/

Vegetarian; $$$; T: Central Square. Ask most diners what region is covered in Mediterranean cuisine and they suggest an arc of countries from Spain to Greece. Ask Ana Sortun, chef-owner of Oleana, and she's more likely to think of a similar arc that runs from Morocco to Turkey. Sortun is the spice mistress of Boston-area chefs. She even wrote a cookbook of dishes grouped by predominant flavors called *Spice: Flavors of the Eastern Mediterranean.* It's tempting to make an entire meal of the meze dishes—like the grape leaves stuffed with lentils, rice, chestnuts, and prunes, or the beans and chickpeas with green chard and orange aioli—but then you'd miss some of the great entrees. These dishes vary with the season but might well include flattened lemon chicken with zaatar spices and Turkish cheese pancakes, or fish roasted with grapes and olives and served with salami and a polenta cake. For those inclined to nibble, Oleana offers a vegetable tasting menu of five meze and dessert.

Petit Robert Bistro, 468 Commonwealth Ave., Fenway, Boston, MA 02215; (617) 375-0699; T: Kenmore; 480 Columbus Ave., South End, Boston, MA 02118; (617) 867-0600; T: Back Bay Station; Petit Robert Central, 101 Arch St., Downtown, Boston, MA 02110; (617) 737-1777; T: Downtown Crossing; petitrobertcentral .com; French; $$. Jacky Robert may be the scion of the Robert clan that brought fine French dining to Boston nearly two generations ago, but Jacky's heart is in the neighborhoods. He launched his first budget bistro in Kenmore Square (Boston University students have all the luck), serving perfect date food at perfect student date prices. Then he replicated the menu and feel in the South End. Both are great spots to settle in for coq au vin or *steak-frites* with a carafe of wine and soulful glances. Over time the menu has evolved, so vegetarians can order something like the quinoa, farro, and lentil cake while Francophiles can still tuck into the cassoulet with lamb, pork sausage, duck confit, and navy beans. Right in Downtown Crossing, Petit Robert Central is more a brasserie than a bistro. The big bar area fills up after work with wine-sippers. But tables and booths can be quite intimate, in case you'd like to conduct a romantic tête-à-tête over plates of beef short rib bourgui-gnon, cassoulet, or hake fillet with baby clams, mussels, scallops, and shrimp. Bistro pricing ensures that Petit Robert Central is an excellent spot for pursuing romance without finance.

Pho Pasteur, 682 Washington St., Chinatown, Boston, MA 02111; (617) 482-7467; Vietnamese; $; T: Chinatown. This soup house intro-duced *pho* to Boston back in the days when the only people who had tasted *pho* were either Vietnamese immigrants or veterans of the Viet-nam War. The Vietnamese are such great cooks that they conquered the French (with some of the best inexpensive restaurants in Paris) and Pho Pasteur certainly has a strong foothold in Chinatown. The food is terrific: warming soup, nicely sliced meat, and gigantic heaps of bean sprouts and basil to add. Service is minimal, but it gets the job done.

Porter Exchange Building, 1815 Massachusetts Ave., Porter Square, Cambridge, MA 02140; Japanese; $; T: Porter Square. The Art Deco brick exterior of this former Sears, Roebuck does not even hint at the bustle inside, where a group of casual eateries so resemble a Japanese street market that they attract homesick students from greater Boston's many universities. Sample noodle soups (with miso broth, Chinese vegetables, and pork, for example) at Sapporo Ramen, sushi and sashimi at Blue Fin Restaurant, and all manner of Korean street food (very popular in Japan) at Cho Cho's. Or venture into Tam-popo for rice bowls and udon noodle dishes. Then stop at Tapicha for a "pearl drink." Pick a tea (black, green, or chai); add flavorings such as mango, peach, or lychee; and then ask the server to throw in "bubbles" of tapioca or coconut jelly.

Posto, 187 Elm St., Davis Square, Somerville, MA 02144; (617) 625-0600; pizzeriaposto.com; Italian/Pizza; $$; T: Davis Square. Americans consider pizza the ultimate casual food, but the Associazione Verace Pizza Napoletana begs to differ. Founded in 1984, the "True Neapolitan Pizza Association" has specific guidelines for any parlor that hopes to call itself an "official Neapolitan pizzeria." Posto is the only establishment in New England to pass muster and you'll need a reservation if you want to check out the hand-kneaded pies that are baked at 485 degrees centigrade for 60 to 90 seconds in a wood-fired, domed oven. If your table decides to share a pizza as an appetizer, you can select from a range of pastas (lobster and scallop tortellini, rabbit ravioli) and entrees (wood roasted chicken, wild striped bass with oven-braised fennel) for your main course.

Prezza, 24 Fleet St., North End, Boston, MA 02113; (617) 227-1577; prezza.com; Italian; $$$; T: Haymarket. Chef-Owner Anthony Caturano may have named Prezza for his grandmother's home town, but his elegant dishes are a long way from Nonna's cooking. The pasta is made in-house, as are the soft pillows of gnocchi. Caturano likes to cook over flaming wood, so many of the main dishes come from the grill, including swordfish served with saffron rice, lobster broth, and mussels. Meat eaters get their fill with oven-roasted meatballs, sausage, and ribs served with creamy polenta and roasted tomato.

Q Restaurant, 660 Washington St., Chinatown, Boston, MA 02111; (857) 350-3968; thequsa.com; Chinese/Vegetarian; $$; T: Chinatown. Superbly cut and beautifully presented sushi is one extreme at Q, while the other is Mongolian hot pot, where you cook your own meat or seafood in a nearly bubbling broth. "We make 12 different kinds of broth," says restaurateur Ming Zhu, "Spicy *mala* and blackbone chicken are the most popular. Since the food arrives at the table raw, it all has to be very fresh and healthy." There's also a choice of a vegetarian platter and vegetarian broth. All this is served at bargain Chinatown prices in an upscale setting on the ground level of a luxury apartment complex.

Redbones Barbecue, 55 Chester St., Davis Square, Somerville, MA 02144; (617) 628-2200; redbones.com; Barbecue; $; T: Davis Square. Redbones is as close to a Texas barbecue roadhouse as you can find in the land of the bean and the cod. All the meats are cooked slow and low except for the grilled sausage and the fried catfish, and the sides are a list of the greatest hits of Southern cuisine, from hush puppies and cat fingers to corn fritters, mac and cheese, succotash, and sweet potato fries. All-meat Texas chili is available, but you can also get a gentle cup of pot likker—the broth from braising greens. Redbones is at its best with big Texas beef ribs, slabs of country-style Arkansas pork ribs, and traditional dry-rub Memphis pork spareribs. In fact, you can order a Barbecue Belt and get some of each along with a serving of smoked beef brisket. All the barbecue is available for takeout, but it's more fun to eat on site, keeping the gullet lubricated with a string of longnecks.

Regina Pizza, 11½ Thacher St., North End, Boston, MA 02113; (617) 227-0765; reginapizza.com; Pizza; $–$$; T: Haymarket. The vertical neon sign beckons on tiny Thacher Street—probably the only way most newcomers will ever find the North End pizza shop, established in 1926, that gave birth to the Regina's chain. Day or night, there will probably be a line of people waiting to get into the tiny establishment. We have never, ever scored one of the wooden booths here, but seats at the bar are just dandy. The pizza style is closer to Neapolitan than American, relying on a yeasty dough and light, slightly spicy sauce. Minimal toppings will keep the crust crisp on the bottom and chewy instead of soggy on top.

Rendezvous, 502 Massachusetts Ave., Central Square, Cambridge, MA 02139; (617) 576-1900; rendezvouscentralsquare.com; Mediterranean; $$$; T: Central Square. Chef-Owner Steve Johnson gets his food locally and his inspiration from Italy, coastal France, Spain, and North Africa. He'll break down a 6-pound locally foraged hen of the woods mushroom into smaller pieces to sauté and serve with fried orecchiette, sauteed black kale, and Piave cheese (or with fried pasta and his signature braised pork and veal meatballs). His winter dish of crispy roast chicken with brussels sprouts, butternut squash, apples, and fried sage is a classic in Gascony and nearby Catalunya, but the ingredients are pure New England. His Sunday night prix fixe deals are local legend.

Rialto, Charles Hotel, 1 Bennett St., Harvard Square, Cambridge, MA 02138; (617) 661-5050; rialto-restaurant.com; Mediterranean; $$$–$$$$; T: Harvard Square. Jody Adams' taste has kept marching east across the Mediterranean from France to Italy. Her most recent inspirations are fish dishes from Sardinia and the earthy flavors of Sicily. She has an impeccable palate, and mixes and matches flavors from different regions with great panache. Thus, her grilled swordfish might come with a Friulian bean stew, braised cabbage, and some house-cured bacon, but it also gets a palate-refreshing blast of juniper berry. The slow-roasted duck with braised escarole is unctuous, but sharp Sicilian green olives cut through the heaviness.

Santarpio's Pizza, 111 Chelsea St., East Boston, MA 02128; (617) 567-9871; santarpiospizza.com; Pizza; $: T: Maverick. Founded in 1903 and now practically hidden under an East Boston highway ramp to Logan Airport, Santarpio's is one of the shrines of Neapolitan-style pizza in the United States. Hard-core fans generally order the cheese and garlic pizza with extra garlic and place a second order for the homemade sausages or the lamb skewers. Be prepared for a long line on weekends, especially Sunday afternoon and evening. Cash only.

Taberna de Haro, 999 Beacon St., Brookline, MA 02446; (617) 277-8272; tabernaboston.com; Spanish; $$; T: St. Mary's Street. Almost everything on the menu in this tavern named for one of La Rioja's most famous wine towns is a *pincho* or *racion* small plate, giving diners lots of different tastes as they compile a meal. That might include such classic Spanish tapas as potato omelet, garlic soup with a poached egg, or ham croquettes. The menu also has a few more substantive plates, such as roasted sea bass; chicken stewed with sherry, saffron, almonds, and Spanish ham; or grilled, organically raised rib eye steak. More than 240 Spanish wines are available.

Taranta, 210 Hanover St., North End, Boston, MA 02113; (617) 720-0052; tarantarist.com; Italian/Peruvian; $$$; T: Haymarket. Peruvian-born chef-owner Jose Duarte grew up in an Italian community in Venezuela, so his marriage of Peruvian flavors with Southern Italian cuisine comes naturally. To get an idea of how well the two go together, try his orechiette con salsicchia, cooked with South American aji peppers, Abruzzi sausage, broccoli rabe, and cherry tomatoes. He also makes gnocchi with cassava root (yuca) and serves them with a spicy green lamb *ragù* and shaved Parmigiano cheese. Pasta portions tend to be restrained, while the more expensive meat and fish dishes are often huge. The brined double-cut pork chop coated with a glaze of sugar cane and rocoto pepper is enough for two, especially because it is accompanied by a sauté of Peruvian giant corn, caramelized onions, and spinach.

Tavolo, 1918 Dorchester Ave., Dorchester, Boston, MA 02124; (617) 822-1918; tavolopizza.com; Italian; $$; T: Ashmont. Chef Nuno Alves invents dishes that seem so logical that you'd think they were part of the Italian canon. On Wednesday night Tavolo offers a regional pasta tour—a three-course, set-price meal focusing on a pasta characteristic of a given region. For Sardinia, Alves invented a dish of Squid Three Ways: squid ink malloreddus pasta (a short ridged pasta); tender squid bodies stuffed with bread crumbs, herbs, and mint; and crisply fried tentacles. With a few dollops of tomato *sugo,* it was a dish to have made a Sardinian grandmother proud. Do not miss the *frico* appetizer. This "pancake" of crisped Montasio cheese, potato, and onion is served with arugula and a dollop of applesauce. Alves works similar magic with pastas, tossing pappardelle noodles with braised lamb, preserved lemon, fennel, and sweet, bright green Castelvetrano olives.

Teatro, 177 Tremont St., Downtown, Boston, MA 02111; (617) 778-6841; teatroboston.com; Italian; $$; T: Boylston. A good spot for dinner before or after a Theater District show, Teatro produces contemporary revivals of Italian culinary classics. Four pizzas are available along with seven different dishes using pasta made in-house. Pastas and risottos are all available in appetizer or main dish portions. We're partial to the shells (*conchiglie*) with Maine lobster and Vermont butter, and the wild mushroom and truffle oil risotto. Terrific antipasti range from simple but inspired truffled deviled eggs to a hot dish of grilled octopus, sopressata sausage, and crispy potatoes.

Topacio, 120 Meridian St., East Boston, MA 02128; (617) 567-9523; Salvadoran/Seafood; $; T: Maverick. Many customers at this principally Spanish-speaking restaurant order the roasted chicken or the *plato montañero* (grilled steak, fried eggs, beans, rice, and tortillas), but the real house specialty is the seafood feast called *sopa de mariscos,* or shellfish soup. Think of it as a Central American take on *bouillabaisse,* filled with bits and pieces of New England finfish, clams, shrimp, and lobster.

Toro, 1704 Washington St., South End, Boston, MA 02118; (617) 536-4300; toro-restaurant.com; Spanish; $; T: Massachusetts

Avenue (Orange Line) or Worcester Square (Silver Line). No single dish is very expensive at this classy reinterpretation of a tapas bar, but you'll spend plenty by the time you're full. Nonetheless, you get what you pay for, with hot tapas like smoked duck drumettes with a quince glaze, grilled corn with aioli and aged cheese, or jonah crab with piquillo peppers. Like genuine Spanish food, it tends to be a bit salty—all the better to encourage you to drink. The wine list (save one Madeira) is strictly Spanish and includes one of our favorite Tempranillos from the town of Toro.

Trade, 540 Atlantic Ave., Waterfront, Boston, MA 02210; (617) 451-1234; trade-boston.com; New American; $$–$$$; T: South Station. This big airy brasserie does a land-rush lunch business. The food is eclectic and bold and service is so good that you can squeeze in a real lunch (say Arctic char with saffron quinoa or a flatbread topped with mushrooms, figs, Gorgonzola, sage pesto, and walnuts) and still get back to the office on time. Trade also flourishes in the evening. The restaurant is the brainchild of Jody Adams, but she gives the kitchen staff leeway to interpret the menu. The site used to be Griffith Wharf, famous for the Boston Tea Party, and the "Trade" concept plays with the idea that spices and foodstuffs come from all over the world. Ironically, most of the ingredients are local and are pulled together in Adams' signature style of a protein paired with a strongly flavored complement— seared chicken with burnt orange, dates, pistachios, and quinoa, for example. No one will throw these treats into the harbor.

Tremont 647, 647 Tremont St., South End, Boston, MA 02118; (617) 266-4600; tremont647.com; New American; $$; T: Back Bay Station. This neighborhood restaurant from Chef-Owner Andy Husbands is almost fanatical about using local produce, fish, and meat. It's hard to order badly when the menu features the likes of the house signature hoisin-glazed pan-seared hake, a lemon-garlic spit-roasted half chicken, or fried catfish with bacony collard greens. Husbands is locally famed for his tater tots stuffed with blue cheese. On Saturday and Sunday, the restaurant has a "pajama brunch" that extends to its adjunct room next door, Sister Sorel. And yes, people do show up in their pj's.

Tupelo, **1193 Cambridge St., Inman Square, Cambridge, MA 02139; (617) 868-0004; tupelo02139.com; Southern; $$.** Leave room for dessert, since Renee "Petsi" McLeod of **Petsi Pies** (see p. 174) also co-owns Tupelo, which features her delicious pies for dessert. Chef Rembs Layman, however, is the one who idolizes Elvis (from Tupelo) and has a mama from New Orleans. That no doubt plays a role in the authenticity of the Cajun gumbo, the "red" jambalaya with smoked andouille sausage and tiger shrimp, and the Cajun-spiced blackened catfish over creamy cheddar grits. Consider starting with Southern spiced turkey meatballs (with French bread for mopping up), or fried oysters with green Tabasco aioli and house pickle.

T.W. Kitchen, **377 Walden St., Huron Village, Cambridge, MA 02138; (617) 864-4745; twfoodrestaurant.com; New American; $$$.** Chef Tim Wiechmann is so obsessed with ingredients that he makes other locavore chefs look like they shop at the airport. The technique is pure French (he cooked under Joël Robuchon in Paris), but the ingredients are so local that it's hard to call the dishes anything but American. The restaurant only serves New England fish, which means Wiechmann has to get creative with lemon sole and winter flounder across the cold months (Moroccan spices are one answer), and that he can come out blasting with a bold bluefish and mustard sauce in the summer. Winter menus are full of earthy vegetables like kohlrabi, rutabaga, and celeriac, while summer menus burst first with green peas and keep going through tomatoes and corn right into the squashes of autumn.

Union Oyster House, 41 Union St., Downtown, Boston, MA 02108; (617) 227-2750; unionoysterhouse.com; Traditional American/Seafood; $$$; T: Haymarket. Claiming to be America's oldest restaurant (established in 1826), Union Oyster House has fed many famous figures, from Daniel Webster (who drank brandy and water with his daily plates of raw oysters) to John F. Kennedy, who used to read the Sunday papers in a booth on the second floor. The best seats in the house, however, are on the horseshoe oyster bar at the entrance. The oysters come from many different spots, and you can spend a happy afternoon trying them all.

Upstairs on the Square, 91 Winthrop St., Harvard Square, Cambridge, MA 02138; (617) 864-1933; upstairsonthesquare.com; New American; $$$–$$$$; T: Harvard Square. This exuberant restaurant looks like it was designed by the team of Hieronymus Bosch and Salvador Dalí. To rein in the cost, eat in the downstairs **Monday Club Bar,** where dishes like tagliatelle with pork jowl Bolognese are available in small and entree-size portions. Monday Club has all the over-the-top desserts for which Upstairs is known—like the Zebra Cake of chocolate layer cake, dulce de leche buttercream, and malted chocolate ice cream. Dinner is bigger and bolder upstairs in the **Soirée** dining room, where a charcoal-grilled sirloin might be served with coconut-scented parsnips and a gratin of macomber turnip. Tasting menus (including an all-vegetarian) are available, with and without selected wine pairings.

Zaftig's Delicatessen, 335 Harvard St., Brookline, MA 02446; (617) 975-0075; zaftigs.com; Casual American/Jewish; $; T: Coolidge Corner. Zaftig's is a little bit of Brooklyn in Brookline, serving the favorites of Ashkenazi Jewish-American cuisine. So, yes, you can have blintzes, and latkes, and kugel for breakfast, matzo ball chicken soup at lunch, and braised brisket for supper. You can also get cheese fries with

LEARN TO COOK

Boston Center for Adult Education, 122 Arlington St., Boston, MA 02116; (617) 267-4430; bcae.org; T: Arlington. Food and wine classes are so popular that the BCAE built state-of-the-art new kitchens several years ago. Offerings range from basic and advanced cooking techniques to explorations of world cuisines.

Boston University Programs in Food, Wine, and the Arts, 808 Commonwealth Ave., Boston, MA 02215; (617) 353-9852; bu.edu/foodandwine; T: Kenmore Square. In addition to a semester-long culinary arts education program cofounded by Julia Child and Jacques Pépin, B.U. offers courses, classes, and one-off events for the general public.

Cambridge Center for Adult Education, 42 Brattle St., Cambridge, MA 02138; (617) 547-6789; ccae.org; T: Harvard Square. Course offerings focus on cuisines of the world as well as more practical matters, such as cooking basics, cooking with natural foods, or creating sandwiches and salads. A number of offerings take students out of the kitchen to explore the food scene in various neighborhoods.

Cambridge School of Culinary Arts, 2020 Massachusetts Ave., Cambridge, MA 02140; (617) 354-2020; cambridge culinary.com. Primarily a professional school of culinary arts, Cambridge Culinary also offers a wide variety of recreational classes, often taught by the same professional faculty.

Stir, 102 Waltham St., Boston, MA 02118; (617) 423-7847; stirboston.com; T: Back Bay Station. Master Chef Barbara Lynch and wine guru Cat Silirie head the instructional team for 1- and 2-day workshops, tastings, and dinners in the tiny demo kitchen in the South End. Stir also holds regular book club dinners with lively discussion over a small meal inspired by the book.

turkey gravy, *salade niçoise,* and french toast all day. There have been lines out the door since Zaftig's first opened in 5757 (that's a.d. 1996).

Specialty Stores, Markets & Producers

Baltic European Deli, 632 Dorchester Ave., South Boston, MA 02127; (617) 268-2435; balticeuropeandeli.com; Grocery; T: **Andrew.** Baltic Deli sits in the once-vibrant "Polish Triangle," which swelled with immigrants after both world wars. The market continues to provide a vital link to the foods of the old country. Refrigerator and freezer cases are stocked with soups (sour pickle, beef tripe, chicken, borscht), pierogi (potato and cheese, plum, mushroom), and blintzes (cheese, blueberry, strawberry). The deli case includes smoked and plain kielbasa or liver sausage, hard salami, and countless other hams and sausages. You can sample them in sandwiches, such as kielbasa with sauerkraut or the popular pork loaf. Pick up some dark rye bread and jars of sauerkraut, grated beets, and pickled mushrooms to round out a meal.

Boston Beer Company, 30 Germania St., Jamaica Plain, MA 02130; (617) 482-1332; samadams.com; Brewery; T: Stony Brook. Founded in 1984, Boston Beer Company practically invented the category of craft beer. Now it has become the 800-pound gorilla of craft breweries, the maker of the relentlessly promoted Sam Adams line of beers. While major production is farmed out to contract brewers across the country, new brews are developed at the original Jamaica Plain facility, which also offers tours. Sam Adams beers are available in Boston pretty much wherever beer is sold.

Bova's Bakery, 134 Salem St., North End, Boston, MA 02109; (617) 523-5601; bovabakeryboston.com; Bakery; T: Haymarket. Part of the charm of Bova is that it's changed little since it was founded in 1932. The best-selling items are the various forms of puffy white Italian bread. But breads are only part of the story. Bova has a window on Salem Street for takeaway pizza slices and the bakery makes fine anise cookies, sugar cookies in a variety of shapes, cakes,  pies, and several types of cheesecake. Best of all, Bova is open around the clock, in case you need to pick up some cannoli after the bars close.

The Butcherie, 428 Harvard St., Brookline, MA 02446; (617) 731-9888; butcherie.com; Grocery; T: Harvard Avenue/Coolidge Corner. The Rabbinical Council of New England supervises this glatt kosher shop where the shelves are piled high with US and Israeli kosher canned and dry goods. But what really packs in the customers is the deli area with fresh kosher meats, sausages, fish, latkes, and blended grain and vegetable salads. Knishes are available in turkey, vegetarian, sweet potato, and potato. The Butcherie also sells several varieties and grades of caviar, sliced smoked salmon, and a tremendous variety of frozen kosher hors d'oeuvres. Closed Sat.

Cafe Vanille, 70 Charles St., Beacon Hill, Boston, MA 02108; (617) 523-9200; cafevanilleboston.com; Bakery Cafe; T: Charles Street. In France, many families enjoy a *bûche de Noël,* or Yule log, every Sunday during the month of December. Parisian-born and -trained chefs Philippe Odier and Bruno Biagianti carry on the tradition by creating beautifully decorated chocolate logs (as well as one other rotating flavor) during the holidays. The rest of the year, you can enjoy napoleons, éclairs, fruit tarts, buttery croissants and brioche, quiches, and freshly baked baguettes and multigrain loaves. A slice of quiche or veggie *tourte* makes a great lunch as does a sandwich of salmon, cream cheese, and cucumber on a baguette, or egg salad, bacon, lettuce, and tomato on a croissant.

Caffè Vittoria, 290–296 Hanover St., North End, Boston, MA 02113; (617) 227-7606; vittoriacaffe.com; Coffee; T: Haymarket. This caffè has been part of the scene in the North End since 1929, and

every old-timer has a tale to tell about a semi-famous criminal or a visiting opera singer. We take them all with a grain of salt. The two separate entrances to the caffè used to define the smoking and (much smaller) nonsmoking sections; since Massachusetts banned smoking in food and drink establishments, the stairway between the two rooms leads upstairs to Stanza dei Sigari, a cigar parlor in the space of a former speakeasy.

Capone Foods, 14 Bow St., Union Square, Somerville, MA 02143; (617) 629-2296; 2285 Massachusetts Ave., Porter Square, Cambridge, MA 02140; (617) 354-0599; T: Porter Square; capone foods.com; Grocery. Albert Capone and his staff use 3,000 pounds of durum wheat every week to make plain, flavored, and filled pastas that range from squid ink fettuccine or black pepper pappardelle to artichoke ravioli or tomato tortellini. Add in all the sauces (Alfredo, roasted pepper pesto, white clam, tomato and sausage . . .) and the variations are almost limitless. Capone also makes a richly flavored ricotta and stocks a small assortment of cheeses. He especially likes to introduce customers to his array of olive oils and vinegars, mostly from Italy and Spain.

Cardullo's Gourmet Shoppe, 6 Brattle St., Harvard Square, Cambridge, MA 02138; (617) 491-8888; cardullos.com; Grocery; T: Harvard Square. Opened in 1950, Cardullo's remains the go-to place for tins of caviar or duck leg confit, Italian truffle sauce, Swedish lingon-berry preserves, Spanish smoked paprika, or sweet Bavarian mustard. We've never failed to find a chocolate assortment to suit any gift-giving occasion, but often just pop in for a Cadbury Flake or other hard-to-find British candy bar. As might be expected, many of the sandwiches made to order in the deli rise above the ordinary, including country pâté with fig spread or Spanish cured ham with Manchego cheese and quince paste. Cardullo's also has a small wine selection of good, if obscure, bottles in the moderate price range and its own line of Italian products, such as pastas, sauces, and olives.

Central Bottle Wine + Provisions, 196 Massachusetts Ave., Central Square, Cambridge, MA 02139; (617) 225-0040; centralbottle .com; Wine, Beer & Spirits; T: Central Square. Central Bottle is a wine store for people who either have taste or would like to develop it. This shop focuses on interesting yet reasonably priced fine wines from all over Europe and California, with a few nods to the southern hemisphere. The real strength tends to be in southern French and Italian producers, but the buyers do a great job of rooting out some of the less-expected regions of Spain as well. The "provisions" part of the name is also taken seriously: Look for top-notch artisanal cheeses (many of them regional) along with charcuterie from near and far.

Christina's Homemade Ice Cream, 1255 Cambridge St., Inman Square, Cambridge, MA 02139; (617) 492-7021; christinas icecream.com; Ice Cream/Yogurt. There are always about 50 flavors of ice cream waiting to be scooped at Christina's, and staff experiment with new flavor combinations all the time. Coffee Oreo, burnt sugar, and pistachio are among the favorites, along with fresh rose, a delicate specialty offered only when rose petals are available. You'll certainly find cookie dough, maple walnut, and other standards, but many of

TASTE OF THE STREETS

Boston's Little Italy and Chinatown are two of the tastiest parts of the city. To find out where the Italian locals shop, sign up for the **North End Market Tour,** a half-day of walking and tasting with Italian food expert Michele Topor. She's on a first-name basis with all the shop owners, who will almost certainly offer you samples. Mandarin-speaking chef Jim Becker pulls back the curtains of the Asian community with his **Boston Chinatown Market Tour,** which concludes with a dim sum lunch. Reservations are essential for both tours; check website for schedule.

L'Arte di Cucinare, 6 Charter St., Boston, MA 02113; (617) 523-6032; cucinare.com.

Christina's rich ice creams have more subtle flavorings, such as ginger molasses, green tea, honey lavender, adzuki bean, or fresh mint. **Christina's Spice & Specialty Foods** (a good source for spices and dried chile peppers) shares the same address, but has a separate entrance. Cash only.

V. Cirace & Son, Inc., 173 North St., North End, Boston, MA 02109; (617) 227-3193; vcirace.com; Wine, Beer & Spirits; T: Haymarket. Founded in 1906 and now operated by the third generation of the family, this shop does a lot of its own importing. That translates into some fabulous deals on northern Italian wines, especially Barbera and Barbaresco, as well as one of the largest selections of grappas and aquavitae we have ever encountered on this side of the Atlantic or even in Italy. The Cirace family also owns the Herbe di Amalfi brand of herb- and flower-infused liqueurs, and even has its own brand of limoncello.

City Feed and Supply, 672 Centre St., Jamaica Plain, MA 02130; (617) 524-1700; cityfeedandsupply.com; Grocery; T: Green

Street. Shelf tags advising "Keep it local" abound, pointing out mustard from Raye's Mustard Mill in Maine, smoked wild kippers from Bar Harbor, and whole wheat and white pita from **Samira's Homemade** (see p. 212) in Belmont. Almost all the cheeses and sausages come from farms or smokehouses we profiled in this book or *Food Lovers' Guide to Vermont & New Hampshire.* But that's just the supply side of CFS. The "feed" aspect pops up in the deli line, where you can order fresh sandwiches, salads, and soups as well as baked goods, coffee, tea, and herbal infusions.

Courthouse Seafood Fish Market and Restaurant, **484 Cambridge St., East Cambridge, Cambridge, MA 02141; (617) 876-6716; courthouseseafood.com; Fishmonger; T: Lechmere.** This venerable fish market definitely caters to the Portuguese neighborhood clientele. It carries all the fresh catch from New England ports, and flies in fresh sardines, stickleback, as well as cockles and other European shellfish from Portugal. If you want to make an authentic bouillabaisse, this is the spot to source the prescribed Mediterranean and eastern Atlantic fish. The

adjacent Courthouse Seafood Restaurant (617-491-1213) is a casual lunch place with fried, steamed, and broiled fish and a few stir-fries. Pick a fillet at the fish market and the cooks will prepare it while you wait.

Dave's Fresh Pasta, 81 Holland St., Davis Square, Somerville, MA 02144; (617) 623-0867; davesfreshpasta.com; Grocery; T: Davis Square. Dave Jick may have started this store as a fresh ravioli shop, but all the other gourmet foods have long since taken over. You can still buy nice ravioli (including the pumpkin ravioli found on half the restaurant menus in town) and sheets of fresh pasta for assembling your own lasagna, but you'll also find seasonal roasted vegetables (beets, brussels sprouts, carrots), the popular artichoke and lemon pesto, and a large array of specialty cheeses and artisanal chocolates. Dave's even has a good selection of unpretentious wines and craft brews.

DePasquale's Homemade Pasta Shoppe, 66A Cross St., North End, Boston, MA 02113; (617) 248-9629; homemade-pasta .com; Specialty Shop; T: Haymarket. At her flour-covered workbench in front of a big picture window, Zoya Kogan turns out about 50 different types of pasta. She's not the only one who's busy. Cheesemaker Joseph Locilento makes fresh mozzarella almost every day and "sometimes twice a day," he says, "especially in the summer when we have fresh tomatoes." Locilento also dries some of the mozzarella for three or four days for pizzas and baked pastas. He is happy to advise on the best sauce for squid ink and tomato pappardelle or for braised short rib and escarole ravioli. To round out a meal, the shop also carries a variety of cold cuts and cheeses.

Flour Bakery & Cafe, 1595 Washington St., South End, Boston, MA 02118; (617) 267-4300; T: Washington St. at E. Newton St. (Silver Line); 12 Farnsworth St., Waterfront, Boston, MA 02210; (617) 338-4333; T: Courthouse; 190 Massachusetts Ave., Central Square, Cambridge, MA 02139; (617) 225-2525; T: Central Square; flourbakery.com; Bakery Cafe. Joanne Chang may have studied applied mathematics and economics at Harvard, but her true calling lies in the kitchen. Anyone who can dream up Midnight Chocolate Cake and Lemon Lust Tarts owes it to humanity to share her talents. Breakfast treats include oatmeal maple scones, chocolate brioche, sticky caramel buns, and sour cream coffee cake. Lunchtime sandwiches feature elegant fillings such as roasted lamb, tomato chutney, and goat cheese or smoked turkey with cheddar and cranberry chutney. Be sure to leave room for a Belgian chocolate brownie or chocolate chip macaroon or take home a whole Boston cream pie or caramel nut tart for a great dinner-party dessert.

Formaggio Kitchen, 244 Huron Ave., Huron Village, Cambridge, MA 02138; (617) 354-4750; South End Formaggio, 268 Shawmut Ave., South End, Boston, MA 02118; (617) 350-6996; formaggiokitchen.com; Cheese. Ihsan Gurdal has devoted his life to the pursuit of exotic cheeses, and these two shops are widely considered among the world's best. The Cambridge location has an aging cellar, allowing Gurdal to purchase cheeses when they are available and sell them when they are ready. At any given time, the shops will have maybe 50 cheeses in the cases, ranging from unpretentious Canadian and New England cheddars to such rarities as a Bleu de Termignon, made by hand by an elderly lady in the French Alps. Both shops also have fresh breads, pasta, desserts, spices, and a small number of sausages and cold cuts of the same quality as the cheeses.

Greenhills Traditional Irish Bakery, 780 Adams St., Dorchester, Boston, MA 02124; (617) 825-8187; greenhillsbakery .com; Bakery Cafe; T: Ashmont. Operated by Dermot and Cindy Quinn since 1991, Greenhills is one-stop shopping for Boston's many Irish immigrants. True to its name, the bakery is known for its Irish soda breads, made with white or whole wheat flour. They are available plain, with raisins, with raisins and caraway, or made with treacle, a dark sugar syrup. The bakery turns out a number of other breads and rolls that are also used for breakfast and lunch sandwiches. Perhaps the most traditional—and filling—is the Irish breakfast sandwich of Irish or American bacon, Irish sausage, white and black pudding, and scrambled egg on a roll.

Haley House Bakery Cafe, 12 Dade St., Roxbury, Boston, MA 02119; (617) 445-0900; haleyhouse.org; Bakery Cafe; T: Dudley Square (Silver Line). Haley House runs a farm, a food pantry, and a soup kitchen, but the bakery cafe is its commercial face. The pastries (cookies, small crumb-topped fruit pies, cupcakes, muffins), sandwiches (jerk chicken quesadilla, for example), and soups (spicy chicken and potato) all set a high standard. Although the cafe is open until late afternoon, breakfast is one of the most popular meals, with many customers favoring the Haley House Slop. That's a plate of cheesy grits, scrambled eggs, and chicken sausage.

Harpoon Brewery, 306 Northern Ave., South Boston, MA 02210; (617) 574-9551; harpoonbrewery.com; Brewery; T: Northern Avenue & Harbor Street (Silver Line SL2). Some area bars, especially in South Boston, have Harpoon's ales on draft, but everyone sells them by the bottle. Harpoon makes eight year-round beers, four seasonal brews, and occasional specials in its 100-barrel limited edition series and its high-alcohol Leviathan series. Complimentary tastings are held twice each weekday afternoon, while guided tours and tastings for a fee are offered on weekends.

Hong Kong Supermarket, 1 Brighton Ave., Allston, Boston, MA 02134; (617) 787-2288; Grocery; T: Packards Corner. Shopping here is a bit like cruising all the little markets of Chinatown under one roof. Fortunately, the aisles are clearly marked, so it's easy to find the specialty ingredients from Japan, China, Thailand, or Vietnam, for example, or to locate entire aisles of tea and coffee, oil and vinegar, or snack foods. Fresh vegetables are up front, while the back wall is devoted to meat and fish, including a broader selection of fin fish than most Chinese grocers carry. For a little punch of flavor, we like to pick up some of the small jars of rice seasonings, such as sesame seed and seaweed, kimchi, salmon, or roasted wasabi.

James Hook + Co., 15–17 Northern Ave., Waterfront, Boston, MA 02210; (617) 423-5501; jameshooklobster.com; Fishmonger; T: South Station. In business since 1925, the Hook family ships more than 50,000 pounds of lobster a day to wholesalers, restaurants, and individuals around the country. But it's much more satisfying to shop in the no-nonsense retail market that manages to hold its own even as skyscrapers rise around it. You can enjoy a lobster roll on the spot and pick up some live lobsters to take home, along with such prepared fish classics as clam chowder, lobster bisque, lobster pie, lobster Newburg, and lobster mac and cheese. To make things easy in the kitchen, Hook also offers frying clams, minced clams, and shucked oysters.

Iggy's Bread of the World, 130 Fawcett St., Alewife, Cambridge, MA 02138; (617) 924-0949; iggysbread.com; Bakery. You'll find Iggy's breads and rolls in many grocery stores and specialty shops throughout greater Boston, but it's worth seeking out this shop at the baking facilities in a small industrial park for the fullest and freshest selection, including the sweet pastries (apple pie, bread pudding) and cookies (caramel, linzer) not distributed to the company's wholesale customers. At lunch there are also slices of pizza and such sandwiches as speck and brie, or ham with sun-dried tomatoes. There are usually about a half dozen loaves cut for samples, so you might be able to taste the dark rye, cranberry pecan, or olive bread. Probably the most popular breads are the pillowy-soft brioche dinner rolls and the salt-crusted francese loaves.

J.P. Licks, 659 Centre St., Jamaica Plain, MA 02130; (617) 524-6740; jplicks.com; Ice Cream/Yogurt; T: Green Street. Think of this shop as ice cream and frozen yogurt with a distinctly local flavor. One of the few survivors of the Premium Ice Cream Wars of the 1980s, J.P.

Licks got some of its original offbeat character from the hordes of tattooed, pierced, and ultimately polite art-school kids who worked at this first store. The ice cream and hard frozen yogurt show admirable restraint by rarely mixing more than two flavors (mint chip, say, or coffee Oreo), and the shop now roasts its own coffee and serves a variety of pastries, including spinach and cheese croissants. This is home for the local chain.

Kam Man Market, 101 Allstate Rd., Dorchester, MA 02125; (617) 541-2288; Grocery; T: Andrew. When we enter this large grocery store with wide, well-marked aisles, we usually head straight to the freezer cases in the rear to assemble a DIY dim sum feast of frozen dumplings (crabmeat, chicken and lotus root, lamb with oyster sauce), potstickers (shrimp, vegetable, beef), and steamed buns. Then we head to the sauce aisle to pick up dipping sauces that range from plum to peanut, chile-garlic to lemongrass. But we have to admit that we are most fascinated by the corner of the store devoted to more variations of noodles than we have ever imagined: stick, pan fried, lo mein, udon, wonton, soft tofu, silken tofu, Shanghai, Vietnamese. The fish display is one of the most extensive (and best) in the city, and the range and quality of the produce are outstanding.

KO Catering and Pies, 87 A St., South Boston, Boston, MA 02127; (617) 269-4500; T: Broadway; KO at the Shipyard, 256 Marginal St., Building 16, East Boston, Boston, MA 02128; (617) 418-5234; T: Maverick; kocateringandpies.com; Bakery Cafe. Sam Jackson opened KO to introduce the meat pies of his native Australia to Boston. The delicious, single-serving pies feature a short crust base filled with braised lamb shank, Irish beef stew, beef and cheese, or curried vegetables, and then topped with puff pastry. For an authentic experience, douse your perfect little pie in ketchup. "It's an Australian thing," Jackson says with a shrug. So are his sausage rolls, spicy shrimp on the barbie over rice, and grilled fish sandwiches. In 2012, Jackson opened the second spot on the East Boston waterfront.

Kupel's Bakery, 421 Harvard St., Brookline, MA 02446; (617) 566-9528; kupelsbakery.com; Bakery; T: Harvard Avenue/Coolidge Corner. Kupel's is best known in this traditionally Jewish neighborhood for its stupendous certified kosher bagels—light rye, pumpernickel, sissel, marble rye, and corn. You can also pick up the bakery's own bagel spreads, ranging from flavored cream cheeses to salmon mousse. In addition to bagels, Kupel's also makes sourdough, sissel, pumpernickel, cinnamon raisin, spinach, and oat bran breads, as well as flaky, bite-size rugelach. Closed Sat.

L.A. Burdick Chocolates, 52D Brattle St., Harvard Square, Cambridge, MA 02138; (617) 491-4340; burdickchocolate.com; Chocolatier; T: Harvard Square. This outlet of the Walpole, New Hampshire–based chocolatier offers pastries to eat in the shop or take home, along with chocolate bonbons (such as cherry and cumin or fig and port), truffles (lemon pepper or cognac), and traditional and salted caramels. For all the elegance of his handmade chocolates that use organic ingredients when possible, founder Larry Burdick retains a sense of fun. His signature product is a chocolate mouse with a colorful ribbon tail. Hot chocolate (in milk, dark, or white) is very popular in the winter and is served iced in the summer.

Mike's Pastry, 300 Hanover St., North End, Boston, MA 02113; (617) 742-3050; mikespastry.com; Bakery; T: Haymarket. Sometimes it seems that every other person on the sidewalk is carrying a blue and white box from Mike's Pastry. The North End's largest and most famous bakery meets the demand with no fewer than 17 flavors of cannoli (including pistachio, espresso, strawberry, and pecan caramel) and a range of cupcakes, cookies, brownies, and cakes. Macaroon flavors include almond, raspberry, apricot, green cherry, and red nut. If you are lucky, you might be able to grab one of the small tables and enjoy your treat in the shop rather than at home.

Modern Pastry, 257 Hanover St., North End, Boston, MA 02113; (617) 523-3783; modernpastry.com; Bakery; T: Haymarket. You'll find a full array of cakes, cookies, cannoli, biscotti, and breads made from Old World recipes at this North End shop that has been in the same family for three generations. But locals line up for the shop's torrone, often made by octogenarian Giovanni Picariello. He combines sugar, honey, nuts, and egg whites into a nougat-like treat. It's available in a variety of flavors including peanut butter, chocolate, caramel, espresso, as well as the family's secret recipe vanilla torrone with roasted almonds.

New Saigon Sandwich Banh Mi, 696 Washington St., Chinatown, Boston, MA 02111; (617) 542-6296; Sandwich Shop; T: Chinatown. Every Chinatown needs a great *banh mi* joint to complement the one good *pho* house (see **Pho Pasteur,** p. 152), and New Saigon is it. In fact, the shop was selling Vietnamese sandwiches (which they call French submarines) for decades before they bothered to put up an English sign. It doesn't matter—it's probably the single most popular lunch spot for all the staff and students at nearby Tufts Medical campus. Not only do they love the shredded pork or barbecued beef sandwiches piled high with a veritable salad of vegetables, they also scarf up vegetarian and chicken box lunches with rice.

Petsi Pies, 285 Beacon St., Somerville, MA 02143; (617) 661-7437; T: Porter Square; 31 Putnam Ave., Cambridge, MA 02139; (617) 499-0801; T: Harvard Square; Bakery; petsipies.com. There's a lot to be said for doing one thing so well that the world beats a path to your door. Renee McLeod (whose childhood nickname, pronounced *PEET-see,* gives the bakery its name) is a pie genius. At either location, expect half a dozen sweet pies in three sizes and a few savory pies (like chicken potpie) in two sizes. Of course, she also makes some delicious cookies, brownies, and scones. McLeod is co-owner of **Tupelo** restaurant in Cambridge (see p. 159), which serves her pies for dessert.

Rosie's Bakery, 243 Hampshire St., Inman Square, Cambridge, MA 02139; (617) 491-9488; rosiesbakery.com; Bakery. Judy Rosenberg unapologetically titled her cookbook *The Rosie's Bakery All-Butter, Cream-Filled, Sugar-Packed Baking Book,* which explains what you need to know about the treats at this, her original retail location. Rosenberg built her mini-empire on giving people the goodies they loved as children, from chocolate sour cream cupcakes to peanut butter chocolate chunk cookies. But her fame rests on her very adult chocolate orgasms—rich brownies topped with a smooth and silky chocolate ganache.

Rubin's Kosher, 500 Harvard St., Brookline, MA 02446; (617) 731-8787; rubins boston.com; Grocery; T: Harvard Avenue. Rubin's has served up the taste of home for generations of eastern and central European immigrants since 1927. The full-service deli sells  superb brisket, pastrami, chopped beef or chicken liver, knockwurst, latkes, potato kugel, beet salad, and even the school lunchbox standard of tuna salad. Sit-down meals can range from simple (a cup of borscht and a couple of spinach knishes) to hearty (barbecue brisket sandwich with homemade potato salad) or comforting (a chicken thigh and leg with matzo ball, noodles, and kreplach in broth). The smoked fish sampler of whitefish, sable, smoked salmon, and herring is great for sharing. Closed Sat.

Sakanaya Japanese Fish Market, 75 Linden St., Allston, MA 02134; (617) 254-0009; sakanayaboston.com; Fishmonger; T: Harvard Avenue/Packards Corner. The best  way to learn about good sushi is to eat it, and Sakanaya sells excellent sushi at bargain prices. Whenever you walk in, there will be a sushi chef patiently preparing more. But the next best way to understand sushi is to make it yourself, and Sakanaya has the incredibly good fresh fish to make that easy. A significant portion of the clientele is Japanese.

Salumeria Italiana, 151 Richmond St., North End, Boston, MA 02109; (617) 523-8743; salumeriaitaliana.com; Grocery; T: Haymarket. Italian opera often plays over the sound system, a stack of dried cod meets you just inside the door, and at the holiday season, huge stacks of panettone (a sweet bread studded with dried fruit) practically obscure the rest of the interior. Once you tear yourself away from the shelves laden with green and black olive paste, tapenades, olive oils, and balsamic vinegar, head to the refrigerated cases in the back for dozens of dried sausages, whole Parma hams, prosciutto shanks, and—during the fall and early winter—fresh white truffles. "They're $2,000 a pound," apologizes one of the staff, "but they're just as expensive in Italy. Would you like a sniff?" he asks, holding the jar. Given an affirmative, he jokes, "That's $20," and offers the open jar.

Savenor's, 92 Kirkland St., Inman Square, Cambridge, MA 02138; (617) 576-6328; 160 Charles St., Beacon Hill, Boston, MA 02114; (617) 723-6328; T: Charles Street; savenorsmarket.com; Butcher. Julia Child catapulted this butcher shop into the limelight as the place to go for prime rib, rack of lamb, venison, buffalo, wild boar, goose, pheasant, or *poussin*. Those less at home in the kitchen than the French Chef might opt for the pork loin already stuffed with prosciutto, provolone, and spices, or the leg of lamb with goat cheese, *herbes de*

Provence, garlic, and rosemary. Or pick up some duck *foie gras,* salmon pâté, Stilton cheese, and a crusty loaf of bread for a picnic on the banks of the Charles River.

Serenade Chocolatier, 5 Harvard Square, Brookline, MA 02445; (617) 739-0795; T: Brookline Village; 2 South Station, Waterfront, Boston, MA 02110; (617) 261-9941; T: South Station; serenadechocolatier.com; Chocolatier. The small shop in Brookline carries on the Viennese chocolate-making tradition. Its signature is the Viennese truffle, alternating layers of dark and milk chocolate blended with hazelnut butter. Serenade also creates more conventional truffles as well as dipped fruits, nut clusters, caramel patties, buttercrunch, and a variety of creams. For an elegant Old World treat, nothing is better than Serenade's marzipan truffle or chocolate-covered marzipan. For a more modern twist, try a made-to-order, chocolate-dipped ice cream bar with vanilla or chocolate ice cream or mixed berry yogurt from **J.P. Licks** (see p. 171). The South Station branch has a somewhat more limited selection.

Shalimar Indian Food & Spices, 571 Massachusetts Ave., Central Square, Cambridge, MA 02139; (617) 868-8311; shalimarindianfoods.com; Grocery; T: Central Square. It seems that there is an Indian restaurant on every block in Cambridge's Central Square, and we'd wager that all the chefs count on this well-stocked shop when they find themselves short on cardamom or star anise. If you want to create Indian food at home, check the freezer cases for frozen samosas (with lamb, cheese, or vegetable fillings), as well as naan, roti, paratha, and other Indian breads. Then look for the packaged gourmet spice blends with recipes on the back. Round out your meal with garlic, mint, coconut, tamarind, or coriander chutney. Easier yet, pick up some lamb vindaloo to take home at the small fast-food counter at the rear of the market.

Sofra Bakery and Cafe, 1 Belmont St., West Cambridge, Cambridge, MA 02138; (617) 661-3161; sofrabakery.com; Bakery Cafe. *Sofra* is an old Arabic word denoting both a picnic and a kilim rug—a synonym for hospitality. The young crowd (often with babies in 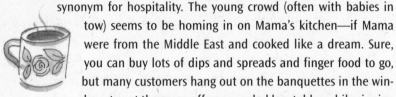 tow) seems to be homing in on Mama's kitchen—if Mama were from the Middle East and cooked like a dream. Sure, you can buy lots of dips and spreads and finger food to go, but many customers hang out on the banquettes in the windows to eat the meze off copper-clad low tables while sipping coffee, tea, or juice. Stuffed flatbreads are especially popular at lunch, especially those filled with spinach, three cheeses, and herbs, though it's hard to resist the green olive and walnut salad, or the dish of smoky eggplant with pine nuts.

Syrian Grocery Importing Company, 270 Shawmut Ave., South End, Boston, MA 02118; (617) 426-1458; Grocery; T: Back Bay Station. Syrian Grocery has fed neighborhood Middle Eastern immigrants since 1940. In Ramon Mansour's family since 1967, it stocks such essentials as Arabic allspice, a blend of seven spices that is used in stews and is the "secret spice" in kibbe, and *mahlab,* which is used in sweet breads instead of vanilla. Mansour always carries beautiful clay tagines, preserved lemons, and Morocco's all-purpose seasoning blend, *ras al hanout.*

Tatte Fine Cookies and Cakes, 1003 Beacon St., Brookline, MA 02446; (617) 232-2200; tattecookies.com; Bakery Cafe; T: St. Mary's Street. Baker Tzurit Or and her assistants are geniuses at baking with nuts. Starting with family recipes, Or has expanded her repertoire to include nut-studded XXL biscotti, butter pistachio cookies, crisp almond biscuits, cashew or hazelnut tarts, walnut coffee cake, and her trademark nuts box of buttery pastry with a caramelized filling and toasted nut topping. She also makes a wonderful strawberry walnut roll, beautiful fruit tarts, an elegant peach bundt cake, and a homey cherry *clafouti*. Her chocolate halvah bomb is just that—chocolate layers enveloping a halvah center.

Taza Chocolate, 561 Windsor St., Union Square, Somerville, MA 02143; (617) 284-2232; tazachocolate.com; Chocolatier. Launched in 2006, Taza takes the chocolate-making process from bean to bar. Founders Alex Whitmore and Larry Skolnick travel to cacao-growing regions (mostly the Dominican Republic and Costa Rica) to buy the top of the crop directly from certified organic growers. Big windows in the factory store offer a view of the work area, including stone mills similar to the ones that inspired Whitmore on a trip to Mexico. Better yet, you can sample the end result and discern the differences between the 60, 70, 80, and 87 percent dark chocolate bars. Taza also makes discs of Mexican-style chocolate, either plain or with flavors including cinnamon, coffee, orange, and chile. If you decide to take the tour (see website for schedule), be sure to wear closed-toe shoes and avoid perfume, since it might mask the sultry smell of chocolate.

Toscanini's, 899 Main St., Central Square, Cambridge, MA 02139; (617) 491-5877; tosci.com; Ice Cream/Yogurt; T: Central Square. We have friends who stock their freezer with Toscanini's deeply-flavored burnt caramel ice cream in fear that they will arrive at the shop and find that it is sold out. Others find perfection in the simple French vanilla or the seasonal strawberry. But we like to keep an open mind. You could close your eyes and point to the chalkboard list of flavors and not be disappointed, whether your finger fell on Kenyan *khulfee,* salty caramel, lemon espresso, or goat cheese brownie. In a twist of Euro-perfection, there is a Belgian chocolate to go with that French vanilla.

Tropical Foods Supermarket, 2101 Washington St., Roxbury, MA 02119; (617) 442-7439; tropicalfoods.net; Grocery; T: Dudley

CITY FARMERS

Boston is just starting to join the national urban farming movement, and while most of the microfarms sell only through commercial channels, a few have full-fledged CSA (community-supported agriculture) programs and farm stands.

Allandale Farm, 259 Allandale Rd., Brookline, MA 02467; (617) 524-1531; allandalefarm.com. Located behind the Arnold Arboretum just over the line into Brookline, Allandale is a survivor—the last old-time working farm in the central city. Open April into November, Allandale devotes its primary efforts to CSA. Consumers buy shares in the season and pick up harvests from June into October. The farm stand carries the surplus, as well as some products from other local farms and suppliers.

ReVision Urban Farm, 1062 Blue Hill Ave., Dorchester, MA 02124; (617) 822-3276; vpi.org/revision. This farm run by and for ReVision Family Home, a shelter for pregnant and parenting women, provides food for the homeless of Dorchester, a CSA program from June through October, and a farm stand that is open July through October. The farm stand takes SNAP/EBT and participates in the city's Bounty Bucks program that doubles the value of SNAP/EBT for produce purchases up to $20. The farm also sells at the **Dorchester House Farmers' Market** (see p. 183), where it also accepts WIC vouchers.

Square. Tropical has been Roxbury's neighborhood supermarket since 1974, making sure that its African-American and Caribbean clientele are equally well fed. The frozen food aisle appeals to both with black-eyed peas, okra, mustard greens, chopped collard greens, and butter beans. Puerto Rican frozen specialties include fried plantains (*tostones*), baked ripe plantains, chicken croquettes, and empanadas. Goya's Hispanic products abound, including a wide range of sausages and the whole line of soup bases and seasonings. In the dry goods, one side of an aisle is devoted to dried beans, peas, and other pulses, and a vegetables section is devoted to root crops, ranging from yautia and cassava to African and Japanese yams. Tropical is the place to pick up smoked goat meat or cross-sectioned oxtail for making an unctuous stew. The meat case holds every edible part of the pig: chitterlings, ears, trotters, and snout, as well as the usual chops, roasts, fatback, and bacon.

Wulf's Fish Market, 407 Harvard St., Brookline, MA 02146; (617) 277-2506; Fishmonger; T: Harvard Street/Coolidge Corner. This fishmonger cuts all its fillets from whole fish bought fresh daily from Fish Pier. The salt smell of the sea pervades the shop and the whole fish laid out on beds of ice are as clear-eyed a lot as you'll find anywhere. One of the great pleasures of shopping at Wulf's, which dates from 1926, is watching the gents in white aprons cut your order.

Farmers' Markets

Haymarket is a throwback to the era of outdoor central markets. Vendors set up their tables along Blackstone Street in Boston, in front of the halal markets on the back side of Faneuil Hall Marketplace on Friday afternoon and all day on Saturday. The amazing bargains get more amazing as the end of the day approaches—especially if you're willing to take an entire case of broccoli, a flat of strawberries, or a basket of peaches. Because most of the food at Haymarket is highly perishable produce, the vendors want to move it at discount prices. At this writing, plans are under way for a year-round public market along the lines of Philadelphia's Reading Terminal Market or Seattle's Pike Place Market. It will be located at 136 Blackstone St. and is scheduled to open in summer 2014.

Boston Medical Center Farmers' Market, 840 Harrison Ave., Boston. Fri from 11:30 a.m. to 2:30 p.m., mid-June through mid-Oct.

Boston Prudential Center Farmers' Market, 800 Boylston St., Boston. Thurs from 11 a.m. to 6 p.m., late May through Oct.

Boston/South Station/Dewey Square Farmers' Market, Dewey Square at South Station, Boston. Tues and Thurs from 11:30 a.m. to 6:30 p.m., late May through Oct.

Boston/South Station/Dewey Square Winter Farmers' Market, Dewey Square at South Station, Boston. Tues and Thurs from 11:30 a.m. to 2:30 p.m., late Nov to late Dec.

Cambridge Center Market, Cambridge Center Plaza, Main Street, Cambridge. Wed from 11 a.m. to 6 p.m., mid-May through late Oct.

Cambridge/Central Square Farmers' Market, parking lot No. 5, Bishop Allen Drive, Central Square, Cambridge. Mon from noon to 6 p.m., late May through mid-Nov.

Cambridge/Charles Square Farmers' Market, Charles Hotel Courtyard, Harvard Square, Cambridge. Fri from noon to 6 p.m., early June to mid-Nov; Sun from 10 a.m. to 3 p.m., late May through mid-Nov.

Cambridge/Harvard University Farmers' Market, corner of Oxford and Kirkland Streets, Cambridge. Tues from noon to 6 p.m., mid-June through Oct.

Cambridge/Kendall Square Farmers' Market, 500 Kendall St., Cambridge. Thurs from 11 a.m. to 2 p.m., June through early Sept.

Cambridge Winter Farmers' Market, 5 Callender St., Cambridge Community Center, Cambridge. Sat from 10 a.m. to 2 p.m., Jan through Apr.

Cambridgeport Farmers' Market, Morse School parking lot, Magazine Street and Memorial Drive, Cambridge. Sat from 10 a.m. to 2 p.m., June through late Oct.

Charlestown Farmers' Market, Thompson Square, Charlestown. Wed from 2 p.m. to 7 p.m., July through Oct.

City Hall Plaza Farmers' Market, City Hall Plaza, Government Center, Boston. Mon and Wed from 11 a.m. to 6 p.m., late May to late Nov (closes 5 p.m. in Nov).

Dorchester/Bowdoin Geneva Farmers' Market, Bowdoin Street Health Center, Bowdoin Street, Dorchester. Thur from 3 to 6:30 p.m., July through Oct.

Dorchester/Codman Square Farmers' Market, Codman Commons at Washington Street and Talbott Avenue, Dorchester. Thur from 1 to 6 p.m., late June through Oct.

Dorchester/Dorchester House Farmers' Market, 1353 Dorchester Ave., Dorchester. Tues from 11:30 a.m. to 1:30 p.m., July through Sept.

Dorchester/Fields Corner Farmers' Market, Park Street Shopping Center, Dorchester. Sat from 9 a.m. to noon, July through Sept.

Dorchester/Grove Hall Farmers' Market, next to 461 Blue Hill Ave., Dorchester. Tues from 3 to 7 p.m., mid-July through mid-Oct.

Dorchester/Peabody Square Farmers' Market, Ashmont Station Plaza, Dorchester. Fri from 3 to 7 p.m., early July through mid-Oct.

Dorchester Winter Farmers' Market, 6 Norfolk St., Codman Square Health Center, Dorchester. Sun from noon to 3 p.m., early Jan through late Mar.

Jamaica Plain Community Servings Farmers' Market, 18 Marbury Terrace, Jamaica Plain. Wed from 4 to 7 p.m., mid-July to mid-Oct.

Jamaica Plain Farmers' Market, 677 Centre St., Jamaica Plain. Tues from noon to 5 p.m. and Sat from noon to 3 p.m., May through late Nov.

Jamaica Plain/Loring-Greenough Farmers' Market, 12 South St., Jamaica Plain. Thurs from noon to dusk, early July to late Oct.

Mission Hill Farmers' Market, Brigham Circle, intersection of Huntington Avenue and Tremont Street, Roxbury. Thurs from 11 a.m. to 6 p.m., June through Oct.

Roxbury/Dudley Farmers' Market, Town Common, Dudley Street and Blue Hill Avenue, Roxbury. Tues and Thurs from 3 to 7 p.m., June through Oct.

Roxbury/Frederick Douglass Square Farmers' Market, corner of Tremont and Hammond Streets, Roxbury. Sat from 11 a.m. to 5 p.m., July through Oct.

Somerville/Davis Square Farmers' Market, Day and Herbert Streets parking lot, Davis Square, Somerville. Wed from noon to 6 p.m., late May to late Nov (closes 5 p.m. in Nov).

Somerville/Union Square Farmers' Market, Union Square Plaza, Somerville. Sat from 9 a.m. to 1 p.m., June through late Oct.

Somerville Winter Farmers' Market, Center for the Arts at the Armory, 191 Highland Ave., Somerville. Sat from 10 a.m. to 2 p.m., mid-Nov through late May.

South Boston Farmers' Market, W. Broadway municipal parking lot, South Boston. Mon from noon to 6 p.m., May through late Nov.

South End Farmers' Market, South End Open Market, end of Thayer Street, Boston. Sun from 10 a.m. to 4 p.m., May through Oct (closed holiday weekends).

South End Winter Farmers' Market, 485 Harrison Ave., Boston. Sun from 10 a.m. to 2 p.m., late Nov to late Apr.

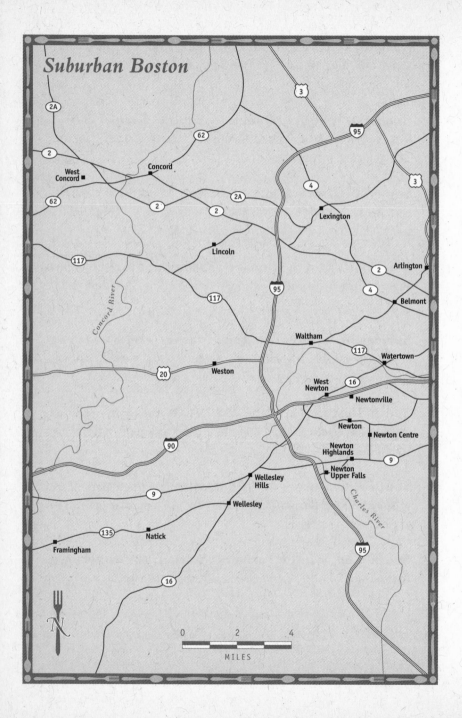

Suburban Boston

2A

2

West
Concord ■

62

2

Concord ■

62

2A

2

2

Lincoln ■

117

117

Concord River

20

Weston ■

90

9

135

Natick ■

Framingham ■

16

3

95

4

Lexington ■

2

Arlington ■

4

Belmont ■

Waltham ■

117

Watertown ■

West
Newton ■

16

Newtonville ■

Newton ■

Newton Centre ■

Newton
Highlands ■

9

Newton
Upper Falls ■

Wellesley
Hills ■

Wellesley ■

Charles River

95

3

95

N

0   2   4

MILES

Suburban Boston

A few years ago, some friends relocated from Back Bay to one of the posher suburbs of MetroWest. Dedicated foodies, they had barely unpacked before they started to explore the gastronomic landscape in the land without sidewalks. It wasn't long before they announced that they no longer needed to come into the city to shop or even to go out to dinner. Like a New Yorker who stumbles onto something worthwhile in one of the flyover states, they discovered a rich gastronomic life in the 'burbs.

Young chefs have also discovered that the rents are a lot lower in the suburbs, so many nascent talents are setting up shop—only to build an appreciative clientele that keeps them from fleeing back into the city even after they make their reputations. In fact, we'd argue, some of the most relaxed fine dining in eastern Massachusetts can be found in communities ringing the city. Suburb means anything but subpar. Some spots are so popular that they lure Bostonians; MBTA trolley and commuter rail stops are given where appropriate.

This chapter covers the communities that ring central Boston—from the immediate outliers like Watertown, Belmont, and Arlington to commuter rail communities like the many villages of Newton as well as Lexington, Concord, Waltham, and even Framingham. Close to Boston, they are often characterized by a rich lode of ethnic shops and dining. Farther west lies open farmland and even a dairy herd or two.

AKA Bistro, 145 Lincoln Rd., Lincoln, MA 01773; (781) 259-9920; akabistrolincoln.com; French/Japanese; $$–$$$; T: Lincoln. Very few chefs can say that a childhood meal gave direction to their lives, but Executive Chef–Co-owner Chris Chung is one of them. A family dinner at one of star chef Joël Robuchon's restaurants convinced him at the age of 8 that he was destined to make his career in haute cuisine. Chung learned his Japanese chops on Oahu, where he was raised, but came by a love of French cuisine naturally from his mother, a native of Marseilles. AKA (pronounced *ah-kah*) marries French bistro fare at bargain prices (spring lamb stew, slow-roasted cod, *moules frites*) with exquisite sashimi that can get pricey by the time you order a few plates. Adventurous diners should show up on Wednesday night for Maki Madness, when Chung tries out a flurry of creative rolls.

Alta Strada Restaurant, Pizzeria & Market, 92 Central St., Wellesley, MA 02482; (781) 237-6100; altastradarestaurant.com; Italian; $$–$$$. Michael Schlow made this "High Street" in Wellesley his first venture into a more casual, community-centric restaurant, and struck a bull's-eye. The Italian menu emphasizes whatever is freshest in the market, and whatever works best in the kitchen's humongous ovens. Even the salads are enough to make most patrons salivate, and the midday pizzas are light and crisp and full of flavors. The reasonably priced pasta plates are always richly flavored: homemade fettuccine with wild mushrooms, rosemary, and Parmesan, for example, or hand-rolled cavatelli with spicy fennel sausage and baby broccoli. The *secondi* meat and fish plates at dinner are hearty and simple, like a grilled pork chop, smoky ribs, and *agrodolce* peppers. For patrons who want to eat the same great food at home (or to pick up some of the great ingredients the restaurant uses), there's a downstairs market with an entrance from the rear parking lot. The entire menu is available for takeout, and customers have been known to dash in wearing pajamas. For those willing to dress, the Sunday brunch is very popular.

B Street, 796 Beacon St., Newton, MA 02459; (617) 332-8743; bstreetnewton.com; New American; $$; T: Newton Centre. Europeans justly celebrate the hamburger as the star of American cuisine. This funky small-town American bistro lets the burger star, though it shares center stage with grilled lamb chops, pan-seared scallops, and spaghetti and meatballs. It's unlikely you'll encounter anything terribly exotic at B Street, but familiarity is part of the appeal. You might be surprised by little touches (the chipotle ketchup and house-made pickle with the burger, for example) that keep you from wondering why you didn't cook the same food at home. Chances are you'd never make the pistachio madeleines that accompany the orange crème brûlée, anyway.

The Biltmore Bar & Grille, 1205 Chestnut St., Newton, MA 02464; (617) 527-2550; thebiltmoregrill.com; New American; $$. We've never quite understood why so many folks equate old-fashioned American dining with Southern food, but the Biltmore nails the look and sound. Tin ceilings and gas station memorabilia meet their match in rockabilly, soul, and retro roots music on the jukebox as well as in the chicken and waffles dish on the late-night menu. Fortunately, the Biltmore only takes the Alabama roadhouse theme so far, stopping this side of greasy collards. In fact, the updated tavern food includes an austere roasted Arctic char with chickpea salad and broccolini and beer-can game hen with sweet potato fries. There's even a separate menu for great cheeses and some local charcuterie. Elvis may have left the building, but the spirit of James Beard has come for dinner.

Blue Ginger, 583 Washington St., Wellesley, MA 02482; (781) 283-5790; ming.com/blueginger; Asian/New American; $$$$.

Chef-Owner Ming Tsai, Food Network star and cookbook author, has made Blue Ginger his home base since 1998. Ming is actually in the kitchen on many nights, overseeing the operations of the executive chef. Known for his matchmaking of Asian and European cuisines, Tsai composes dishes where all the boundaries blur and fabulous flavors emerge. Rack of lamb, for example, is glazed with pomegranate molasses and is served with apple-endive salad, Chinese black-bean creamed spinach, and mashed potatoes. Tsai is also a leader in serving sustainable fish, and his sablefish dishes are invariably big hits. One version marinates the fish (also known as "black cod" and sometimes as "butterfish") in miso and sake, and pairs it with a vegetarian soba noodle sushi. To enjoy the cuisine on a more limited budget, make a lunch reservation (weekdays only).

Blue Ribbon Bar-B-Q, 908 Massachusetts Ave., Arlington, MA 02476; (781) 648-7427; 1375 Washington St., West Newton, MA 02465; (617) 332-2583; blueribbonbbq.com; Barbecue; $; T: West Newton. When it comes to barbecue, we are not purists. Your birth certificate need not read North Carolina, Tennessee, Texas, or Missouri

to make good barbecue. We do ask that you don't parboil the meat and that you roast everything long and slow over a smoky fire. That said, we like *all* the barbecue at Blue Ribbon, though we're probably most partial to the Carolina-style pulled pork, which takes a good 14 hours to roast before it's pulled apart and simmered in a vinegar sauce.

We're also fans of the Kansas City–style burnt ends: slightly charred beef chunks cut from the tougher top of the brisket and simmered in a tomato-based sauce until they disintegrate. Most customers come for takeout. Just make sure there's a cold six-pack of PBR at home.

Casey's Diner, 36 South Ave., Natick, MA 01760; (508) 655-3761; Casual American; $. Proof that good things come in small packages, 10-stool Casey's is so compact that the entry is through a sliding door and there are no booths. There is, however, a window on one end, and, according to the staff, "Even when it's 5 degrees outside, people are lined up at the take-out window." Chances are that they're ordering either the diner's famed steamed hot dogs or its juicy burgers.

The diminutive diner was built in 1922 and purchased in 1925 by the Casey family, who have been running it ever since. Alas, over the years the exterior has been reclad in wood, but the interior gleams with the patina of 85 years of good grub.

CK Shanghai, 15–17 Washington St., Wellesley Hills, MA 02481; (781) 237-7500; ckshanghai.com; Chinese; $–$$. Most of Boston's top chefs doff their toques to C.K. Sau as the Chinese master. So you can eat modern East-West fusion at **AKA Bistro** (see p. 188) or **Blue Ginger** (see p. 189), or come here and let Chef-Owner Sau introduce you to the pleasures of world-class traditional Chinese cuisine. The menu is as inscrutable as at any lower-rent Chinese restaurant, but Sau's interpretations are exquisite. Focus on the section of the menu called "Shanghai's Specialty Seafood, Meat, and Poultry," which covers the best dishes. Apart from the lobster or the Peking duck, they're remarkably inexpensive. Another good strategy is to fold up the menu, ask what's fresh, and request that the chef cook you a memorable meal. Don't be surprised if it includes Hunan-style whole fish (Sau's special sauce really makes the dish) and some wok-fried scallops with black peppercorn sauce.

Deluxe Town Diner, 627 Mount Auburn St., Watertown, MA 02472; (617) 926-8400; deluxetowndiner.com; Casual American; $. It's great to see American folkways handed down fork by fork. Young parents from Cambridge, Belmont, and Watertown bring their kids here to introduce them to the great American dining car experience, so it's often loud with the sound of excited children. Consider the soundtrack part of the charm. Deluxe serves breakfast for all three meals, which, as any traveling salesman or truck driver will tell you, is the safest way to eat on the road. Nobody messes up breakfast. But not everyone does it as well as Deluxe, with dishes such as challah french toast and crab cakes Benedict. Club sandwiches are the stars of the lunch menu, although a pretty authentic New York–style hot pastrami might warrant consideration. The blue plate specials feature diner standards like meat loaf dinner or roast turkey. Deluxe steps everything up a notch for dinner, when a fine-dining chef serves the likes of braised short ribs, corn fritters, and bacon-wrapped plantains.

80 Thoreau, 80 Thoreau St., Concord, MA 01742; (978) 318-0008; 80thoreau.com; New American; $$–$$$; T: Concord. With **Rialto** (see p. 155) alumna Carolyn Johnson in the kitchen, 80 Thoreau proves that Concord residents don't need to go into the city to get a great meal—only as far as a commuter rail station. Johnson lets seasonal ingredients shine in her cleanly conceived, intensely flavored dishes. Winter starters, for example, favor such plates as a scallop crudo, with the raw shellfish supported by blood orange, fried shallot, and sea salt. Her tagliatelle with lamb *ragù* comes with braised fennel seasoned with juniper berries and accented by black olives. In the summer, local farms supply all the vegetables. The wooden floors, high-beamed ceiling, and solid white walls bounce noise, so 80 Thoreau often sounds even fuller than it is. Good luck getting even a seat in the bar unless you arrive before the commuter train from North Station does.

Elephant Walk, 663 Main St., Waltham, MA 021451; (781) 899-2244; elephantwalk.com; Cambodian/French; $$. With other locations in Boston and Cambridge (see p. 138), Elephant Walk reflects the culinary side of French imperialist adventures in Indochina. The restaurant serves upscale Cambodian food, including the house specialty of *amok*—a coconut milk custard scented with aromatic Khmer spices and filled with crab, shellfish, and catfish fillets. Yet the same menu includes a broad choice of Parisian bistro plates along with a list of vegetarian and gluten-free dishes. Should you wish, you can hopscotch courses between Southeast Asia and the French countryside. This Waltham branch belongs to the Benefit Restaurant Project, donating 3 percent of sales to a charity selected each month.

51 Lincoln, 51 Lincoln St., Newton Highlands, MA 02461; (617) 965-3100; 51lincolnnewton.com; New American: $$$; T: Newton Highlands. Chef-Owner Jeffrey F. Fournier certainly has all the local bona fides a young chef could ask for, including a stint with Lydia Shire, but he also spent some of his early days in the trade in and around Santa Monica, giving him a well-rounded and thoughtful approach to contemporary market-driven cooking. So while he poaches lobster in butter and Sauternes, he also serves steamed Asian-style buns and prepares a lovely seared fluke fillet with sweet pea risotto. Many locals pop in for impromptu dinner at the bar, savoring the excellent but affordable burger or the fish tacos. Intimate and casual, 51 Lincoln is very much a neighborhood trattoria for Green Line commuters.

Flora, 190 Massachusetts Ave., Arlington, MA 02474; (781) 641-1664; florarestaurant.com; New American; $$–$$$. During the explosive last-century days of Boston fine dining, Bob Sargent was chef at a slew of top restaurants. Then in 1996, he and wife Mary Jo opened this relaxed, friendly bistro in the former Arlington Five Cents Savings Bank, where they've been providing a warm welcome and memorable meals ever since. Plates are available in three sizes. Appetizers range from simple salads to carrot-ginger soup to a house charcuterie plate. So-called "medium plates" are good for sharing as an appetizer or ordering as a modest main dish. That might include a dish of clams with white beans, braised escarole, and sausage—or a single lamb T-bone chop with green beans, red peppers, and French feta fondue. Entree plates are large and meaty. Sunday brunch is special at Flora—the light streaming in the big windows highlights the elegance of the white linens and gleaming table settings.

Gustazo Cuban Cafe, 289 Belmont St., Belmont, MA 02478; (855) 487-8296; gustazo-cubancafe.com; Cuban; $. Apart from the Cubano sandwich, Cuban food has a low profile in greater Boston. Gustazo does a very authentic version of the Cubano, aside from having to  put it on French bread because Miami-style Cuban bread is unavailable. Miami expats also favor the *pan con léchon,* a sandwich of slow-roasted pork served with an avocado-pineapple salad. For a heartier plate, try the classic *ropa vieja* ("old clothes"), a Canary Islands recipe that evolved into the Cuban national dish. It's a hearty plate of shredded skirt steak cooked with *sofrito* (onion, garlic, and diced pepper) in a mild tomato sauce. It's served with white rice, fried plantains, and black beans.

Il Capriccio, 888 Main St., Waltham, MA 02453; (781) 894-2234; ilcapricciowaltham.com; Italian; $$$. Founded decades ago by a Milanese expat, Il Capriccio was one of the flag bearers for northern Italian cuisine in greater Boston even before meat-centric Tuscan menus became the vogue. The pastas are all available as entrees, but stick with the smaller servings for a first course and enjoy a full meal here. The house *salumi* makes a good starter for sharing, but you'll want your own black risotto with lobster or gnocchi with Ipswich clams before contemplating the meat and fish *secondi*. The semolina-crusted trout stuffed with braised cabbage and speck (and served with mustard sauce and lentils) is a great argument for drinking red (Barbaresco) with fish. The wine list is one of the most extensive in the region, and certainly one of the most discerning. The organization of the list—clumping a group of whites or reds under a single price, then listing by region and grape—is a big help for diners who have an idea how much they can spend and want to see what the selection might be at that price point. Most wines are from northern Italy or France, but Il Capriccio also serves a few from Turtle Creek, a *garagiste* in nearby Lincoln.

Il Casale, 50 Leonard St., Belmont, MA 02478; (617) 209-4942; ilcasalebelmont.com; Italian; $$–$$$. This casual spot in Chef Dante de Magistris's hometown focuses squarely on his grandmother's recipes for Italian comfort food. Even the name (which translates as "the country house") suggests home cooking. Of course, few of us ever lived in a huge former firehouse with brick walls and dashing chandeliers. You could just graze on the *sfizi*—little appetizer plates that include terrific meatballs in a tomato *ragù* and *arancini* made from porcini mushroom risotto. Many pasta dishes are available as appetizers or main dishes. You can dine like Italians and order a bunch of dishes for the table and have them all served family style. The food may be rustic but the kitchen prepares it with exquisite finesse. The "naked ravioli" (*ignudi*), for example, are made by rolling ricotta and Parmigiano cheese into balls, then breading them with egg white and flour, and very gently boiling them so that the filling has a barely perceptible skin holding it together. Family-style tasting dinners are available in a modestly priced choice (the Fiat) or a deluxe version (the Ferrari).

Inna's Kitchen, 19 Pelham St., Newton Centre, MA 02459; (617) 244-5345; innaskitchen.com; Jewish/Casual American; $; T: Newton Centre. If you want to order a chicken, brisket, salmon, or vegetarian Shabbat dinner for six, you'll have to order two days ahead. But you can always stop in the busy shop for a bowl of chicken matzo soup, a hot pastrami sandwich, a spinach and feta knish, and a slice of apple strudel. You can get cheese blintzes for breakfast or challah French toast for Saturday brunch and take home some stuffed cabbage, latkes, and beet salad for later. Mother and son Inna and Alex Khitrik hold themselves to high standards. Though the shop is not under kosher supervision, they use glatt kosher meat along with organic and local products whenever possible.

The Local, 1391 Washington St., West Newton, MA 02465; (617) 340-2160; thelocalnewton.com; New American; $$; T: West New-  ton. This is tavern dining the way it was meant to be—small plates of casual food prepared with considerable care from mostly local ingredients. There are no reservations, so count on a substantial wait on weekend evenings as everyone in Newton seems to love the cult-status fried pickles; the fries liberally dusted with parsley, rosemary, and thyme; and the "flatbread pizza things." Craft beers abound.

Lumière, 1293 Washington St., West Newton, MA 02465; (617) 244-9199; lumiererestaurant.com; French; $$$; T: West Newton. Chef-Owner Michael Leviton is one of the good guys—a member of the board of overseers of Chefs Collaborative and a passionate proponent of local and sustainable foods. He's also a fabulous cook with a flair for classical French bistro fare. The local shift to fishing for hake instead of cod suits him perfectly, as he can get day boat–fresh Gloucester hake to serve with a lentil ragout, just as the French would do. The restaurant prepares its own charcuterie, which makes a perfect starter—assuming you can pass up the artichoke soup with crème fraîche or a small plate of miso-glazed scallops. The room is classically elegant, even a little formal, which makes it wonderful for a date or special occasion. While Leviton clearly loves fine French wines, he peppers his wine list with outstanding Spanish, Italian, and American finds.

Main Streets Market and Cafe, 42 Main St., Concord, MA 01742; (978) 369-9948; mainstreetsmarketandcafe.com; Bakery Cafe; $$. You can eat all day at Main Streets, starting with three-egg omelets and breakfast sandwiches in the morning followed by wraps and a bowl of bean-free beef chili at lunch. The most tempting items might be the afternoon sweet snacks, like red velvet cupcakes, individual Boston cream pies, and old-fashioned lemon bars. In the evening, the menu becomes more tavern-oriented with shrimp and scallop risotto, *steak-frites*, and lobster mac and cheese. Choices of beer on tap include an ale brewed exclusively for Main Streets. Acoustic musicians entertain Wed through Sat night.

Pasha, 669A Massachusetts Ave., Arlington, MA 02476; (781) 648-5888; pashaturkish.com; Turkish; $–$$. Pasha is perhaps the prettiest of the Boston area's Turkish restaurants, and it also has the most extensive list of dishes and of Turkish wines. The wines are still a work in progress (the modern wine industry is very young), but the food is easy to like. Start with a little of everything by ordering the plate of mixed appetizers, which includes hummus, stuffed grape leaves, shredded beets in homemade yogurt, and baba ganoush. We tend to skip kebabs at Turkish restaurants—while they are invariably good, we're usually more curious about sauteed and baked dishes. A good bet at Pasha is the *manti,* described on the menu as Turkish-style ravioli. They are more like tiny tortellini stuffed with a mixture of ground lamb and ground beef and served over creamy yogurt with a butter sauce on top. In Turkey, a friend told us, "*manti* are what your mother makes for you when you're sick."

Strip-T's, 93 School St., Watertown, MA 02472; (617) 923-4330; stripts.com; Casual American/New American; $$. Paul Maslow and a friend opened a simple lunch spot in 1986, but everything was kicked up a notch in 2011, when Paul's son Tim joined the fold, fresh from cooking with New York star chef David Chang. Instead of subs, the lunchtime sandwich menu features the likes of Japanese eggplant *banh mi,* a fried fish sandwich with kimchi squash, or slow-roasted lamb shoulder with roasted onion and yogurt. The evening menu is hardcore American bistro—roasted skate, grilled bavette steak, glazed veal breast, and (in season) roasted Cape Cod bluefish with buttery grits. There's no changing the limited seating (29 chairs plus the take-out room) and the barebones decor, but this strip shop doesn't tease: It delivers.

Sweet Chili, 470–472 Massachusetts Ave., Arlington, MA 02474; (781) 646-2400; sweetchilitogo.com; Thai; $. Thai restaurants abound in greater Boston, but few rise to the level of this Arlington standby that's been around since the 1990s. Some of the best dishes are the village curries like the Randang curry, with a choice of chicken or beef, or the Panang curried duck, which is served as a half duck roasted with vegetables. Fans of spicy Thai food might consider the soft-shell crab with a hot basil chile sauce, or the squid stir-fried in a (basil-free) hot chile sauce. If you're tempted to order pad thai, opt for the more authentic (and fiery) country-style.

Tryst, 689 Massachusetts Ave., Arlington, MA 02476; (781) 641-2227; trystrestaurant.com; New American; $$–$$$. Just the right balance of upscale elegance with relaxed style makes Tryst an affair to remember. (The menu is full of such references. Appetizers are labeled "Just a Fling," while small plates are "Not Fully Committed," salads are "Getting Fresh," and main dishes are "Getting Serious.") For all the cutesy whimsy, the dishes are serious bistro comfort food, ranging from slowly braised coq au vin served with Parmesan polenta to tagliatelle Bolognese, or spicy roast duck with black pepper spaetzle. Solo diners can grab a spot at the communal high-top table in the bar. The wine list includes numerous wines by the glass.

Tuscan Grill, 361 Moody St., Waltham, MA 02453; (781) 891-5486; tuscangrillwaltham.com; Italian; $$. This restaurant built around a simple wood-fired spit put Waltham on the dining map when it opened in 1991, and it's anchored the Moody Street dining scene ever

LEARN TO COOK

Thanks to all the cooking shows on broadcast and cable television these days, even kids are interested in learning their way around the kitchen. Here are two spots in Newton where you (and your kids) can earn your toque.

Create-a-Cook, 53 Winchester St., Newton, MA 02461; (617) 795-2223; createacook.com. Create-a-Cook offers four-session cooking courses and Monday night advanced workshops for adults, but classes for children are the real lure. Classes in the five seven-week terms are broken into six age groups for kids from 3 to 15. The staff are all professional chefs, and they also offer a special program of three-hour adult cooking parties that include a chef, recipes, food, the professional kitchen, and all the cleanup.

Newton Community Education, 140 Brandeis Rd., Newton Center, MA 02459; (617) 559-6999; newtoncommunityed.org. Newton is a cook's town, and this education program offers a host of classes from basic wine appreciation to creamy desserts to detailed courses in such ethnic cuisines as Persian, Moroccan, Caribbean, East African, and Indian.

since. The most inventive starter is the shrimp and corn *arancini,* but you won't go wrong sticking to the grill and ordering the grilled calamari with spicy tomato broth. The wood grill dominates the entrees, with the marinated lamb steak, broccoli rabe pesto, and garlic-roasted potatoes leading the way.

Via Lago Cafe & Catering, 1845 Massachusetts Ave., Lexington, MA 02420; (781) 861-6174; vialagocatering.com; Eclectic; $$.

One of the most dependable "nice" spots for lunches ranging from a good juicy hamburger (or less juicy veggie burger) to a plate of coq au vin or pork cassoulet with roast pork, Polish sausage, and duck confit, Via Lago is downtown Lexington's midday go-to when you're hungry but don't want to commit to a full restaurant experience. Most of the day you order from the line and someone will deliver the food to your table. In the evening, the tables are clad in white linens, waitstaff take your order, and the menu ratchets up a notch with daily specials like grilled grass-fed rib eye steak or peppercorn-crusted rack of lamb. Via Lago may look like a high-ceilinged bar room, but the broad comfort food menu makes it more a place to eat than drink.

Watch City Brewing Company, 256 Moody St., Waltham, MA 02453; (781) 647-4000; watchcitybrew.com; Brewery; $$. A brew-pub that matches its beers nicely with the food, Watch City has built its reputation on copper-colored, fruity American ale with a bit more hops bite than most, now being made as Mongrel Red IPA. We prefer the Moody Street Stout, with its overtones of coffee, chocolate, and nuts and its creamy richness. Compared to the sweetness of Guinness, Moody Street is dry stout, which gives a greater clarity to its overtones. While Watch City has the usual bar-food suspects (buffalo wings, popcorn shrimp), it also serves grilled steak tips, skillet-roasted marinated salmon, and pan-seared tuna with orange-ginger sauce.

Specialty Stores, Markets, & Producers

Arax Market, 585 Mount Auburn St., Watertown, MA 02472; (617) 924-3399; Grocery. Located along the "Armenian highway" of shops leading into downtown Watertown from Cambridge, Arax stocks a full line of specialty and imported Middle Eastern foods, carrying more produce than its neighboring competitors. Arax also specializes in hookahs and all their paraphernalia, which brings the shop business from around the region.

A. Russo & Sons, 560 Pleasant St., Watertown, MA 02472; (617) 923-1500; russos.com; Grocery. A pioneer in specialty produce,

Russo is principally a wholesaler of fruits and vegetables to some of the Boston area's leading restaurants. But this large farm stand (or small market, depending on how you look at it) on the Waltham line in Watertown is chock-full of delights for the home cook, too. Russo carries more wild and exotic mushrooms (both fresh and dried) than any other supplier to the public in the region. If something is in season somewhere, it's available at Russo, making the store an essential stop if, say, you develop a sudden craving for blackberries in January. Boston area cooks also appreciate the broad selection, generous packaging, and low prices on fresh herbs.

Baza Market, 30 Tower Rd., Newton Upper Falls, MA 02464; (617) 986-8510; Grocery. In case you wondered where Boston's Russian immigrants shop, wonder no more. One look at high-fat sour cream, soft cheeses, and butters from around the world will give you a pretty good idea why Russian food can taste so good. Try some stuffed cabbage or roasted duck at the hot bar or pick up a beautiful loaf of coriander or sunflower bread, some chicken or veal-stuffed dumplings, smoked sturgeon, herring in sour cream, and pickled beets for a feast at home.

Big Sky Bread Bakery & Cafe, 142 Main St., Watertown, MA 02472; (617) 332-4445; bigskybreads.com; Bakery Cafe. Descended from the American school of high-rising bread with tender crusts, Big Sky produces some of the most sophisticated loaves this side of the European-style bakers. The honey whole wheat is a standby sandwich bread in any number of good delis, and the dark and marble rye breads are the perfect complement to hearty soups. While a limited number of Big Sky breads are available in other markets and at many farmers' markets, this shop carries the whole line along with small pastries, cakes, and a full line of challah breads.

Bread & Chocolate Bakery Cafe, 4 Hartford St., Newton Highlands, MA 02461; (617) 795-0500; T: Newton Highlands; 108 Madison Ave., Newtonville, MA 02460; (617) 243-0500; T: Newtonville; breadnchocolate.com; Bakery Cafe. Both locations have the full range of pastries created by Eunice Feller, a professionally trained artist who now turns her creative eye to delicious baked goods. She's especially known for her Kugelhopf Morning Bun, her Boston Cream Pie cupcake, and her Hong Kong Ding Dong of green tea sponge cake, marshmallow center, and dark chocolate ganache. The Newton Highlands shop has the larger cafe area for sitting down with a bowl of soup of the day and a slice of quiche or a pesto chicken salad sandwich on ciabatta bread. For Eunice Feller's recipe for **Lemon Blackberry Pound Cake,** see p. 303.

Captain Marden's Seafoods, 279 Linden St., Wellesley, MA 02482; (781) 235-0860; captainmardens.com; Fishmonger. Possibly the Boston-area's most respected wholesale fishmonger—there's hardly a fine restaurant or gourmet shop they don't supply—Captain Marden's also has a comprehensive retail operation. The seafood party platters are especially popular. And you don't have to tell company that you didn't make the lobster quiche from scratch.

The Concord Cheese Shop, 29 Walden St., Concord, MA 01742; (978) 369-5778; concordcheeseshop.com; **Cheesemonger.** Proprietor Peter Lovis credits both the locavore movement and the interest in organic foods with sparking the production of great artisanal cheeses and laments that he has room to stock only about 150 to 200 cheeses—domestic and imported—at a time. "But over the course of a year, we sell about 1,000 different cheeses. And some of them were milk in a goat only 10 days before," he says. Perhaps the most anticipated cheese is the 400-pound wheel of Crucolo that is delivered to the store and rolled in on a red carpet on the first Thursday after Thanksgiving. The cow's milk cheese made in the Italian Alps has become so popular that Lovis now has to order two of the giant wheels for the holidays. (He stocks 30-pound wheels the rest of the year.) "It's my favorite for a grilled cheese sandwich, with tomato, bacon, and butter on both sides of the bread," he says. Lovis and his staff can give advice for serving all the cheeses, or for pairing them with the shop's wine selection. For Peter Lovis's recipe for **Chèvre Pound Cake,** see p. 301.

China Fair, 70 Needham St., Newton Highlands, MA 02461; (617) 332-1250; chinafairinc.com; **Housewares.** If you're equipping a kitchen from scratch, you could do worse than to start at China Fair, which carries an extensive line of generic pots and pans, kitchen utensils, and specialty items such as cookie cutters in unusual shapes (dinosaur, coffeepot, house, saw, hammer, cowboy boots, sailboat, palm tree . . .), quesadilla presses, pressure cookers, pizzelle makers, waffle makers, and sandwich presses. You'll also find shelf after shelf of casserole dishes, gratin plates, and pie plates. Once you've outfitted the kitchen, you can move on to the dining room, as China Fair sells a great deal of casual dinnerware. In fact, many local restaurants come here for their table settings. The paper goods annex has anything you'd ever need for a big party, from invitations to banners and noisemakers to paper cups and plates.

Concord Teacakes, 59 Commonwealth Ave., West Concord, MA 01742; (978) 369-7644; concordteacakes.com; **Bakery Cafe.** The chocolate and lemon cakes that Judy Ferth used to launch the business are still part of her repertoire, but now customers can choose among seven cake flavors and nine fillings for custom cakes. The favorite, by the way, is chocolate cake with white buttercream icing. But the shop, with a few tables for those who can't wait to eat their treats at home, is also known for its cupcakes, scones, coffeecakes, and chocolate brownies. There are also breakfast sandwiches to start the day, prepared sandwiches for a quick lunch, and comfort food classics (chicken potpie, mac and cheese, spinach quiche) to heat at home.

Craft Beer Cellar, 51 Leonard St., Belmont, MA 02478; (617) 932-1885; bostoncraftbeercellar.com; **Wine, Beer & Spirits.** Suzanne Schalow and Kate Baker are pretty sure that there's nothing quite like their store in the US, and we certainly can't think of any other place that stocks around 1,000 different craft beers at such fair prices. Schalow is proud to call herself a beer geek, and she can recite the entire pedigree of every beer (and brewer) represented in the place. Whether your taste runs to a simple pale ale or a Belgian triple, this is the place to go. Schalow and Baker bring beer sommeliers' palates to the task of guiding your purchases to match your preferences. Check for tastings on Thurs, Fri, and Sat.

Danish Pastry House, 205 Arlington St. #4, Watertown, MA 02472; (617) 926-2747; danishpastryhouse.com; **Bakery.** Enriched with egg and full of butter, true Danish pastry dough is somewhat like croissant dough, but less flaky. You can taste how good it is in the Danish specialty pastries sold in this small shop at the baking facility. The Spandauer, what most of us think of as a "Danish," comes with apple, raspberry, and custard fillings. Thebirkes mixes the dough with poppy seeds and marzipan to great effect, but perhaps the shop's most extraordinary creation is the Kringle, a perfect combination of pastry, marzipan, and almonds. You can buy it by the slice or take a whole one home to bake in the oven for five minutes and share with friends for breakfast. For dessert, try a Chocolate Snail, which swirls the dough around a big chunk of chocolate. Warm slightly and top with ice cream. For the related cafe in Medford, see p. 109.

Debra's Natural Gourmet, 98 Commonwealth Ave., West Concord, MA 01742; (978) 371-7573; debrasnaturalgourmet.com; Grocery. Debra Stark opened her namesake store in 1989 and is one of the founders of Stark Sisters Granola (sold at the store, naturally). Debra's stocks as much local product as possible, assuming it meets the store's standards, which tend to exceed the USDA requirements for "organic" or the FDA requirements for "natural." You'll find almost every food group you'd find in a conventional grocery, but the brands may be unfamiliar. Special events highlight herbal medicine, potions and lotions, and frequent product tastings.

DePasquale's Sausage Co., 325 Watertown St., Newton, MA 02458; (617) 244-7633; Grocery. Sweet and hot Italian sausages are the mainstays of this small shop, along with Chinese sausages, which, says the proprietor, "taste like Chinese spareribs." All the sausages are made in the small kitchen in the back and when you stop in you might also find breakfast sausages and others flavored with maple, tomato and basil, or the extremely popular combination of cheese and garlic. A wall of Italian foodstuffs—pastas, sauces, olive oil, and the like—makes for one-stop shopping.

Fastachi, 598 Mount Auburn St., Watertown, MA 02472; (617) 924-8787; fastachi.com; Specialty Shop. We're nuts for Fastachi. The big machines visible through the plate glass windows at the back of this little shop are nut roasters that turn out the almonds, pistachios, cashews, hazelnuts, pecans, macadamia nuts, and peanuts that are lightly dusted with sea salt and combined into various mixes. The most popular is the tart and salty cranberry nut mix, though purists may stick to their favorite nut sans embellishment, enjoy it ground into a delicious butter, or savor it enrobed in chocolate. (We're big fans of the pistachio butter, which we sometimes combine with fresh basil to make pesto.) The most popular bark features almonds and dark chocolate, but we're partial to the elegant white chocolate bark with macadamias and lemon peel.

George Howell Coffee, 311 Walnut St., Newtonville, MA 02460; (617) 332-6886; georgehowellcoffee.com; Coffee. Once the no-compete clause that George Howell signed when he sold his beloved Coffee Connection chain to Starbucks expired, Howell  promptly got back in the game. He started importing beans again under the name Terroir (now George Howell Coffee), and in early 2012 made his coffee shop comeback with this small Newtonville location. The baristas are anything but fast, but the coffee is worth waiting for. It's the taste of a legend. You can take it to go, but as staff are quick to say, "it's too good for a paper cup." Delicious croissants and simple sandwiches (fig jam and brie, for example, or turkey with basil pesto) are just a bonus.

Gordon's Fine Wines & Liquors, 894 Main St., Waltham, MA 02451; (781) 893-1900; gordonswine.com; Wine, Beer & Spirits. One of the top wine shops in New England for more than 75 years, Gordon's is operated by the third generation of the founding family and the depth of its offerings is matched by very few shops in the region. Moreover, Gordon's makes learning about wine fun. First Friday tastings (first Friday of each month) are free and feature 15 or so wines in a two-hour event complete with live jazz and hors d'oeuvres. (It's a great chance to dress up a bit, as cocktail attire is encouraged.) Want to know more? The wine education center offers classes ranging from the basics of tasting wine to events highlighting a specific region or style of wine. The third Thursday of every month, two sommeliers square off serving eight wines paired with four courses of food. Attendees choose the winner of the SomSmack.

Keltic Krust, 1371 Washington St., West Newton, MA 02465; (617) 332-9343; keltickrust.com; Bakery Cafe; T: West Newton. As the name suggests, the bakery specializes in Irish-style breads, including, of course, wheat or raisin soda bread, along with less familiar specialties such as yeasted barm brack bread with raisins and orange and lemon peels, and eccles cakes, a flaky pastry filled with raisins and cinnamon. Best bet for a light lunch? A sausage roll of house-made sausage wrapped in pastry dough. Celiacs and others on restricted diets adore Keltic Krust's healthy breakfast bars of nuts, dried fruits, and berries, which are vegan as well as gluten-free.

T.F. Kinnealey, 227 Linden St., Wellesley, MA 02482; (781) 235-8322; kinnealey.com; Butcher. Like adjacent **Captain Marden's Seafoods** (see p. 202), Kinnealey has been a key player in the wholesale industry in New England since the mid-20th century. The bulk of the trade is with high-end restaurants, country clubs, and hotels, and most of the meat Kinnealey carries is graded USDA Prime—literally a cut above the best available in supermarkets. Kinnealey acquired the John Dewar stores (including this one) in 2006 and uses them to showcase its best meats and specialty products for discerning home cooks.

Lakota Bakery, 1375 Massachusetts Ave., Arlington, MA 02476; (781) 646-0121; lakotabakery.com; Bakery. If you're a cookie freak, you've probably encountered Lakota's splendid cookies at select gourmet shops, coffee emporia, and delis. They run the gamut from orange chocolate chip and "old-school peanut butter" (glazed with

chocolate and chopped peanuts) to traditional ginger and less-traditional chocolate ginger cookies. Linzer cookies feature the traditional raspberry as well as strawberry and apricot fillings. But Lakota's biggest hits are sandwich cookies that catapult the Oreo into another dimension. They include lemon, mint, vanilla, and mocha buttercream between the cookie layers. Lakota sometimes bakes a pie or two, but the shop is really a cookie specialist.

Lee's Place Burgers, 216 Sumner St., Newton Centre, MA 02459; (617) 795-2022; Burgers. "Sometimes you just need a good burger," say the proprietors of this mom-and-pop eatery, and they will happily grill one for you even if you arrive a little before they open or a little after they normally close. The 6-ounce sirloin burgers are excellent as is, but even better with the somewhat spicy house-made special sauce. It's also good on the veggie and turkey burgers, or on the grilled chicken breast sandwich.

Lizzy's Homemade Ice Cream, 367 Moody St., Waltham, MA 02453; (781) 893-6677; lizzysicecream.com; Ice Cream/Yogurt. Most of the year, Coffee Oreo tends to be the flavor of choice at this homemade ice cream emporium, although Charles River Crunch, a dark chocolate ice cream with almond toffee, has its adherents as well. Come August, and customers line up for the treat of fresh peach ice cream, made with fruit from a local farm. Lizzy's prides itself on its hot fudge sundaes and even offers a Grab 'n' Go Sundae Party Kit to enjoy at home.

Macaron Sweeterie, 848 Massachusetts Ave., Lexington, MA 02420; (781) 863-0848; macaronsweeterie.com; Bakery Cafe. Sella Abalian, the proprietor of this sweet little shop, is originally from Montreal and knows her *macarons*. The delicate meringue-based cookies migrated from France to French Canada and continue to gain ground here in the States. The pastel colored delights include apricot, lavender, passion fruit, pistachio, coconut, lemon, and rose—filled with buttercream or jam. For a bit of Paris meets Rome, Abalian also serves equally colorful Italian gelatos. Try a scoop of chocolate/hazelnut *bacio* with a salted caramel *macaron* or order an *affogato* (a cup of espresso and vanilla gelato) to sip along with a black currant *macaron*.

Marty's, 675 Washington St., Newton, MA 02460; (617) 332-1230; martysfinewine.com; Wine, Beer & Spirits. One of the mega-merchants of wine, beer, and especially spirits, Marty's carries everything from bargain jug wines to $200 bottles of Ornellaia and $500 bottles of Sauternes. Marty's also stocks an extensive line of gourmet foods, including dozens of olive oils and balsamic vinegars, all manner of dried pastas and pickled vegetables, and even a line of prepared foods like quiche, meat loaf, or roasted duck leg should you be unable to wait to uncork your latest wine purchase.

Massis Bakery, 569 Mount Auburn St., Watertown, MA 02472; (617) 924-0537; massisbakery.com; Grocery. Massis puts a Greek accent on the Middle Eastern–Balkan–Armenian fare so popular in East Watertown. While it carries many of the same breads, baklava, and imported goods (grape leaves, for example) as the others, it also has a good selection of feta cheeses and a mind-boggling assortment of spices in various package sizes.

The Meat House, 1398 Massachusetts Ave. #4, Arlington, MA 02476; (781) 643-6328; themeathouse.com; Butcher. Most of the meat at this chain shop comes from Pineland Farms in New Gloucester, Maine, and while it does not arrive as whole carcass, it does come in primal cuts that the staff breaks down to request. Want a porterhouse that's 2 inches thick? No problem. The cases are filled with marinated meats ready for grilling, and the store carries an extensive line of prepared foods that might range from Red Bliss potato salad to grilled asparagus to barbecue baked beans. Almost everyone on staff, at least at this outlet (of 10 nationwide), has a culinary school degree, so cooking advice comes from people who know what they're talking about.

Nashoba Brook Bakery, 152 Commonwealth Ave., West Concord, MA 01742; (978) 318-1999; slowrise.com; Bakery Cafe. You'll encounter Nashoba Brook's loaves of bread at health food stores and conventional groceries all over eastern Massachusetts. You'll also find them in many sandwich shops and delis as an alternative to **Iggy's** (see p. 171). One of the striking aspects of their slow-rise breads is that none of the sandwich breads use oils, milk, sugar, or eggs, so they tend to have strong, grainy flavors. The brioche hot dog buns (which by definition have to use both eggs and butter) might be an exception, but they sure beat spongy white bread for holding frankfurters. The cafe at the bakery carries fresh soups and salads as well as sandwiches. There are also four to five kinds of cookies available as well as blondies, brownies, and other sweet treats.

Penzey's, 1293 Massachusetts Ave., Arlington, MA 02476; (781) 646-7707; penzeys.com; Specialty Shop. Penzey's does a huge mail-order business, but it's a treat to sniff the differences between Turkish and Mexican oregano or between Spanish and Hungarian paprika at the shop. It's also a great place to pick up double-strength vanilla or hard-to-find ingredients such as Middle Eastern zaatar or *charnushka* (the tiny black seeds often found on Jewish rye bread). So far, this Arlington shop is the only Massachusetts outpost of the Wisconsin-based retailer.

Priscilla Hand Made Candies, 19 Walden St., Concord, MA 01970; (978) 371-0585; Chocolatier. This adjunct to the famous Gardner shop (see p. 79) sells all sorts of milk and dark chocolates with nuts, chewy centers, and soft centers—including the signature French Roll, which has a chocolate center that has been flattened, dipped in milk chocolate, and rolled in crushed cashews.

Quebrada Baking Co., 208 Massachusetts Ave., Arlington, MA 02474; (781) 648-0700; 272 Washington St., Wellesley, MA 02481; (781) 237-2111; quebradabakingco.com; Bakery Cafe. The folks at Quebrada realize that sometimes you only need a little taste of something sweet, and we're grateful that we can stop in for a mini mocha bean cupcake, blueberry scone, chocolate chip muffin, éclair, or fresh fruit tart. Kids love the whimsically decorated cookies, and the beautifully decorated cakes and cupcakes steal the show. But the fresh-baked breads are the quiet stars, including plain, poppy, sesame, and raisin braided challah, and a slightly sweet Irish soda bread with raisins and caraway seeds. On Friday, customers stock up on the Swedish-style cardamom coffee bread so that they can enjoy it as a toasted breakfast treat on the weekend.

Rancatore's, 36 Leonard St., Belmont, MA 02478; (617) 489-5090; 1752 Massachusetts Ave., Lexington, MA 02420; (781) 862-5090; rancs.com; Ice Cream/Yogurt. Before opening his first shop in Belmont in 1985, Joe Rancatore learned the premium ice cream ropes from his brother Gus at **Toscanini's** in Cambridge (see p. 179). Among the most popular flavors are Hydrox cookie and ginger snap molasses ice creams, mango sorbet, and khulfi yogurt. Rancatore likes to encourage creativity. An employee competition to make the best ice cream yielded the Cocoa Joel, a decadent concoction of milk chocolate and bittersweet chocolate ice cream, chocolate mousse yogurt, crushed Hydrox cookies, and chocolate chips.

Ride Studio Cafe, 1720 Massachusetts Ave., Lexington, MA 02420; (339) 970-0187; ridestudiocafe.com; Coffee. Ever wonder where bike messengers get the energy to buzz around like that? Maybe they're all coffee aficionados. This shop sells high-end bicycles and serious coffee. Lattes and cafe crème are made with organic milk or cream from High Lawn Farms in western Massachusetts. Espresso beans hail from Stumptown Roasters in Portland, Oregon, and the beans for pour-over brews come from the George Howell Coffee Company in Acton.

Rosenfeld's Bagels, 1280 Centre St., Newton Centre, MA 02459; (617) 527-8080; Bakery; T: Newton Centre. There are two salient pieces of information about Rosenfeld's Bagels: The folks in Newton

swear by them, and the shop is closed on Monday and Tuesday. Since no one can resist immediately eating all the bagels they purchase on Sunday, the two-day closure causes severe withdrawal symptoms in some patrons—but not severe enough to make them buy supermarket bagels. Rosenfeld's also makes challah. Cash only.

Samira's Homemade, 203 Belmont St., Belmont, MA 02478; (617) 489-3400; samirashomemade.com; Specialty Shop. Samira Hamdoun got raves when she brought her homemade dips to parties at Harvard. So in 2011, Samira, who is Lebanese, and her husband Ragab, who is Egyptian, founded their business to make authentic foods the way their mothers and grandmothers made them. They began with hummus and soon put their own stamp on the traditional chickpea-based dip by adding flavors such as roasted red pepper, kalamata olive, and jalapeno. They also make *ful medammes,* a hummus-like dish made with fava beans. "It's the Egyptian national dish," says Samira, explaining that their version is creamier than the traditional, somewhat watery original. "It's called the 'Egyptian meat,'" she says. "They even have it for breakfast. It's very filling and high protein." She prefers it as a sandwich for lunch with tomatoes and cucumbers. (It's also low calorie.) The couple's other products include *muhammara,* an almost addictive spicy spread of roasted red pepper, walnuts, and pomegranate molasses, and a deliciously smoky baba ganoush.

Sevan's Bakery, 599 Mount Auburn St., Watertown, MA 02472; (617) 924-3243; sevanboston.com; Grocery. The shops catering to East Watertown's extensive Armenian community are packed with imported goods from Armenia and similar items from Greece and the Middle East—especially olives, oils, and seasonings that cut across several cultures. Sevan's is known for its fresh *lamejun* and pita breads as well as a delicate, only lightly smoky baba ganoush. Unlike some of its competitors, Sevan's also carries goods from Turkey.

Sophia's Greek Pantry, 265 Belmont St., Belmont, MA 02478; (617) 489-1371; Grocery. No one in eastern Massachusetts makes yogurt like Sophia Georgoulopoulos, who uses her grandmother's recipe for a thick and creamy version using both goat and sheep's milk. She makes both 2% and nonfat versions as well as one mixed with honey. "I put it over fresh fruit with some nuts," she says, "It's my dinner." She lets her imagination run wild when she dreams up flavor combinations for each day's batch of frozen yogurt. One of the customer favorites is taro, though we find the watermelon to be especially refreshing in the summer and also like the complex flavor of the blueberry, honeydew melon, and green apple blend. Georgoulopoulos's yogurt is used by a number of Boston's top chefs, as is the olive oil from her family's olive press imported by Extra Virgin Foods. (Importer Paul Hatziiliades actually has an olive oil tasting bar at Sophia's. The oils come from his family's and her family's trees.) She also makes all the Greek dishes in the cold cases—pastitsio, stuffed grape leaves, moussaka, stuffed peppers and tomatoes, and octopus salad.

Stoddard's, 360 Watertown St., Newton, MA 02458; (617) 244-4187; stoddards.com; Housewares. Boston's leading cutlery shop since 1800, Stoddard's has seen every fad in knives come and go. Cooks who prefer to work with their hands instead of food processors will be in seventh heaven here, where the selection runs from perfectly functional, plastic-handled, stamped Victorinox chef's knives found in every restaurant kitchen around the world to the perfectly balanced, frighteningly sharp Kikuichi carbon-steel knives. Other small items, like exquisite tweezers, traditional razors and shaving paraphernalia, and mirrors and bath soaps round out the selections. Stoddard's also offers classes in knife techniques and in care and maintenance of fine knives.

Sweet Thyme Bakery, 1837 Massachusetts Ave., Lexington, MA 02420; (781) 860-8818; sweetthymebakery.com; Bakery. Sweet Thyme brings an Asian taste palate to European-style pastries. The

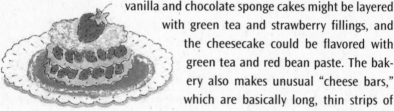

vanilla and chocolate sponge cakes might be layered with green tea and strawberry fillings, and the cheesecake could be flavored with green tea and red bean paste. The bakery also makes unusual "cheese bars," which are basically long, thin strips of cheesecake wrapped in paper. The bars come in a range of equally unique flavors, including rose cranberry and mango chocolate. They can be frozen and eaten like an ice cream bar. The shop also makes breads such as raisin, sesame, and seven-grain and offers sandwiches at lunchtime. The Asian-style sweet rice cakes are made with rice flour and flavored with apple or red bean paste for a sticky, chewy treat.

Vicki Lee's, 105 Trapelo Rd., Belmont, MA 02478; (617) 489-5007; vickilees.com; Bakery Cafe. It takes advance planning to make "aram sandwiches," one of Vicki Lee's signature specialties. *Lavosh* cracker bread has to be moistened with water and rolled overnight so that it will be soft enough to wrap around beef or ham or turkey with lettuce, or around salmon. But all the foodstuffs in this elegant shop require a similar attention to detail—from the homemade toasted granola to the chocolate symphony torte covered in dark chocolate ganache and decorated with handmade chocolate flowers. Vicki Lee's is a favorite for weekday lunches and Sunday brunch. We also imagine that many people in Belmont plan their week around the nightly take-home entrees.

Waltham India Market, 315 Moody St., Waltham, MA 02453; (781) 899-6016; Grocery. If you're prone to making impulsive purchases on an empty stomach, first head downstairs for a beef or lamb kebab and a glass of fresh juice in the Food Bazaar. It will take you quite a while to peruse the street-level grocery, which is actually larger and more comprehensive than most supermarkets in India, where the shoppers would know exactly what to do with snake gourds and long beans, not to mention vegetables with names like *tinda, karela,* and *guvar.* A whole aisle is devoted to dried pulses; dairy cases to cheeses, yogurt, and yogurt drinks; numerous shelves to relishes, chutneys, and hot sauces. One of the best ways to expand your palate and your knowledge of Indian food is to purchase the packaged spice mixes so that you can try your hand at making beef biryani, chicken masala, or fish curry at home.

Wasik's, the Cheese Shop, 61 Central St., Wellesley, MA 02482; (781) 237-0916; wasiks.com; Cheesemonger. Wasik's does a lot of its own *affinage,* buying young cheeses at a good price and bringing them along to optimal ripeness before selling them. Cheeses here hail from around the world, though an increasing number come from small artisanal New England producers. Wasik's also makes its own cheese spreads and chutneys, and has a terrific selection of cheese gift baskets.

Belkin Family Lookout Farm, 89 Pleasant St. South, Natick, MA 01760; (508) 653-0653; lookoutfarm.com. The land of Lookout Farm has been tilled since 1651, making it one of the oldest working farms in North America. With more than 180 acres of grape arbors, orchards, berry patches, and vegetables, Lookout has a vast array of produce throughout the growing season, including you-pick strawberries, peaches, plums, nectarines, several varieties of apples, and fall pumpkins. Open late Apr through Oct.

Eastleigh Farm, 1062 Edmands Rd., Framingham, MA 01701; (508) 877-1753; eastleighfarm.com. Sign a release and you can buy rich and delicious raw milk at the farm store. The 300-head herd consists mostly of Jersey and Guernsey cows with a few Brown Swiss mixed in, so the milk tends to be high in butterfat. Nobscot Artisan Cheese (508-433-0662; nobscotcheese.com) is made on the premises with Eastleigh milk and is available at the farm store as fresh cheese (several flavors) and a semi-hard washed-rind Alpine-style that's been lightly aged for about three months. The store also carries local honey, locally baked bread, and some fruit and vegetables in season.

Hutchins Farm, 754 Monument St., Concord, MA 01742; (978) 369-5041; hutchinsfarm.com. You can find Hutchins Farm produce at some farmers' markets in Cambridge, Somerville, and Belmont, but it's more fun to visit the farm stand during the growing season. The family farm was a pioneer of conscientious organic farming (since 1973) and all vegetables and herbs are grown from seed or from the farm's own "mother" plants. You'll find the New England basics of carrots and corn, along with more unusual crops such as daikon and rapini. A website chart indicates availability of the more than 50 herbs, fruits, and vegetables. Farm stand open June through Oct. Self-serve on the porch, Apr, May, and Nov.

Land's Sake, Inc., Newton and Wellesley Streets, Weston, MA 02193; (781) 893-1162; landssake.org. Once an outlier of the Arnold Arboretum in Boston, this preserve of suburban forest and farmland is a public experiment in land management combined with environmental education. Pick up a tree map and go for a walk, and take advantage of the certified organic farm, which offers pick-your-own blueberries, raspberries, strawberries, vegetables, and herbs. Open mid-June through Oct.

Verrill Farm, 11 Wheeler Rd., Concord, MA 01742; (978) 369-4494; verrillfarm.com. The spacious farm stand has more than enough room for produce from Verrill's 100 acres of farmland, along with local honey, jam, marmalade, and other products. Sandwiches and salads are available from the deli, and the bakery turns out a range of cakes, fruit tarts, pies, and *crostatas,* free-form pastries filled with fruits of the season. You could probably eat Verrill's ready-to-heat meals for a month without repeating a dish. They range from vegetarian lasagna to beef stroganoff, lemon dill salmon to veal wiener schnitzel. Check the website for the schedule of field-to-fork dinners. For the recipe for **Verrill Farm Corn and Tomato Tart,** see p. 289.

Wilson Farm, 10 Pleasant St., Lexington, MA 02421; (781) 862-3900; wilsonfarm.com. We imagine that the Irish immigrants who founded Wilson Farm in the late 19th century would be dumbfounded if they saw it today. From their original purchase of 16 acres of farmland, the family now grows more than 125 different crops on 33 acres in Lexington and another 500 acres in Litchfield, New Hampshire. The farm stand, which is bigger than many grocery stores, offers the full progression of fresh produce across the seasons, along with artisanal and farmhouse cheeses, fresh meats and seafood, delicious baked goods, soups, salads, and heat-and-eat meals.

Farmers' Markets

Arlington Farmers' Market, Russell Common parking lot, Arlington center. Wed from 2 to 6:30 p.m., mid-June to late Oct.

Belmont Farmers' Market, Municipal parking lot, Cross Street and Channing Road, Belmont. Thurs from 1:30 to 7 p.m. (6 p.m. after Labor Day), early June to late Oct.

Framingham Farmers' Market I, St. Tarcisius Church parking lot, Waverly Street, Framingham. Wed from 3 to 6 p.m. and Sat from 9 a.m. to noon, mid-July to Oct.

Framingham Farmers' Market II, Village Green, Edgel Road, Framingham. Thurs from 12:30 to 5:30 p.m., mid-June through Oct.

Framingham Winter Market, 24 Vernon St., Framingham. First Thurs from noon to 5:30 p.m., Dec through May.

Lexington Farmers' Market, Massachusetts and Fletcher Avenues, Lexington. Tues from 2 to 6:30 p.m., late May through Oct.

Natick Farmers' Market, Natick Common, downtown Natick. Sat from 9 a.m. to 1 p.m., mid-May through mid-Nov.

Natick Winter Farmers' Market, Common Street Community Church, Natick. Sat from 9 a.m. to 1 p.m., late Nov through mid-Apr.

Newton Farmers' Market, Cold Spring Park, 1200 Beacon St., Newton Highlands. Tues from 1:30 to 6 p.m., early July to late Oct.

Newton Highlands Winter Farmers' Market, Hyde Community Center, 90 Lincoln St., Newton Highlands. Tues from 1:30 to 6 p.m., mid-Nov through late June.

Newton/Post 440 Farmers' Market, American Legion Post 440, 295 California St., Newton. Tues from noon to 5 p.m., late May to late June. Fri from noon to 5 p.m., mid-June to early Oct.

Waltham Farmers' Market, Santander Bank parking lot, Main and Moody Streets, Waltham. Sat from 9:30 a.m. to 2:30 p.m., mid-June to early Nov.

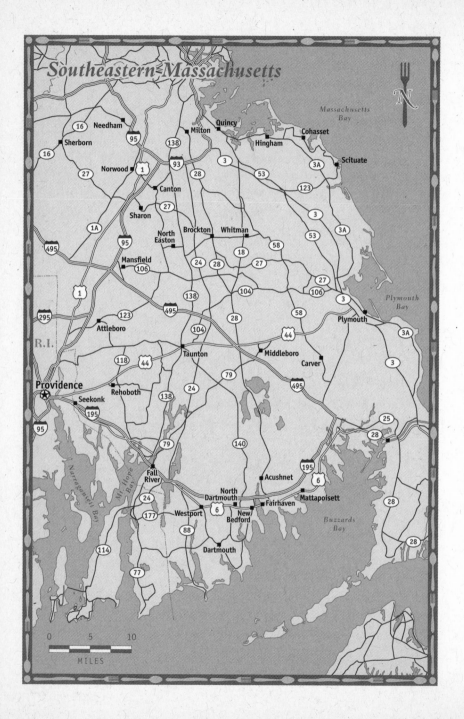

Southeastern Massachusetts

Many Bay Staters don't even think of Norfolk, Bristol, and Plymouth Counties when their attention turns to food, considering the region between Boston and Cape Cod to be a ring of southern suburbs followed by a long stretch of highway to reach the bridges to the Cape. Yet this area embraces the great fishing port of New Bedford—one of America's richest—as well as boulder-strewn peninsular farms where vegetables seem to spring up with no more effort than calling their names.

It is also a region of substantial cultural diversity. Devotees of the Food Channel may know that star chef Emeril Lagasse rose to fame in New Orleans, but his roots are in Fall River and he frequently makes reference to the French-Canadian traditions he learned in the family kitchen. Even more dramatic is the culinary influence of the Portuguese, who have made up a substantial segment of New Bedford's fishing fleet since the early-19th-century whaling days. It is said that the Portuguese have 365 ways to cook codfish, or *bacalhau,* one for every day of the year; you can taste many of them in area restaurants.

Despite the population pressures imposed by the proximity to Boston (which gets closer every day through improved public transportation), much of southeastern Massachusetts remains farmland and orchards. The acidic but sandy peat bogs of Plymouth County produce much of the nation's cranberry crop. The alluvial loam of Westport's peninsulas yields an almost embarrassing abundance of crops, from spring lettuce to fall pumpkins. Gentle microclimates abound, especially among the towns that border on Buzzards Bay, permitting the cultivation of European wine grapes and other crops that normally require a growing season longer than most of the state enjoys.

Gargantuan fishing boats bring a deep-sea harvest of flaky fish and sea scallops into New Bedford. In addition, enterprising clam diggers and mussel and oyster gatherers stock the restaurants and fish shacks of the area, and many of them also set up impromptu roadside stands to unload their extra catch. The estuaries of Buzzards Bay rival the North Shore for their extensive flats.

While much of the southeastern Massachusetts bounty is siphoned off to the restaurants of Boston and New York, many small farmers and fishermen have turned to direct retailing to gain an economic edge in businesses with traditionally thin margins. Look for the symbol of the Southeastern Massachusetts Agricultural Partnership (SEMAP) at farm stands, stores, and restaurants. These are businesses that support local producers, guaranteeing the freshest food and a sustainable harvest.

Foodie Faves

Alma Nove, 22 Shipyard Dr., Hingham, MA 02043; (781) 749-3353; almanovehingham.com; Italian; $$$. This Hingham waterfront restaurant is Wahlberg central. Donnie and Mark are co-owners with big brother Paul and a family friend, and the place is named for Ma Wahlberg and her nine kids. Chef Paul leaves the spotlight to his brothers and concentrates on the flavor-intensive modern menu. You could easily make a meal of the extensive list of antipasti—braised pork meatballs with polenta, Island Creek oysters with roasted red pepper cocktail sauce, sautéed mussels with almond butter—but then you'd miss the homemade gnocchi or the wood-grilled swordfish. Pastas, by the way, can be ordered in half servings. When the weather permits, everyone wants to eat by the outdoor fire pit.

Antonio's Restaurant and Cafe, 267 Coggeshall St., New Bedford, MA 02746; (508) 990-3636; antoniosnewbedford.com; **Portuguese; $–$$.** This Portuguese-American classic has been a favorite in New Bedford since 1989. It's prized as much for its big (enough for lunch the next day) portions as for its baked stuffed shrimp, grilled Portuguese sardines, or boiled cod. The best deal in the house is the Steak Antonio's Style. It's a 16-ounce sirloin grilled and topped with ham, fried eggs, and a Portuguese beef sauce. Light eaters and bargain hunters can get fried fish or pork steak sandwiches with fries or rice for about the same price as fast food from beneath the golden arches. Order ahead if you'd like takeout in foil hotel pans designed to serve 14 to 18.

The Back Eddy, 1 Bridge Rd., Westport, MA 02790; (508) 636-6500; thebackeddy.com; **New American; $$.** Founded by legendary grill chef Chris Schlesinger, this casual bistro overlooking the town harbor is famous for its use of local products: native produce, locally harvested seafood, and regional cheeses, wine, beer, and breads. Many diners start with the native littlenecks or locally cultivated oysters from the raw bar. The wood grill is pressed into service for such signature entrees as yellowfin tuna steak served Japanese style with house-made kimchi. For a more traditional New England dish, try the fried New Bedford sea scallops with hand-cut fries and cole slaw. Open late Mar through New Year's Day.

Bia Bistro, 35 S. Main St., Cohasset, MA 02025; (781) 383-0464; biabistro.com; **New American; $$–$$$.** Brian and Tristen Houlihan's village bistro strikes just the right American interpretation of a

French-Italian Riviera menu. You can opt for big plates like seared duck breast and confit leg or barbecued beef short ribs with a summer vegetable succotash or lighter dishes such as Brian's version of a Portuguese fisherman's stew with chouriço amid the shellfish and bits of white fish trim. Bia is as casual as a real bistro, so it's common to see folks in jeans and Top-Siders who've just stepped off their boats, ordering a bargain burger or one of the pizzas and a glass of wine.

Blount Clam Shack and Soup Store, 840 Bedford St., Fall River, MA 02723; (774) 888-0050; blountretail.com; Seafood; $–$$. Based in Rhode Island, Blount Fine Foods claims to be the largest producer of clam chowder in New England and the largest producer of lobster bisque in the country. And that's just the tip of the iceberg. You can try many of their products at the soup bar at the company's faux fish shack restaurant, along with such seafood classics as a lobster roll or a whole-belly clam roll. The chefs put haddock to particularly good use in a fried haddock sandwich, a haddock Reuben (with swiss cheese, coleslaw, and tartar sauce), or a wrap with salsa and cheddar cheese. When you've finished your meal, stop at the soup store to select from a dizzying array of choices (butternut squash and apple, scallop and bacon chowder, or fire-roasted vegetable, just to name a few) to heat up at home.

Cafe Paprika, 734 Washington St., Norwood, MA 02062; (781) 440-0060; paprika-online.webs.com; Mediterranean; $. Some of the plates here are Italian (chicken Milanese, for example) and some are Spanish (garlic shrimp, paella), but the owner and the best dishes are Moroccan. Lahcen Abaichi offers no fewer than four different tagines every night, including one with saffron-scented marinated fish and preserved lemons and another featuring tiny, bite-sized meatballs in a tomato sauce with *ras al hanout* and eggs. Order these with couscous, not rice, for an authentic flavor. If there's one category of Moroccan dishes missing, it's the array of small chopped salads. But you can compensate with a dish of *zaalouk:* roasted eggplant mixed with tomato, grilled peppers, and Moroccan spices and drizzled with olive oil. Cafe Paprika also serves Spanish and Italian sandwiches at lunch.

Cinderella Restaurant, 85 Columbia St., Fall River, MA 02721; (508) 675-0002; cinderella1983.com; Portuguese; $$. One of the dressiest Portuguese restaurants in southeastern Massachusetts, Cinderella has been waving the red and green of the homeland flag since 1983. To eat authentically, you can start with a *caldo verde* (kale-potato soup with bits of sausage) or the homemade codfish cakes before moving on to a dish of pork with littleneck clams or grilled Norway *bacalhau* (cod). Perhaps in deference to Portuguese-American taste, Cinderella also offers a number of dishes featuring butterflied giant tiger shrimp. The list of Portuguese wines concentrates on table wines of the Douro and Dão regions with a nice choice of after-dinner ports.

5 South Main, 5 S. Main St., Cohasset, MA 02025; (781) 383-3555; 5southmain.com; Casual American/Vegetarian; $. There's nothing fancy or esoteric here—just good simple food with a cheery smile. This cozy cafe (22 seats inside plus warm-weather patio overflow) has made itself into the social center of Cohasset for breakfast and lunch. All the usual egg dishes are available at breakfast but most diners come for the signature french toast of grilled thick-sliced cinnamon bread dusted with cinnamon sugar. Owner Jennifer Warshaw offers a slew of choices if you want to build your own grilled cheese sandwich, but it's hard to resist her BLT with lobster salad. Among the veggie offerings is one she calls the Endless Summer Sandwich. It contains cucumbers, tomatoes, sprouts, cheddar cheese, mayonnaise, and salt and pepper on choice of bread. (She recommends the sourdough.)

Freestones City Grill, 41 William St., New Bedford; (508) 993-7477; freestonescitygrill.com; Casual American; $$. A big, bright room that feels like a cross between a men's club and a pub, Freestones occupies a building originally constructed in 1877 as a bank. It's a toss-up which side of the menu is more popular—the steak and burger side, which includes an excellent grilled meatloaf dinner, or the seafood section, with three treatments each for local cod and local scallops. (New Bedford is the world's top port in scallop landings.) Scallops are also available deep-fried, but the delicate flavor doesn't hold up well to that treatment. Better to stick with the whole-belly fried clams. Burgers and clam or scallop plates are especially good (and inexpensive) options at lunch.

Mimo Restaurant, 1526–1530 Acushnet Ave., New Bedford, MA 02746; (508) 997-8779; Portuguese; $. Take a look at the wine list before you even read the menu and you'll understand that this casual restaurant is serious about Portuguese cuisine. The list of roughly 80 wines is broken down by region of Portugal (Alentejo, Dão, Douro, Ribatejo, Setúbal, Bucelas, etc.). A short list of wines appears, almost as an afterthought, under "United States," and an even shorter list under "Rest of the World." The food ranges even more widely, pulling in some of the former Portuguese colonies (*camarão á Moçambique,* or shrimp Mozambique, for example, and a Brazilian version of stewed salt cod), as well as the classics of the home country (*puerco Alentejana,* or marinated pork cubes in a brown sauce with clams). The lunch menu, by contrast, leans heavily on simple sausage dishes and sandwiches.

Oro, 162 Front St., Scituate, MA 02066; (781) 378-2465; restaurant oro.com; New American; $$–$$$. Chef Robin and wife Julie King have all the bona fides to be cooking and running the front of the house pretty much anywhere. In fact, they met at Kevin Costner's locavore Santa Barbara restaurant, Epiphany, and both have worked with some of the Boston area's best restaurateurs. But they call Scituate home, and they've brought the fresh-market, locavore sensibility to the Scituate waterfront. Lobster cakes are one of Robin's signature dishes. They are coated in panko crumbs, plated on a puddle of lobster bisque, and topped with a tangle of crunchy deep-fried julienned sweet potatoes. We also like the daily duck tasting (seared breast, confit leg, and Madeira duck jus). Sunday brunch is imaginative— lobster sliders and fries, hot maple doughnuts, blueberry ricotta pancakes. The Kings seem to be cooking for their friends and neighbors.

Patrizia Italy Trattoria, 170 Water St, Plymouth, MA 02360; (508) 747-0015; patriziasitaly.com; Italian; $$$. We give Patrizia extra points for responding to queries about how to dress as "smart casual." Food this good deserves a little respect. The menu skips around the Italian peninsula a bit, with great northern pastas like tagliatelle with a real veal-pork-beef Bolognese sauce and pappardelle with a ragout of porcini mushrooms and speck (a northern Italian ham), followed by *secondi* that range from a Roman-style veal scallopini to a Sicilian treatment of swordfish. But the menu is really only an outline, as the choices and treatments change depending on what catch was landed and what produce is being picked. Patrizia also features an excellent wine list that balances Italians with Californians.

Petit Robert, 45 Chapel St., Needham, MA 02492; (781) 559-0532; prbneedham.com; French; $$. Every town should have a budget bistro that serves real French food, but only Needham is lucky enough to have Jacky Robert's one venture outside Metro Boston (see p. 151). Like the others, this is a great spot to settle in for coq au vin or *steak-frites* with a carafe of wine and soulful glances. Vegetarians can order something like the quinoa, farro, and lentil cake while Francophiles can still tuck into the cassoulet with lamb, pork sausage, duck confit, and navy beans.

Toll House: The First Chip

In 1997 the Massachusetts legislature designated the chocolate chip cookie the official cookie of the Commonwealth, despite strong lobbying on behalf of the Fig Newton. In the 1930s, Ruth Wakefield made culinary history when she added pieces of a cut-up Nestle chocolate bar to some butter cookies she was baking for guests at the Toll House Inn, which Ruth and husband Kenneth ran in an 18th-century toll house outside of Whitman. The "toll house" cookies were an immediate hit, and Ruth eventually allowed Nestle to publish her recipe in return for a lifetime supply of chocolate (and other considerations—stock in the company, we hope). To make it even easier for cooks to whip up a batch, Nestle introduced prechopped Semi-Sweet Chocolate Morsels (with the recipe on the bag) in 1939 and set the cookie on the road to becoming the country's favorite.

Riva, 116 Front St., Scituate, MA 02066; (781) 545-5881; rivarestaurant.net; Italian; $$–$$$. This casual trattoria on Scituate harbor brings the market-driven approach of fine Italian cuisine to the South Shore by embracing the incredible local produce, fish, and shellfish. Chef Michael Tondorf, a Scituate native, worked here as a teenager before going off to get his culinary degree at New England Culinary Institute and then train under superchef Todd English. In late 2012, Michael and his sister Kara bought the place. The Tondorfs have maintained Riva's generous portions but have spiffed up the menu with slightly more sophisticated preparations. One of the dependable local dishes is the pancetta-wrapped day-boat cod served with a root vegetable hash and lobster cream. Tondorf's version of scallop risotto includes red pears and spinach and a sprinkle of toasted pumpkin seeds. Desserts are what we think of as savory chef's desserts—crème brûlée, bread pudding, cheesecake, and a great version of fallen chocolate cake with a fresh raspberry center.

Sagres Restaurant, 177 Columbia St., Fall River, MA 02721; (508) 675-7018; sagresrestaurant.com; Portuguese; $$. This venerable traditional Portuguese restaurant is well-loved in Fall River for dishes like the Portuguese steak (with beef gravy and a fried egg) and a Cornish hen version of rotisserie chicken with a spicy sauce and both rice and french fries. Several salt cod dishes are offered every night, though the most popular is *bacalhau à Gomes de Sá*—boneless salt cod baked with potatoes, onion, and olive oil and garnished with black olives and chopped hard-boiled egg. The Portuguese version of Spanish paella blends the flavors of the Alentejo with some of the shellfish of New England: lobster, shrimp, littlenecks, cod, calamari, mussels, chicken, and chouriço simmered with rice, carrots, and peas.

Scarlet Oak Tavern, 1217 Main St., Hingham, MA 02043; (781) 749-8200; scarletoaktavern.com; New American; $$–$$$. The core of this historic tavern is a 250-year-old farmhouse that, in true New England tradition, has sprouted new wings and additions every half-century or so. As a result, there is an atmospheric tavern downstairs and several dining rooms of different sizes upstairs, several of which do double-duty as function rooms or private dining for special occasions. A sister restaurant to **Gibbet Hill Grill** in Groton (see p. 96), Scarlet Oak follows a similar farm-to-table approach. Succulent Black Angus steaks and platters of South Shore seafood are house specialties, and much of the seasonal produce hails from the farm on the Gibbet Hill property.

Shawmut Diner, 943 Shawmut Ave., New Bedford, MA 02746; (508) 993-3073; Casual American; $. The neon Indian atop the Shawmut glows, his reflection flashing off this large aluminum diner like a clarion call from America's roadside past. This New Bedford landmark is perpetually jammed in the mornings, but it serves breakfast food all day as well as grilled sandwiches, burgers, hot dogs, and such diner specialties as American chop suey at lunch. Open daily until 2:30 p.m., Fri and Sat all night.

Sichuan Gourmet, 386–388 S. Main St., Sharon, MA 02067; (781) 784-6698; laosichuan.com; Chinese; $. This Sharon outpost of authentic Sichuan cooking is Chef Lujin Liu's latest effort to bring the carefully prepared, complex cooking of his native Chengdu to the Bay State. Although most Boston-area Chinese restaurants serve the Cantonese cuisine of southern China, Liu is a great believer in the strong flavors and contrasting textures of Sichuan food. Although the cuisine is generally considered spicy (it does use both hot peppers and Sichuan peppercorns), in Liu's hands it becomes subtle and sophisticated. Even a classic Chinese restaurant dish of "kung pao chicken" (properly rendered as *gong bao*) trades in the usual gloppy presentation for a delicate dish of perfectly cubed chicken, hot red peppers, and peanuts.

Spicy Lime, 522 Pleasant St., New Bedford, MA 02740; (508) 992-3330; Thai; $–$$. This tiny downtown storefront run by Thailand-born Linda Sawang features her mother, Yai Sawang, in the kitchen. Mother and daughter alike support local farmers and fishermen, so they have adapted traditional Thai dishes to southeastern Massachusetts provender. In fact, some local gardeners even trade produce for meals. The light, fresh cuisine is a hit in New Bedford—almost an antidote to the fried food of other ethnic offerings. A salad of shredded green papaya, lime, tomatoes, and green peanuts, tossed in the restaurant's signature dressing, is one of the greatest hits. The crisp white tablecloths on the 11 tables give the room a crisp elegance rarely seen at this price point.

Steel & Rye, 95 Eliot St., Milton, MA 02186; (617) 690-2787; steel andrye.com; New American; $$–$$$. Boasting an industrial look (the building was once a car dealership), Steel & Rye serves straightforward, no-nonsense food with an emphasis on local product. The appetizer menu features an "oyster of the day" as well as Pat's Wellfleet clams roasted on a bed of salt. Chef-Owner Chris Parsons carries through with pastas made in-house—gemelli with braised lamb and bitter greens, tiny gnocchi with lobster in a morel mushroom sauce—and homey dishes like his broccoli casserole with wild mushrooms, Comté cheese, and a Ritz-type cracker made in the Steel & Rye kitchen. If you just want to nibble at the bar, you could do a lot worse than ordering the duck rillettes with fennel and dried fruit *mostarda,* the pickled quail eggs, or what Parsons simply calls "Today's Cheese."

Sweet Basil, 942 Great Plain Ave., Needham, MA 02492; (781) 444-9600; sweetbasilneedham.com; Italian; $$. Chef-Owner Dave Becker has all the qualifications for an Italian chef. He cooked in Napa Valley, worked for one of the contemporary Italian restaurants in Boston, and spent time in Liguria learning to make pasta. His house specialties veer from Italian-American standbys like chicken parmigiana to a classic Bolognese meat sauce over pappardelle to a very contemporary dish of *chifferi* pasta (sort of ridged elbow macaroni) tossed with a *ragù* of fava beans and spring vegetables.  An amateur potter, Becker also makes the brown and blue dinnerware. Note that neither reservations nor credit cards are accepted, and Sweet Basil is BYOB.

Taiyou Shabu & Sushi, 235A Quincy Ave., Quincy, MA 02169; (617) 773-6888; taiyoushabu.com; Japanese; $–$$. Owned by Chinese brothers Huihua Li and Honghua Li, Taiyou serves Japanese dishes as interpreted via California. The restaurant attracts Quincy's extensive Chinese community, but plenty of non-Asians come in to swish paper thin slices of meat, seafood, and even vegetables in hot broth, then dump the remaining broth over rice noodles (or in a very Chinese variation, thick wheat noodles) to get every last drop of *umami*. The sushi includes both the usual suspects—variants of the California roll, lots of spicy tuna—and many house specialty maki rolls that veer far from tradition but delight nonetheless.

Tosca, 14 North St, Hingham, MA 02043; (781) 740-0080; tosca hingham.com; Italian; $$$. It figures that a restaurant named for Puccini's most inventive opera would cook almost everything over a wood-fire grill or in a big wood-fired oven and serve it with theatrical flair. Opened in 1993, Tosca signaled the resurgence of destination dining at the Hingham waterfront, and it remains a keystone of the dining scene. Big spenders might consider the "Butcher's Reserve" menu of grilled meats, which can be accompanied by trophy-level red wines. A large part of the regular menu is gluten-free (dishes are clearly identified), and the pastry chef offers a minimum of seven lavish desserts every night. The extensive wine list includes several splits of red for light drinkers or those wishing to switch wines with each course.

Wahlburgers, 19 Shipyard Dr., Hingham, MA 02043; (855) 924-5246; wahlburgers.com; Casual American; $. Actors/singers Donnie and Mark and Chef Paul Wahlberg are behind this fun, family-friendly spot that makes a casual alternative to adjacent **Alma Nove**

(see p. 222). Bring the kids for fresh-ground beef burgers or for specialties, such as the Thanksgiving Burger of ground turkey, stuffing, orange-cranberry sauce, roasted butternut squash, and mayo on a bun. For a real retro touch, order that sandwich with tater tots (or for a modern twist on retro, sweet potato tater tots). The bar serves a house unfiltered pale ale crafted for the restaurant by **Harpoon** in South Boston (see p. 170).

**Amaral's Bakery, 241 Globe St., Fall River, MA 02724; (508)
674-8988; amaralsbakery.com; Bakery.** You'll find Amaral's Portuguese sweet bread, biscuits, and muffins (sort of like English muffins
but sweeter and more substantive) in little shops all over eastern
Massachusetts wherever there is a substantial Portuguese or Brazilian
population. But if you go directly to the bakery (open Mon through Fri
from 5 a.m. to 4 p.m. and Sat from 5 a.m. to 3 p.m.), you can get the
sweet bread rings fresh from the ovens where the Amaral family has
been making them for more than a half-century.

**Amaral's Market, 488 Belleville Ave., New Bedford, MA 02746;
(508) 996-1222; Fishmonger.** Portuguese life in America is distilled
at this excellent market that specializes in fresh and frozen fish. The
cases of fish on crushed ice take up a large corner of the store, and
here you'll find fish that never make it to the Anglo markets, such as
chinchards (North African horse mackerel that are usually grilled) and
large herring, as well as some that do, such as sea bass, haddock, hake,
fresh squid, perch, pollock, and sea bream. Look into the frozen food
cases and the selection expands to include frozen octopus (whole and
sectioned). Several brands of salt cod (*bacalhau*) are also available. This
is one of the rare places where you can find freshly rendered cooking
lard (a huge improvement over the usual waxy grease sold as lard) and
a refrigerator case where chocolate chip cookie dough is sold next to
blood sausages. Amaral's also carries Martin's cheese, a Portuguese-
style fresh cheese made locally.

**Bloomy Rind, 21 Main St., Hingham, MA 02043; (781) 740-1001;
bloomyrind.com; Cheese.** Mary Gonzalves is the cheesemonger at this
terrific little gourmet shop that also sells prosciutto, artisanal sausages,

spreads, salsas, olive oil . . . and all manner of things that go well with cheese. Her husband Robert is the house chef (he used to cook at **L'Espalier,** see p. 145, and with Todd English) and he makes takeaway dishes like farro salad or green pea guacamole (in season only), as well as the soups and sandwiches available at lunch. Tastes of almost everything are available, and Mary tends to get customers hooked on sensational cheeses they've never tried before.

The Butcherie II, 15 Washington St., Canton, MA 02021; (781) 828-3530; Grocery. Looking for potato latkes like your bubbie used to make? Beef knishes? Carrot kugel? You'll find them in the refrigerated cases at The Butcherie II, a one-stop kosher grocer for the suburbs south of Boston. That same section also offers several brands of New York half-sour pickles, along with ready-to-heat chicken noodle soup, split pea soup, hearty cabbage soup, tzimmes, potato kugel, five-vegetable knishes, mushroom knishes, and scallion latkes. The shelves are filled with canned goods and dry goods from Israel and the large kosher foods companies of New York and New Jersey. Empire-brand kosher poultry is available, as are whole corned briskets and tongues. Closed Sat.

Buzzards Bay Brewing Company, 98 Horseneck Rd., Westport, MA 02790; (877) 287-2421 or (508) 636-2288; buzzardsbrew .com; Brewery. Allied with Westport Rivers Winery, this microbrewery sits on a 140-acre family farm. You'll see hops growing along the drive to the three-story barn that houses the brewery and retail shop. In 2012, the brewers rejiggered their approach to use almost entirely North American malts and hops. The Buzzards Bay IPA remains the flagship—forward malts and bold hops. Many of the other brews are equally hoppy, with the smooth exception of the Moby D easy-drinking

THAT FIRST CUP

With its orange and purple decor, the busy shop looks like all the others in the Dunkin' Donuts chain—except for the small plaque inside the door proclaiming, "On this site the original Dunkin' Donuts opened its doors in May 1950." When Dorchester native and eighth-grade dropout William Rosenberg set up shop in a former awning store, he charged a nickel for a doughnut and ten cents for the cup of coffee to dunk it in. His simple formula proved a huge success. According to corporate headquarters, Dunkin' Donuts is the world's leading baked goods and coffee chain, serving more than five million customers per day.

Dunkin' Donuts, 543 Southern Artery, Quincy, MA 02169; (617) 472-9502; dunkin donuts.com.

pale ale. Retail store open Sat from Apr through Dec for tastings, growler sales, and tours.

Cape Quality Seafood, 657 Dartmouth St., Dartmouth, MA 02748; (508) 996-6725; capequalityseafood.com; Fishmonger. Here's another outstanding fish market that caters to the more catholic tastes of the ethnic populations of southeastern Massachusetts. It's one of the few spots where you'll find periwinkles next to littleneck, steamer, and chowder clams. Cape Quality also sells large (5- to 7-pound) lobsters, shucked-out lobster tails and claws, and the full range of finfish caught by local fishermen. Many ready-to-heat items are available, including stuffed quahogs. If you want to sit down and eat, there is a separate entrance to the dining area, where broiled, baked, steamed, and fried fish and shellfish are served, along with a few grilled steaks.

Dorothy Cox's Chocolates, 63 Alden Rd., Fairhaven, MA 02719; (508) 996-2465; dorothycox.com; **Chocolatier.** This family-owned and -operated business has been creating gourmet chocolates for more than three-quarters of a century; one of the current owners is, in fact, the namesake of her grandmother. The company produces 110 varieties of chocolate candies, but it is best known for its buttercrunch, made with equal quantities of butter and sugar. The company claims to have introduced chocolate-covered dried cranberries and it certainly makes

some of the best. Call during slower seasons to see if tours are being offered.

Gaspar's Sausage Company Factory Outlet, 384 Faunce Corner Rd., North Dartmouth, MA 02747; (508) 998-2012 or (800) 542-2038; linguica.com; **Butcher.** Since the late 1920s, Gaspar's has been the largest producer of smoked Portuguese sausages in the country. The line emphasizes linguiça and chouriço spiced pork sausages (pronounced *ling-GWEE-sah* and *shoor-REES*) made by Portuguese Americans in southeastern Massachusetts. The chouriço, which is noticeably hotter than the linguiça, is often used in casseroles and fried dishes, while linguiça is frequently grilled and served on a bun. A *morcela* (blood sausage) is also available seasonally. Look for Gaspar's products in Portuguese markets or visit the factory store. For Gaspar's recipe for **Kale Soup,** see p. 288.

Gypsy Kitchen, 1241 Hancock St., Quincy, MA 02169; (617) 847-1846; gypsykitchenquincy.com; **Specialty Shop.** Formerly a sauce stand in Boston's Quincy Market, Gypsy Kitchen has expanded its horizons and its product lines in this handsome downtown Quincy storefront. It's still a prime resource for all varieties of hot sauce from around the globe, including owner Lisa Lamme's own recipe Gypsy

Juice, which Lamme uses to give a little zing to guacamole. She also stocks many other spices, coffees, and gift baskets, as well as imported cheeses and wines from France, Italy, Spain, and California.

How on Earth, The Store, 62 Marion Rd. (Route 62), Mattapoisett, MA 02739; (508) 758-1341; howonearth.net; Grocery. The motto at the nonprofit How on Earth project of the Marion Institute is "Know your farmer, know your food." The Store carries a bounty of local produce in season. They also stock local and organic dairy products, pasture-raised eggs, pasture-raised meats, and breads from local bakers. You can also choose from a large assortment of bulk grains, beans, nuts, as well as oils and vinegars. Visit at lunch time to enjoy a turkey meatloaf sandwich or chicken salad with walnuts and dried cranberries.

O'Brien's Bakery, 11 Vernon St., Quincy, MA 02169; (617) 472-4025; obriensbakeryquincy.com; Bakery. Owner Brian Jackle comes from a long line of bakers and is especially well-known for his Irish soda breads. But rather than limiting his horizons, he also turns out a range of artisan breads, including Swedish breads, beer bread, and Pullman bread, which is favored for sandwiches. The shop also has a variety of pastries and offers sugar-free and gluten-free breads and pastries. No one need leave O'Brien's hungry. They even turn out their own gourmet dog treats.

Peaceful Meadows Farm, 60 Bedford St. (Route 18), Whitman, MA 02382; (781) 447-3889; 109 W. Grove St., Middleboro, MA 02346; (508) 947-1322; 170 Water St., Plymouth, MA 02360; (508) 746-2362; peacefulmeadows .com; Ice Cream/Yogurt. This dairy farm was established in the 1920s and early customers received deliveries of milk and cream by horse and wagon. The family started making ice cream in 1962 and now offers more than 20 flavors that range from vanilla or chocolate to fresh banana or fudge walnut. The rhythms of farm life keep the ice cream makers attuned to the seasons. Look for monthly specials such as peach in July, blueberry cheesecake in August, and pumpkin in October. If you head to the farm in Whitman, you can stop in the dairy store for milk, local baked goods, eggs, bacon, and maple syrup before heading to the ice cream stand. The ice cream—but not the milk—is also available in Middleboro and Plymouth. All three locations stock the very popular egg nog during the winter holiday season.

Rainbow Turkey Farm, 199 Homestead Ave., Rehoboth, MA 02769; (508) 252-4427; **Butcher.** Judy and Tom Mello raise about 500 turkeys each year for the Thanksgiving and Christmas holidays. Call a few days before you need a bird and you'll be able to pick it up, freshly dressed, at the farm.

Sid Wainer & Sons Specialty Produce and Specialty Foods, 2301 Purchase St., New Bedford, MA 02746; (888) 743-9246; **sidwainer.com; Grocery.** This remarkable company distributes imported and locally grown gourmet products all around the country. Fortunately, they also have this retail market. Forget your mother's advice to never visit a grocery store on an empty stomach. We fast for a day before we hit Sid Wainer, where the shopping experience is a smorgasbord that's as filling as it is educational. On a single Saturday morning, we could sample grilled black olives; roasted yellow, green, and red tomatoes; organic red rice salad; goat cheddar, Manchego, farmhouse cheddar, Pont l'Évêque, and Camembert cheeses; smoked duck breast; artichoke paste from Italy; banana walnut coffee cake from Cape Cod; soft amaretti from Italy; Italian baby fig compote; figs in syrup; pumpkin chestnut whole grain soup made with Zuppa Saracena grain mix; chive, red pepper, and wild berry soft unripened goat cheeses; two Spanish olive

CRAZY ABOUT CRANBERRIES

Cranberries have a long history in Massachusetts. Native Americans ate fresh cranberries and also combined them with cornmeal to make bread or with dried deer meat and fat to make that precursor of the energy bar, pemmican. A recipe for cranberry sauce appears in a 1663 Pilgrim cookbook, but the berries didn't really become popular until the late 19th century, when enough sugar was imported from the West Indies to balance their natural astringency.

Today, Massachusetts produces nearly half of all cranberries grown in the United States, and most of the state's cranberry bogs are located in the swampy flatlands of Plymouth County. If you're driving around southeastern Massachusetts in October, turn off the main road to be treated to the stunning sight of bright red cranberries floating on deep blue water as they wait to be harvested. You might want to time your visit for the mid-October **Cranberry Harvest Celebration** (see Appendix C).

For a more low-key cranberry encounter, stop by **Flax Pond Cranberry Company** (1 Robbins Path, Carver, MA 02330; 508-866-2162; flaxpondfarms.com) in September or October. (Call for hours.) You'll turn down a packed-sand road and pass old, weathered buildings where ancient pickup trucks are parked out front. Farther in are massive rectangular bogs. Jack and Dot Angley talk a bit about cranberry growing and demonstrate the "dry" method of cranberry harvesting. Visitors can try their hand at screening berries and can sample cranberry juice and raw berries "if they dare." There's even a small gift shop selling cranberry taffy, cranberry-land honey, and other merchandise.

oils from Arbequina olives; two Tuscan olive oils; two aged balsamic vinegars from Modena; and anise, raspberry, tangerine, lavender, and lemon honeys. The staff chefs and bakers prepare foods in the demonstration kitchen to show you how to use the products. Walk in at the holiday season and you might see a chef whipping up stuffing with truffles or blue Hubbard squash with fennel.

Westport Lobster Company, 915 Main Rd., Westport, MA 02790; (508) 636-8500; Fishmonger. While it might seem peculiar to find a fishmonger along a main road, keep in mind that this end of Westport is a thin peninsula and fishing boats are moored not more than a hundred yards away. The unassuming brown-shingled 1875 former stable fairly brims over with the ocean's bounty. Deep-sea fish such as swordfish and tuna are usually available, as are more coastal cod, flounder, and haddock. Fresh shellfish varieties include quahogs, littlenecks, mussels, steamer clams, and oysters. As the name suggests, there's never a shortage of lobster (or crabs, for that matter). Westport Lobster also smokes salmon, trout, mussels, haddock, and scallops.

Westport Rivers Vineyard & Winery, 417 Hixbridge Rd., Westport, MA 02790; (508) 636-3423; westportrivers.com; Wine, Beer & Spirits. Established in 1986, Westport Rivers makes the best varietal grape wines in Massachusetts, quite possibly the best in New England. The winery is justifiably famed for its *méthode champenoise* sparkling Chardonnay from grapes grown on the farm. In addition to the sparkling wines, Westport Rivers also produces a still Chardonnay, Pinot Noir, Riesling, Pinot Blanc, Grüner Veltliner, Pinot Noir Rosé, and a small vintage of Rkatsiteli (a variety native to the country of Georgia). The winery also dabbles in an aperitif wine of dry-fermented Chardonnay combined with fresh juice as well as various vermouths available only at the winery. Besides the wines (tastings always available), the winery store carries a few select items for picnicking, including Great Hill Blue cheese, local goat cheese, crackers, and biscotti, as well as glasses, picnic baskets, and corkscrews. On Saturday tours, you walk from the gray-shingled shop to the brown-shingled winery through a grape arbor that frames views of the vineyards. During the year, festivals and special dinners feature local produce, seafood, beef, and specialty foods.

Woods Seafood Market & Restaurant, 15 Town Pier, Plymouth, MA 02360; (508) 746-0261; woodsseafoods.com; Fishmonger. With all the emphasis on turkeys, it's easy to forget that the Pilgrims fished long before they farmed. Woods continues the tradition in style from a large gray building on Town Wharf. One end is the fish market, which carries the usual fresh Cape Cod Bay fish (flounder, cod, haddock), several deep-sea fish (tuna, swordfish, shark), mussels, sea and bay scallops, and all variety of clams. Crustaceans, of course, abound, with both large and small lobsters available. If you feel the need to eat your fish immediately, place an order at the take-out window and carry your sandwiches or fried plates to booths or tables in a large glassed-in room overlooking the ocean.

Farm Stands & PYOs

Ashley's Peaches, 1461 Main St., Acushnet, MA 02743; (508) 763-4329. The stand is open from late July through mid-October, but it's best to call ahead because Ernest and Diane Ventura pick peaches each morning and sell them the same day. If none are ripe, the stand will not open. To try to ensure a steady supply and a long season, this family farm, now in its fifth generation, grows more than 30 varieties of peaches, as well as nectarines, a few varieties of apples, and tomatoes and pumpkins. Although it's hard to imagine anything better than a fresh-picked peach, you'll also find jams and jellies, peach cobblers, apple pies, and muffins.

Dowse Orchards, 98 N. Main St. (Route 27), Sherborn, MA 01770; (508) 653-2639; dowseorchards.com. The motto at Dowse is "America's best crunchin' apples since 1778," but the family has been pressing cider from the apples "only" since 1853. About 50 acres of the farm are planted in apples, and several acres more grow vegetables, flowers, and Christmas trees. The farm stand is open from May until Christmas Eve, beginning with lettuces and garden plants in the spring and wrapping up with the last of the apples (mostly older varieties like Spencer, Baldwin, and Stayment Winesap), pumpkins, and trees in the fall and early winter.

Four Town Farm, 90 George St., Seekonk, MA 02771; (508) 336-5587; 4townfarm.com. Located at the border of Massachusetts and Rhode Island, where the acreage edges into four different municipalities, Four Town has extensive fields of flowers for picking as well as strawberries, raspberries, pumpkins, and the more unusual English peas and fava beans. The farm stand has baked goods, soups, pies, vegetables, cider, and apples. Open mid-Apr through Christmas. Call for pick-your-own days and hours.

Noquochoke Orchards, 594 Drift Rd., Westport, MA 02790; (508) 636-2237. The Smith family has been farming for more than 110 years and their orchards are a regional treasure, producing (at last count) 70 varieties of apples, covering the entire harvest season with both cooking and eating varieties, along with pears, peaches, plums, nectarines, and quinces. They are particularly known for their antique apples such as Winesap, Russet, and York. Although the orchards

WESTPORT MACOMBER

The growing movement to "eat local" has sparked interest in the intensely local Westport Macomber. This cross between a radish, turnip, and cabbage was developed on a farm that had been in the Macomber family since the 17th century. In 1876, brothers Adin and Elihu Macomber planted radishes next to rutabagas (themselves a cross between a cabbage and a turnip) to allow for cross-pollination. The resulting vegetable—with its white flesh, sweet flavor, and aroma of horseradish—became known, logically enough, as the Westport Macomber. Harvested in October and November, Macombers have become popular with local chefs. You might find them used in soups or baked goods or mashed (alone or with carrots or potatoes). If you want to try them yourself, buy Macombers that are solid and fairly dense. Wash and peel them before boiling. Many aficionados believe that Macombers are best after the first frost.

demand the lion's share of attention, the farm also yields strawberries, sweet corn, squash, tomatoes, and the local heirloom root vegetable, the Westport Macomber (see sidebar). Cider has a particularly fresh taste because of the extra care that goes into making it. To avoid the cooked taste of many stable fresh ciders, the apples are hand-washed before pressing and the juice is sterilized with ultraviolet light. Open mid-July to mid-Dec.

Oakdale Farm, 59 Wheaton Ave., Rehoboth, MA 02769; (508) 336-7681; oakdalefarms.com. Richard and Marie Pray's fields and greenhouses yield corn, summer and winter squashes, tomatoes, collards, lettuces, and dozens of types of culinary and medicinal herbs.

Their retail shop sells dried herbs and herb and flower flats, as well as candles, wreaths, and other decorative craft items year-round, fresh produce in season.

Pine Hall Farm, 588 Middle Rd., Acushnet, MA 02743; (508) 995-0041. Pine Hall offers visitors the unusual opportunity to try their hand at gathering cranberries by the dry harvest method. Check with the owners in October. They make the fields available after they have completed their own harvest.

Sampson Farm, 222 Old Bedford Rd., Westport, MA 02790; (508) 674-2733. People unfamiliar with southeastern Massachusetts are often surprised to discover how many farmers grow potatoes. Jerome Sampson has 70 of his 100 acres in potatoes, and while he sells most of the crop to the wholesale market, he maintains a small retail stand where he also offers corn, pumpkins, squash, and other vegetables. Open July through Oct.

Spring Meadow Farm, 109 Marion Rd., Mattapoisett, MA 02739; (508) 758-2678.  The warm exposure on Buzzards Bay means that strawberry picking often begins by the end of May and you can return later in the season for PYO blackberries and flowers, along with other vegetables. Open through mid-Oct.

Volante Farms, 292 Forest St., Needham, MA 02492; (781) 444-2351; volantefarms.com. Building a 9,000-square-foot farm stand in 2012 allowed Volante Farms to stay open all year selling its own and other produce, grass-fed New England meats, as well as ice cream and bakery products. They grow wildly popular baby lettuce and arugula all year. The farm has been in the family since 1917 and at the Needham location for more than a half-century. With the expansion, Volante Farms now has a deli with daily soup and sandwich specials and makes some finished dishes available in the refrigerator cases. For Chef Todd Heberlein's recipe for **Summer Vegetable Pasta with Arugula Pesto,** see p. 292.

Ward's Berry Farm, 614 S. Main St., Sharon, MA 02067; (781) 784-3600; wardsberryfarm.com. The PYO season begins with strawberries in mid-June, progresses to blueberries in July and August, and concludes with pumpkins in September and October. In addition to farm-grown vegetables in season, Ward's offers breads, cheeses, homemade jams, and baked goods, including their legendary (and huge) blueberry muffins made when the berries are fresh and ripe. If you work up an appetite in the fields, you can grab lunch at the sandwich counter.

Farmers' Markets

Attleboro Farmers' Market, Municipal parking lot, 74 N. Main St., Attleboro. Sat from 8 a.m. to noon, June through Oct.

Attleboro/Our Lady of LaSalette Farmers' Market, 947 Park St. (Route 118), Attleboro. Fri from 2 to 6 p.m., June through Oct.

Brockton Fairgrounds Farmers' Market, Brockton Fair Grounds, Brockton. Sat from 9 a.m. to noon, mid-July through Oct.

Brockton City Hall Plaza Farmers' Market, 45 School St., Brockton. Fri from 10:30 a.m. to 1:30 p.m., July through Oct.

Buzzards Bay Farmers' Market, Main Street, Buzzards Bay Park, Buzzards Bay. Fri from 10 a.m. to 2 p.m., July through Oct.

Cohasset Farmers' Market, Cohasset Common, Main Street, Cohasset. Thurs from 2:30 to 6:30 p.m., mid-June to mid-Oct.

Fall River Kennedy Park Farmers' Market, Kennedy Park, Fall River. Sat from 7 a.m. to 1 p.m., mid-May through Nov.

Fall River Lou Sevin Square Farmers' Market, Lou Sevin Square, Old 2nd Street, Fall River. Thurs from 11 a.m. to 6 p.m., June through Oct.

Fall River Ruggles Park Farmers' Market, Ruggles Park, Fall River. Wed from 9 a.m. to 3 p.m., June through Nov.

Fall River Winter Farmers' Market, 72 Bank St., Fall River. Third Sat from 8 a.m. to noon, Nov through Apr.

Hingham Farmers' Market, Bathing Beach parking lot, 96 Otis St. (Route 3A), Hingham. Sat from 10 a.m. to 2 p.m., May through Nov.

Mansfield Farmers' Market, 80 N. Main St., Mansfield. Thurs from 2 to 6 p.m., mid-July to mid-Sept.

Middleboro Farmers' Market, Town Hall lawn, Route 105, Middleboro. Sat from 9 a.m. to 1 p.m., June through Nov.

Milton Farmers' Market, Town Park, Wharf and Adams Streets, Milton Village. Thurs from 1 to 6 p.m., mid-June through Oct.

New Bedford Clasky Common Farmers' Market, Pleasant and Pearl Streets, New Bedford. Sat 9 a.m. to 1 p.m., mid-July to late Oct.

New Bedford Downtown Farmers' Market, Main library lawn on Pleasant Street, New Bedford. Thurs from 2 to 6 p.m., mid-July through Oct.

New Bedford Farmers' Market, Brooklawn Park, Ashley Boulevard and Carlisle Street, New Bedford. Mon from 2 to 7 p.m., July to late Oct.

Norwood Farmers Market, Town Common, Nahatan Street and Route 1A, Norwood. Tues from noon to 6 p.m., mid-June through Oct.

Old Rochester Farmers' Market, Old Rochester Regional School, 135 Marion Rd., Mattapoisett. Tues from 3 to 7 p.m., June to mid-Oct.

Original Easton Farmers' Market, 591 Depot St. at Cross Street, North Easton. Tues from 2 to 6 p.m. and Sat from 10 a.m. to 2 p.m., late May through Oct.

Plymouth Farmers' Market, Stephens Field, Route 3A, Plymouth. Thurs from 2:30 to 6:30 p.m., mid-June through Oct.

Plymouth Farmers' Market, 1820 Courthouse Green, Plymouth. Sat from 10 a.m. to 2 p.m., mid-June through Oct.

Plymouth Winter-Into-Spring Farmers' Market, Plimoth Plantation, 137 Warren Ave., Plymouth. Second Thurs from 2:30 to 6:30 p.m., Nov through May.

Quincy Farmers' Market, John Hancock municipal parking lot, Quincy center. Fri from 11:30 a.m. to 5:30 p.m., late June to mid-Nov.

Taunton Farmers' Market, parking lot behind City Hall, Spring and Summer Streets, Taunton. Thurs from 11 a.m. to 3 p.m., July through Oct.

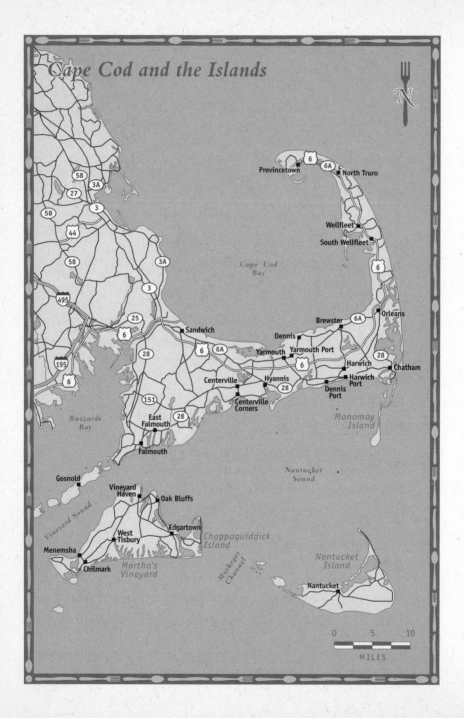

Cape Cod and the Islands

Cape Cod &
the Islands

It's obvious from a map that Martha's Vineyard and Nantucket are islands, but so is Cape Cod, separated from mainland Massachusetts by the Cape Cod Canal. These land masses feel uncommonly evanescent—as they should. Virtually everything you see above the waterline is glacial debris—deposits of rock and grit scraped off the face of New England and left behind when the ice sheets ebbed a hundred centuries ago. Wave action, onshore currents, and rising sea levels are conspiring to put it all underwater again.

Despite the thin glacial soils, native peoples managed to grow corn here for centuries before the English colonists arrived—indeed, their cache of dried corn, pilfered by the Pilgrims in Truro, kept some of the Plymouth colonists from starvation over the winter of 1620–21. As European settlers spread onto the Cape and out to the islands in the 17th century, they eventually turned to the sea for their living.

And so it is today. Although the few farm stands of the Cape and Islands are spectacular, the most prominent thing about the region is not the land, but the ocean. The waters of Cape Cod Bay are no longer so thick with cod that a person could walk from boat to boat on their backs, as some early accounts claimed, but they are rich fishing grounds nonetheless. Sportfishermen speak of striped bass and bluefish runs in these waters as some of the finest in the world. Given careful management, the halibut and tuna fisheries, especially around the Nantucket shoals, show startling resilience.

The real gastronomic success story in the Cape and Islands, however, is shellfishing. Oyster aficionados rank the Wellfleet bluepoint oyster as one of the finest flavored in the world, and the mussel farms on the sandy shoals off Chatham are unparalleled in New England. Order shellfish at the humblest seafood shack, and you're guaranteed a gourmet treat. Visit town hall for a license, and you can gather your own. It is one of the mysteries of summer that no clams taste as good as the ones you dig yourself and steam on a bed of kelp in a pot of seawater.

This corner of Massachusetts is the state's summer beach playground, attracting hundreds of thousands of vacationers. In America, wherever you find tourists, you also find sweets. Cape Cod is one of the great historical centers for the production of saltwater taffy, and old-fashioned purveyors are still turning out these sticky morsels, each wrapped in a twist of waxed paper. The chocolatiers are comparative latecomers, but they have flourished, and temptation calls on almost every block.

Foodie Faves

Abba, 89 Old Colony Way, Orleans, MA 02653; (508) 255-8144; abbarestaurant.com; New American; $$$. A longtime favorite at the crook of the Cape, Abba has evolved over the years from a strong Thai-influenced menu to offering locavore New American dishes, occasionally with a Thai touch. (The lobster and shrimp pad thai that's been on the menu for decades is still one of the most popular dishes.) Whatever the dish, the kitchen maintains the spirit of Thai cooking, with straightforward, clean flavors and some great contrasts in texture. For example, grilled tuna comes with a vegetable nori roll tempura, and filet mignon is paired with a green coconut curry pasta and grilled eggplant. It makes for adventurous eating without feeling that you've been transported to southern California. Native shellfish and the local catch figure extensively on the menu.

Black Cat Tavern, 165 Ocean St., Hyannis, MA 02601; (508) 778-1233; blackcattavern.com; Casual American; $$–$$$. This very old-school tavern–cum–fried seafood spot across the street from the Hy-Line ferry dock is a pleasant spot to eat—especially if the weather allows and you can snag an outdoor table at the Shack Out Back raw bar. The Black Cat's claim to fame, though, is its giant lobster roll, which contains all the meat of a large lobster, nicely diced, moderately dressed, and heaped on a roll. Take the optional knife and fork—you'll need them.

Black Dog Tavern, 20 Beach St. Extension, Vineyard Haven (Martha's Vineyard), MA 02568; (508) 693-9223; Casual American; $$; Black Dog Bakery, 3 Water St., Vineyard Haven, MA 02568; (508) 693-4786; Black Dog Cafe, 509 State Rd., Vineyard Haven, MA 02568; (508) 696-8190; theblackdog.com; $. The tavern, dating all the way back to 1971, has evolved into a Martha's Vineyard landmark, as much for its unrelenting marketing as for its cozy quarters. The Black Dog logo is emblazoned on everything on- and off-island, it seems. Yet it remains a good place for soups and stews, hearty sandwiches, and a friendly pint of root beer. The Black Dog Cafe handles all the baking and serves soups as well as sandwiches on house-made bread. The Black Dog Bakery is more snack-oriented, with muffins, doughnuts, hearth breads, soups, and sandwiches.

Bookstore & Restaurant, 50 Kendrick Ave., Wellfleet, MA 02667; (508) 349-3154; wellfleetoyster.com; Seafood; $$. The name of this peculiar business should also include "& Shellfish Beds," for the littlenecks and oysters raised a short distance away are the main reasons for seeking out this casual beachside restaurant. The best bet is always the raw bar—especially the littlenecks and Wellfleet bluepoint oysters on the half shell. But the kitchen also makes a stirring Portuguese stew of shellfish and linguiça as well as a satisfying plate of baked cod, scallops, and shrimp. In the summer, the sun sets over the water behind Great Island—the best views are from the second-floor dining room. The bookstore at the back of the building contains a bewildering array of used books and magazines, many of which seem to be the sort left behind in summer rental cottages. Open mid-Feb through Dec.

Bramble Inn, 2019 Main St., Brewster, MA 02631; (508) 896-7644; brambleinn.com; New American; $$$. The Cape might be a shorts-and-sandals kind of summer place, but you'll want to put on nicer clothes for dining at the Bramble. The slightly formal rooms and Chef-Owner Ruth Manchester's elegant New American dishes warrant a little extra effort. If a chill wind is blowing in off Cape Cod Bay, you might order the roasted rack of lamb or falling-off-the-bones short ribs. But the local seafood, mostly sourced from the Chatham docks and Wellfleet's shellfish beds, is the real star, whether it's a bowl of mussels steamed with Portuguese sausage and hot pepper rings, or a "harbor stew" of mixed shellfish, and catch of the day in a white wine–saffron broth.

Brazilian Grill, 680 Main St., Hyannis, MA 02601; (508) 771-0109; braziliangrill-capecod.com; Brazilian; $–$$. Brazilian immigrants flood onto Cape Cod to take many of the seasonal service jobs. Sensing a critical mass, Walter Witt and Maximiliano De Paula opened this authentic *churrascaria,* where waiters circulate with long skewers of meat and diners help themselves from a buffet table of soups, salads, and side dishes. The barbecue includes several cuts of beef and pork as well as chicken, linguiça, lamb, quail, and chicken hearts grilled over natural wood charcoal. For a lighter meal, opt for the buffet only.

Meals on Wheels

If you like your meal accompanied by ever-changing scenery, the lunch, dinner, and Sunday brunch excursions of the Cape Cod Central Railroad might be just the ticket. With white-linen service, they are a taste of a bygone era. The dinner service is reserved for those aged 12 and up and even requires a bit of dressing up (no jeans, shorts, or T-shirts). Dining excursions are offered May through October, though schedules vary. Reservations are strongly recommended. Almost all excursions depart from the Hyannis train station at 252 Main St., Hyannis.

Cape Cod Central Railroad, (508) 771-3800 or (888) 797-7245; capetrain.com.

Cape Sea Grille, 31 Sea St., Harwich Port, MA 02646; (508) 432-4745; capeseagrille.com; New American/Seafood; $$$. Set on the marshy shores of Harwich Port, the Cape Sea Grille has the grace and gentility of a fine country home with the whole bottom floor opened up to provide elegant dining. Douglas and Jennifer Ramler took over the well-established restaurant in 2002 and transformed a fine-dining establishment into a gourmet destination for creative New American cuisine with an emphasis on fresh local shellfish and produce. Doug worked in one of Boston's best French provincial kitchens (**Hamersley's Bistro,** see p. 141), so there's a Burgundian accent to such appetizers as crispy duck confit in a swiss chard purse and the house-made country pâté. With such dishes as lobster, shrimp, and scallops tossed with pasta, peas, asparagus, and Pernod cream sauce, his entrees bring Mediterranean style to Cape foodstuffs. A few tables look out the back to gorgeous summer sunsets over the marshes, but that time slot must be reserved far in advance. Open Apr through mid-Dec.

Chillingsworth, 2449 Main St. (Route 6A), Brewster, MA 02631; (508) 896-3640; chillingsworth.com; French/New American; bistro $$, restaurant $$$$. For more than four decades, Chillingsworth has been Cape Cod's top haute-cuisine dining room, although in recent years a casual bistro has offered an a la carte menu of New American dishes simpler than the over-the-top French six-course fixed-price repast in the restaurant. Dine in the bistro in shirtsleeves with an open collar on seared tuna steak with a salad of Asian vegetables, New York *steak-frites* with grilled onions, or roasted pork loin with polenta. Or opt for the dress-up formal service and culinary complexity of the dining room and start with such treats as oysters in puff pastry or asparagus with morel mushrooms before applying the silverware to a seared duck breast and duck confit salad graced with blackberries and a balsamic vinegar sauce. There are even a few rooms upstairs for overnight stays. Open Mother's Day through Thanksgiving.

Cru, 1 Straight Wharf, Nantucket, MA 02554; (508) 228-9278; crunantucket.com; Seafood; $$$. The main reason to walk into Cru and sit down for several hours is to enjoy the salt breeze sweeping across the polished stone bar while you slurp raw shellfish in style. The oysters might hail from Barnstable Sea Farms, from Island Creek in Duxbury, from Martha's Vineyard, and usually from one place farther away (Maine, Prince Edward Island, etc.). A few seafood entrees round out the choices (though there's always a steak, a chicken dish, and a vegetarian option for members of the party who don't or can't eat seafood).

Glass Onion, 37 N. Main St., Falmouth, MA 02540; (508) 540-3730; theglassoniondining.com; New American; $$$. The wainscoting and sea-mist walls combine to give the Glass Onion a recherché look, but the kitchen is thoroughly up to date with its farm-to-table/dock-to-table cooking. Fish dishes are often the best bet, especially in summer and fall when the docks are most active in Chatham and Barnstable, giving the chefs lots of choices for daily specials. We like the Glass Onion's treatment of line-caught swordfish: quickly grilled (ask for seared) and served with a corn-scallion risotto. The wine list is a bit limited.

Home Port Restaurant, 512 North Rd., Menemsha (Martha's Vineyard), MA 02552; (508) 645-2679; homeportmv.com; Seafood; $$–$$$$. The Home Port has been a Menemsha tradition since 1930, and the large dining room is almost always packed. The fishing port's classic dining room, with its wall of mounted fish and weathered wood trim, continues to serve some of the Vineyard's finest fish meals. Many diners opt for the three-course menu with several options for each course—including the classics of lobster bisque or stuffed quahogs to start, boiled lobster or fish for the main course, and blueberry pie for dessert. If you're so foolish as to show up without a reservation (the phone starts ringing in the spring for July tables), you can go to the take-out window and carry your lobster roll or basket of fried fish to nearby Menemsha Beach for glorious alfresco sunset dining. Open late May through mid-Oct. BYOB.

Mac's Shack, 91 Commercial St., Wellfleet, MA 02667; (508) 349-6333; macsseafood.com; Seafood/Casual American; $–$$. You can't miss Mac's Shack. The clapboard house below the village has a lobsterman and dory on its roof and folks milling around outside hoping to get in. (Seating is first come, first served.) When you do get seated, you can go casual with a beer and lobster roll, or get fancy with uni and wild ramp carbonara made with fresh pasta. Fried and grilled fish are always available, though the choice is limited by the local catch. The sister seafood and ice cream shack, Mac's on the Pier (265 Commercial St., Wellfleet, 508-349-9611, BYOB) has picnic tables and is, as the name suggests, right on Wellfleet Town Pier.

Martha's Vineyard Chowder Company, 9 Oak Bluffs Ave., Oak Bluffs (Martha's Vineyard), MA 02557; (508) 696-3000; mvchowder.com; Seafood; $$–$$$. When the silky, light, and quahog-laden namesake chowder won a Martha's Vineyard chowder cookoff for owner J.B. Blau, he celebrated by opening a restaurant with the chowder as a centerpiece. Smart move. Adding clam chowder fritters to the mix (they're called ChoCos) was even smarter, as they are a bit like eating chewy pieces of the sea. Nothing gets too fancy here beyond said fritters, but proven delights like fried oysters, seared scallops, and prosciutto-wrapped cod with gnocchi satisfy most customers. Chicken and beef are available for the party members who shun fish, and there are some classically dense desserts, including flourless chocolate cake and a brownie sundae.

Menemsha Galley, Menemsha Harbor, Menemsha (Martha's Vineyard), MA 02552; (508) 645-9819; menemshagalley.com; Seafood; $. Nestled amid the fishermen's shacks at the end of the harbor, the Galley is the low-cost alternative for waterfront food. The take-out menu is fairly standard, but the Galley is famous for its lobster rolls, which consist of big servings of shredded lobster meat barely held together with a dab of mayonnaise and served on a grilled hot dog bun. Open Memorial Day weekend through Labor Day.

Naked Oyster Bistro & Raw Bar, 410 Main St., Hyannis, MA 02601; (508) 778-6500; nakedoyster.com; Seafood; $$–$$$. Chef-Owner Florence Lowell has her own oyster farm in Barnstable Harbor to keep her raw bar stocked. She pairs the oysters with farmed littlenecks from the same area. For a real treat, order her seafood tower of four each of oysters, littlenecks, and Gulf shrimp along with a chilled lobster tail and tuna sashimi. Oysters are available naked or with mignonette or with any number of other toppings. Lowell likes hers with flying-fish roe, because the pop of the caviar gives the bivalves a little drama without overwhelming the flavor. The cooked dishes reflect a sensitive palate that likes subtlety: lobster ravioli in sage brown butter with toasted hazelnuts or diver scallops wrapped in crisped prosciutto and served with steamed fingerling potatoes and grilled asparagus.

9 Ryder Seaside Dining, 9 Ryder St. Extension, Cabral's Wharf, Provincetown, MA 02657; (508) 487-9990; 9ryder.com; Italian/ Seafood; $$–$$$. Fred Hemley and Francis Iacono have been cooking in P'town for decades—they're the gastronomic heirs of Sal DelDeo and Ciro Cozzi and their tradition of serving fresh seafood and homemade Italian sauces seasoned with fresh herbs. Fred and Francis's latest venture has all the charm (and a few of the drawbacks) of a shack on the water. For charm—you can't get closer to the fish coming off the boats and the nautical setting tells you that the best bet is pasta with fish (probably calamari or flounder). The drawbacks are that the place is small and the kitchen even smaller, so orders have been known to get backed up on busy nights (which is most nights). One way to avoid that is to dine early, as 9 Ryder starts serving earlier than most places in town. Mixologist Sarah Jane Mulcrone fashions artisanal cocktails—you can order dinner at the bar and chat with her as she works.

Nor'East Beer Garden, 206 Commercial St., Provincetown, MA 02657; (508) 487-BEER (2337); noreastbeergarden.com; Casual American; $–$$. Provincetown excels in outdoor drinking and dining, but most such places are situated to watch the passing crowd and show off that you've scored a prime seat. This beer garden, though, manages to cultivate an outdoors but off-road sensibility so that once the gate closes behind you, the summer hubbub fades away. The main attraction is the great assortment of (mostly) New England craft brews (Clown Shoes and Pretty Things among them) along with nicer-than-average pub food. Burgers seem to arise from a garden of tomato slices and big leaves of lettuce, while the buttermilk fried chicken sandwich is a study in glorifying home cooking with a couple of slices of really good bread.

Offshore Ale Company, 30 Kennebec Ave., Oak Bluffs (Martha's Vineyard), MA 02557; (508) 693-2626; offshoreale.com; Brewery; $–$$. This breezy brewpub welcomes visitors all summer and is also just the sort of retreat that islanders need during the quiet winter months. The menu caters to both with lobster rolls, clam chowder, and fish-and-chips, as well as a dressed-up meat loaf with truffle oil and smoked bacon and a homey roasted half chicken. The brick oven pizzas are big and imaginative—roasted duck with pancetta and leeks, for example. Almost everything goes well with Offshore's Nutbrown Ale.

Òran Mór Bistro, 2 S. Beach St., Nantucket, MA 02554; (508) 228-8655; oranmorbistro.com; New American; $$$. Set in the upstairs of a Nantucket historic building (is there any other kind?), this restaurant has a cozy bar and three intimate dining rooms. Lest that sound a little too precious even for Nantucket, chef and co-owner Chris Freeman's menu has plenty of hearty celebration for everyone. No one else we know offers chicken-fried octopus with smoked fennel and chorizo, for example, or pierogi stuffed with duck confit and smoked mushrooms. He has the touch to pair sautéed sea scallops with pork belly and serve the combo with sweet potato lasagna. Wife Heather manages the house, keeping everything flowing smoothly for a memorable evening.

PB Boulangerie Bistro, 15 Lecount Hollow Rd., South Wellfleet, MA 02663; (508) 349-1600; pbboulangeriebistro.com; French; $$–$$$. Founded by French-born chefs Philippe Rispoli and Boris Villatte, whose first names provide the initials for the business, this French anomaly in a sea of fried seafood is a huge plus on the Cape. The bakery alone sells more than 1,500 croissants a day in season

(Memorial Day until sometime in the fall), along with hundreds of loaves of bread. Villatte has moved on to open his own separate bakery in Falmouth (see **Maison Villatte**, p. 272), but the bakery at PB continues to turn out a full range of gorgeous Viennese pastries in addition to the breakfast goodies. The evening bistro offers unabashedly French food, including the escargots of Rispoli's native Burgundy (with parsley and pureed spinach) as well as seared *foie gras* (with an apple tarte tatin). It is possible, however, to simply order a perfect cheeseburger with a spicy mayonnaise and homemade french fries as overseen by a real French chef.

The Pearl, 12 Federal St., Nantucket, MA 02554; (508) 228-9701; thepearlnantucket.com; Asian/Seafood; $$$–$$$$. There was a time not long ago when the very words "Asian fusion" signaled a restaurant hopelessly mired in the past, but the very un-Asian chefs of the Pearl manage to pull off contemporary Asian fusion with panache. The wok-fried salt-and-pepper lobster with lo mein noodles is a strikingly novel way to serve New England's signature crustacean, and the kimchi pan-cake and Asian pear salad that come with pan-seared sea scallops offer great textural contrast and just enough sweetness to bring out the salty tang of the fish. It's easy to imagine the chefs sailing up and down the coast of Asia from the Mekong Delta north to Sapporo, Japan, gathering recipes the whole way. Of course, this being Nantucket and The Pearl being geared to the hedge-fund crowd with its white-on-white Tokyo-by-way-of-Berlin-by-way-of-New-York decor, it's also possible to get a 2.5-pound grilled rib eye for two.

Red Pheasant Inn, 905 Main St. (Route 6A), Dennis, MA 02638; (508) 385-2133; redpheasantinn.com; New American; $$$. Located in an antique barn not far from the Cape Playhouse, Red Pheasant is a good bet for pre-curtain dining. Just be sure to allow time for the somewhat leisurely service. Chef-Owner Bill Atwood Jr. is the second generation to run this mid-Cape favorite since Swiss-trained Bill Sr. opened it in 1977. Atwood is perhaps a little less dependent on the daily catch, since his menu is less fish heavy than at some Cape restaurants. Probably the most popular fish dish is Faroe Island farmed salmon (which just happens to pair nicely with a grilled corncake). True to the name of the inn, Atwood offers a game dish of the night—usually elk or bison. For diners interested in comfort food, he provides a short list of homey plates that include grilled chicken and "Denise's Mom's Meatloaf."

Ruggie's Breakfast & Lunch, 707 Main St., Harwich, MA 02645; (508) 432-0625; ruggiescapecod.com; Casual American; $. Cape Cod is filled with friendly breakfast and lunch places, but when it comes to the Mid-Cape, we've become especially enamored of Ruggie's. We like the cheerful service, great breakfast grill food, and a sandwich menu with tremendous depth on the bench. Its  long counter, big windows, and often crowded tables make Ruggie's look like an umpteenth generation institution, but it's only been open since 2010. We're waiting to see someone order "The Duke." Consume the monster meal of two waffles, six eggs, a quarter-pound each of cheddar and American cheese, hash browns, sausage gravy, two buttermilk pancakes, six bacon strips, three sausage patties, and two pieces of boneless "country style" fried chicken in 30 minutes with just one eight-ounce glass of juice, and it's on the house. (And your picture goes on the wall.)

Scargo Cafe, 799 Main St. (Route 6A), Dennis, MA 02638; (508) 385-8200; scargocafe.com; New American; $$. "Cafe" is the operative word at Scargo—it's more casual than a restaurant and less focused on strong drink than a tavern or a gastropub. Most of the food is true

American bistro cooking—roast Statler chicken breast (with the first joint of the wing attached), potato-crusted baked haddock served atop a sweet corn and bacon chowder, char-grilled hanger steak with caramelized onions and crumbled blue cheese, and the now-ubiquitous lobster mac and cheese. Sometimes the kitchen stretches for a little more pizzazz—pan-seared halibut with mango beurre blanc—but most preparations let the ingredients rather than the chef be the star. Many of the same dishes are available at lunch, but most locals stick to the excellent sandwich menu.

Swan River Seafoods, 5 Lower County Rd., Dennisport, MA 02639; (508) 394-4466; swanriverseafoods.com; Seafood; $$. We've always thought that a restaurant attached to a fish market is probably the best place to get the freshest dinner. That's certainly true at Swan River. "This is where the fishermen unload their catch," explains one of the cheerful young men behind the counter as he trims a large bluefish into fillets. The market offers a complete seafood line from its own day boats. It will also steam lobsters (caught locally, of course) at no extra charge. The location on the grassy marshes at the mouth of Swan River is undeniably picturesque, and you can eat lunch and dinner here gazing out the big back windows to the marsh and river. The menu features the full range of broiled, fried, and sautéed seafood, which comes straight from the boats to the kitchen daily. Open May through Oct.

Ten Tables, 133 Bradford St., Provincetown, MA 02657; (508) 487-0106; tentables.net; New American; $$–$$$. The name refers to a previous restaurant by the same chef in a tiny location. Fear not—there's usually plenty of seating at this American bistro spot that offers unusually good value in often pricey P'town. All the pastas are made in-house, and the beef for the burgers is a custom grind. Ten Tables emphasizes shellfish for its seafood, in part because there are so many reliable suppliers of great clams, mussels, and oysters on the Outer Cape. Wines are very reasonably priced (with a rosé and a *vinho verde* on tap by the carafe), and beers lean toward domestic craft beers and Belgian imports.

Tiny's, 336 Commercial St., Provincetown, MA 02657; (508) 413-9582; tinyslocalfood.com; New American; $$–$$$. Chef Kristyn "Tiny" Samok is one of the hardest-working chefs we know. She starts with breakfast at the near-crack of dawn (8 a.m. is *really* early in Provincetown) and keeps cranking right through dinner service. The second-story space is as tiny as Samok, consisting mainly of an out-

side deck. The lack of cover from occasional precipitation, of course, makes for an interesting dining schedule. She makes an innovative corn-beet hash served at breakfast with eggs any style, and her lunchtime lobster dog is a stroke of genius. If you've ever tried to eat a juicy lobster roll only to have the lobster salad plop out onto the picnic table, or worse, dribble up your arm, you'll appreciate her lobster sausage on a bun with dill slaw. The dinner menu reflects the constant shift of harvests and catches. Fortunately, cod is available most of the season (mid-May into late Oct), so most diners get a shot at her sake-poached cod with ginger beurre blanc.

Toppers, Wauwinet Inn, 120 Wauwinet Rd., Nantucket, MA 02584; (508) 228-8768; wauwinet.com; New American; $$$–$$$$. Back in the mid-1800s, the Wauwinet Inn's predecessor, Wauwinet House, was a shorefront restaurant where patrons arrived by boat. The gastronomy at Toppers is a far cry from the simple shore dinner, but guests who aren't staying at the inn can still arrive on *The Wauwinet Lady,* an open launch that cruises across Nantucket Harbor between the village wharves and the inn from late June to early September. There's even cocktail service on board. Toppers offers elegant New American dining and pays due attention to fish and shellfish with such dishes as butter-poached lobster or roasted local black bass. Carnivores might prefer the short rib with bone marrow custard. There are two sophisticated dining rooms, but lunch guests can opt for a lobster and crab cake or dry aged sirloin *steak-frites* on the west-facing terrace, which is a great spot for sunset drinks. It's also a popular location for Sunday brunch. Open early May through late Oct.

Ventuno, 21 Federal St., Nantucket, MA 02554; (508) 228-4242; ventunorestaurant.com; Italian; $$$. Husband and wife chefs Gabriel Frasca and Amanda Lydon bring a little contemporary Italian flair to Nantucket, transforming Cape Cod clams into *spaghetti alla vongole* with the addition of lots and lots of garlic and some white wine. Wild halibut meets locally grown spring green veggies to become *merluzzo alla vignarola*. It makes for light, ingredient-driven dining. The pairing of chilled local oysters with a Meyer lemon Italian ice is truly inspired.

Specialty Stores, Markets & Producers

All Cape Cook's Supply, 237 Main St., Hyannis, MA 02601; (508) 790-8908; allcapecookssupply.com; Housewares. The shop is located about a block from the Nantucket ferry landing, and Nantucketers often swarm in like locusts with platinum cards when the ship docks. The emphasis here is utility: You can choose among a top-of-the-line professional mandoline, a couple of good, metal, mid-priced mandolines for half the cost, or a cheap but perfectly functional "occasional" plastic mandoline. The shop carries odd sizes of cake pans, baking sheets, tart pans, and pizza pans as well as clam knives, oyster knives, steaming kettles, lobster picks, and a whole wall of kitchen hand tools you didn't know existed but can't live without.

Angel Foods, 467 Commercial Street, Provincetown, MA 02657; (508) 487-6666; angelfoods.com; Grocery/Bakery Cafe. Directly across the street from the Provincetown Art Association and Museum, Angel Foods has just enough groceries to keep summer folks with kitchens from starving plus a deli counter with a good choice of sandwiches and bakery cases with all the molasses cookies, muffins, and scones you could desire.

Atlantic Spice Company, 2 Shore Rd. (junction of Route 6 at Route 6A), North Truro, MA 02652; (508) 487-6100; atlanticspice .com; Specialty Shop. This herb and spice company carries an overwhelming assortment of products for cookery and craft, including culinary herbs and spices, spice blends, baking items, shelled nuts and seeds, bulk tea, essential oils, extracts and flavorings, and bins and bins of ingredients for potpourri. Medicinal herbs are mostly those also used in cooking or as herbal tea.

Blue Willow Fine Foods & Bakery, 1426 Rte. 6 (Post Office Square), South Wellfleet, MA 02667; (508) 349-0900; thebluewillow .webs.com; Bakery Cafe. This tiny shop is right off the Cape Cod Rail Trail, making it a convenient place for cyclists to take a break and fuel up on muffins, scones, and breakfast burritos. Order some take-out sandwiches along with delicious cookies, bars, cakes, and pies to take with you on your ride.

Cabot's Candies of Cape Cod, 276 Commercial St., Provincetown, MA 02657; (508) 487-3550; cabotscandy.com; Specialty Shop. Owned and operated by third-generation candymakers, this old-fashioned shop makes all its saltwater taffy on the premises. Of the 30 different flavors, molasses peanut butter is the most popular. If you visit during production time, you can see the taffy being wrapped on a sturdy 1920s machine. Cabot's also makes fudge and peanut brittle and sells a wide variety of chocolates and hard candies. In a town where contemporary flash and sizzle are the order of the day, Cabot's offers a somehow reassuring window to a more innocent era on old Cape Cod.

Candy Co., 975 Rte. 28, South Yarmouth, MA 02664; (508) 398-0000; Specialty Shop. Making a choice here is a little like, well, being a kid in a candy store. The store makes its own barks and nut clusters, but it also sells all the retro small candies of everyone's youth, whether you're 7 or 70 years old. When's the last time you saw Licorice Allsorts, Mary Janes, or Walnettos? Real German Gummis come in a bewildering variety of creepy shapes (bears, worms, frogs). And if you get the itch to make your own chocolates, Candy Co. also carries melting chocolate and molds for Christmas and Easter, as well as less seasonal themes such as animals and babies.

Cape Abilities Farm to Table, 193 Main St., Chatham, MA 02633; (508) 778-5040; capeabilities.org; Grocery. Seasonal produce from the Cape Abilities Farm takes up most of the display space here, but you can also buy cold drinks and snacks as well as some works by local artists. Cape Abilities is a program that empowers Cape residents with special needs to lead meaningful and active lives. (See p. 278 for farm store.)

Cape Cod Winery, 681 Sandwich Rd., East Falmouth, MA 02536; (508) 457-5592; capecodwinery.com; Wine, Beer & Spirits. Founded in 1994, this ambitious winery is already producing an extensive list of soft, early-drinking wines from its own plantings of French-American hybrid varietals Seyval and Vidal Blanc. The winery also makes wines from its mature plantings of European *vinifera* grapes, including Cabernet Sauvignon, Cabernet Franc, Merlot, Chardonnay, and Pinot Grigio.

CRUNCH!

With the red-and-white lighthouse on the bag, **Cape Cod Potato Chips** are perfect summer picnic fare—and the company itself has become a popular stop for vacationers. About 250,000 people a year take the self-guided tour of the company's state-of-the-art facility to see how potatoes are transformed into kettle-cooked potato chips. At the gift shop at the end, you might get free samples—including experimental products—and can peruse the whole product line. The company opened in 1980 and is keenly attuned to changing tastes in snack foods. Look for reduced-fat chips, whole-grain chips, waffle cut chips (like biting into two chips at once), and chef's recipe chips with gourmet flavor pairings such as feta and rosemary or roasted garlic and red pepper. Open weekdays.

Cape Cod Potato Chip Company, 100 Breed's Hill Rd., Hyannis, MA 02601; (508) 775-3358 or (888) 881-2447; capecod chips.com.

Several grapes are blended with cranberries and peaches to make both dessert and table wines. Open late Apr through Christmas.

Catch of the Day Seafood Market & Grill, 975 Rte. 6, Wellfleet, MA 02663; (508) 349-9090; wellfleetcatch.com; Fishmonger. Located across the highway from the entrance to Marconi Beach on the Cape Cod National Seashore, Catch of the Day features littleneck clams and oysters from shellfish beds at Mayo Beach on Cape Cod Bay. Not only does the market have a breathtaking selection of perfect fish beautifully displayed, the staff will also cut and cook everything to order. Despite the casual feel—wooden picnic tables outside, wooden stools inside—this is definitely not your usual fish shack. Order sesame-seared tuna with a side of crème fraîche, a steamed shellfish sampler, or fish tacos with roasted corn salsa. Of course, you don't have to have anything cooked: The owners will happily prepare sushi from the fish on hand. Open mid-Apr through mid-Oct.

Centerville Pie Company, 1671 Falmouth Rd., Centerville, MA 02632; (774) 470-1406; centervillepies.com; Bakery/Bakery Cafe. A great pie is a thing of lip-smacking beauty, and Centerville manages the nearly impossible feat of making equally great savory, fruit, custard, and cream pies. Part of the secret is the ultra-flaky crust. You can order them cooked or uncooked (in case you want to pretend you did all the work yourself). The chicken pie is a signature item—in fact, demand from family and friends led Laurie Bowen to team up with Kristin Broadley to found the company in 2009. They were nearly immediately discovered by Oprah Winfrey, and the rest, as they say, is history. Sweet specialties include the quivery coconut custard pie, a grandly traditional apple pie, and a classic lemon meringue pie (with gently toasted meringue). During the height of summer, Centerville also offers a lobster pie. An attached cafe serves egg plates in the morning and burgers, tuna melts, and other sandwiches at lunch—and, of course, pie slices.

Chatham Candy Manor, 484 Main St., Chatham, MA 02633; (508) 945-0825; candymanor.com; Chocolatier. This family-run business was founded more than a half-century ago. The "specialty of the Manor" is the Turtle, a homemade caramel thick with pecans, walnuts, cashews, or almonds and drenched in milk or dark chocolate. The shop also produces truffles, chocolate-dipped fruits, caramels, and fudge. But on Friday evenings in July and August, most people come in to pick up a small bag of chocolate creams to eat during the Chatham Band

Concerts, which are held in the park next door (beginning at 8 p.m.). Among the molded chocolates, we are most fond of the "sea themed" lobsters, starfish, scallops, quahogs, and sand dollars.

Chatham Fish & Lobster, 1291 Main St., Chatham, MA 02633; (508) 945-1178; chathamfishandlobster.com; Fishmonger. Chatham has one of the most dynamic small-boat fishing fleets on Cape Cod, and this fishmonger seems to always get the pick of the catch, which means a real treat when the tuna harpooners are working in late summer and early fall. Lobsters range from dainty 1-pounders up to more than 6 pounds—enough to feed a family. You can buy fresh and prepared seafood, such as fish cakes, crab cakes, marinated mussels, and smoked bluefish, as well as bay and sea scallops, littlenecks, quahogs, and whatever finfish have come off the boat that day. The adjacent Marine Cuisine Restaurant offers an even broader choice of prepared food for eating at the tables or taking home. Dishes range from fish tacos to lobster BLTs to a seafood lasagna with layers of scallops and shrimp. Chatham Fish & Lobster also has a second fish market at the **Ring Brothers Marketplace,** 485 Route 134, South Dennis, MA 02660; (508) 394-5004. For a recipe for **Cape Cod Crab Cakes,** see p. 297.

Chatham Jam & Jelly Shop, 10 Vineyard Ave., Chatham, MA 02669; (508) 945-3052; chathamjamandjellyshop.com; Specialty Shop. Wild beach plum jam is a Cape Cod classic and this shop in Carol Cummings' home is a great place to try it. Carol has been carrying on the Cape tradition of making and selling preserves since 1983, doing all the fruit preparation, cooking, and canning in her kitchen. While beach plums may have first captured her interest, she preserves numerous local fruits and berries including cranberries, blueberries, wild blackberries, wild grapes, apples, pears, plums, quince, and crabapples. Products include jams, jellies, marmalades, butters, conserves, and chutneys—many are open so that you can taste before you buy.

Cisco Brewers, 5 Bartlett Farm Rd., Nantucket, MA 02554; (508) 325-5929; ciscobrewers.com; **Wine, Beer & Spirits.** If you assumed that Cisco Brewers makes beer, you would be correct. Their Whale's Tale Pale Ale (their English-style flagship) and Sankaty Light Lager (only 3.8% ABV) are available wherever people drink on Nantucket. Another half-dozen or so brews are also available seasonally. But this multipurpose facility also makes wine (using grapes from California, Washington, and New York) and, as Triple Eight Distillery, fashions vodka, several flavored vodkas, rum, gin, and whiskey. You can try them all in the bar. Check the website for tours.

Connie's Bakery, 205 Commercial St., Provincetown, MA 02657; (508) 487-2167; conniesbakery.com; **Bakery.** Connie O'Meara's bakery has been peripatetic, popping up all over Provincetown at different addresses over the years. Finally establishing a foothold downtown on Commercial Street has been a real boon for business—not that folks didn't seek her out for her muffins, scones, cinnamon rolls, *crostatas* and cookies anyway. She also whips up beautiful cakes to order. A number of homey breads are available daily, and Connie's slices some for luncheon take-out sandwiches.

Cottage Street Bakery, 5 Cottage St., Orleans, MA 02653; (508) 255-2821; cottagestreetbakery.com; **Bakery.** You might be tempted to try the almond croissants, cranberry almond poppyseed muffins, or cinnamon buns. But go for the French Breakfast Puff, the more mellifluous name for the original Dirt Bomb, a heavenly if messy muffin, redolent of nutmeg and cinnamon, that sheds sugar even as you try to break it into manageable pieces. Founder JoAnna Keeley has retired, but her successors continue to cook up a storm. Other sweets include lemon or fig bars, chocolate chip cookies, breads, and fresh fruit tarts. At lunchtime the bakery serves savory soups (Hungarian mushroom, potato leek, pumpkin bisque, and corn chowder) and sandwiches (turkey with cranberry relish, chicken salad, and hummus with vegetables).

Cuttyhunk Shellfish Farms, Fish Dock, Cuttyhunk Island, Gosnold, MA 02713; (508) 990-1317; cuttyhunkshellfish.com; Fishmonger. Most of the oysters and clams that this aquaculture operation raises are sold to restaurants and wholesalers. But from Memorial Day to Columbus Day, you can enjoy lunchtime chowder, stuffed quahogs, and raw bar offerings at the dock. Even more fun, in the late afternoon and early evening, Cuttyhunk has a raw bar on the dock and a floating raw bar that serves the boats in the harbor. You can purchase oysters and clams on the half shell, shrimp cocktail, stuffed quahogs, crab spread, and clam chowder.

Dunbar Tea Shop, 1 Water St. (Route 130), Sandwich, MA 02563; (508) 833-2485; dunbarteashop.com; Specialty Shop. Located in a circa-1740 carriage house across Water Street from the historic Dexter Grist Mill, this tea shop, opened in 1991, has become known as one of America's finest. The front of the shop carries an extensive line of packaged and loose teas, teapots, strainers, and tea services. The tearoom is up a few steps, in a wood-paneled former billiard and gentleman's smoking room. Only the fireplace smokes there now, and only in the winter. Additional summer seating is available on the patio and in the shady tea garden for tea, pies, cakes, shortbreads, scones, and tiny sandwiches. For a recipe for **Honey Pumpkin Tea Bread,** see p. 300.

Four Seas Cape Cod, 360 S. Main St., Centerville Corners, MA 02632; (508) 775-1394; fourseasicecream.com; Ice Cream/Yogurt. Cape Cod's oldest ice cream shop has been operating since 1934 in a small white cottage that was originally a blacksmith shop. Small stools line the counter and booths are clustered on the left side against a wall.

Located near Craigville Beach, it's a charming little roadside stop—the forerunner of the Cape's many ice cream shops, setting the standard for high quality and a wide variety of flavors. Among the more unusual are cantaloupe, penuche (made with brown sugar fudge), coconut, and blueberry frozen yogurt.

Hallet's, 139 Main St. (Route 6A), Yarmouth Port, MA 02675; (508) 362-3362; hallets.com; Grocery. Established in 1889, Hallet's was for many years a pharmacy with a soda fountain. The apothecary is gone, but the soda fountain survives, complete with a marble counter and vintage stools. Belly up to the bar and order ice cream sodas, malteds, frappes, sundaes, and fountain drinks, along with sandwiches (tuna, egg or chicken salad, for example) that would be right at home in a school lunch box. You can also take a little taste of Hallet's along when you leave: They bottle their own sodas, including black cherry, sarsaparilla, raspberry-lime rickey, birch beer, root beer, and cream. Open Apr through Oct; call for winter hours.

Hatch's Fish Market, 310 Main St., Wellfleet, MA 02667; (508) 349-2810; hatchsfishmarket.com; Fishmonger. Over the years, Hatch's has evolved from a simple stand behind town hall into a lean-to and finally into an enclosed building. Whatever the local fishermen are catching or digging, Hatch's is selling. Hatch's also smokes fish and mussels and makes pâté. The lobster pool is always full of the Cape's favorite crustacean, and Hatch's will steam them on the spot. The biggest selection, however, is shellfish, including local bluepoint oysters, prized as some of the finest in the Northeast. During July and August, a produce stand almost obscures the fish market as it overflows with local tomatoes, peppers, summer squash, and corn. Open mid-May through mid-Sept.

Larsen's Fish Market, 56 Basin Rd., Chilmark (Martha's Vineyard), MA 02535; (508) 645-2680; larsensfishmarket.com;

Fishmonger. Although a few fishing boats venture from other ports, Menemsha remains the only true fishing village on Martha's Vineyard, and Larsen's is the place to go for the fresh catch. In addition to the full array of finfish and shellfish, Larsen's also makes crab cakes (to take home or have heated on the spot), hors d'oeuvres, and specialty dips and will cook lobster, steamer clams, and mussels to order. The market also has a raw bar featuring oysters, littlenecks, and cherrystone clams. Sunset, by the way, is a very popular time to visit. Open May through Oct. If you're on Martha's Vineyard but you can't get out to Menemsha, you can purchase the same fish (cooked or not) at **Edgartown Seafood Market** (138 Cooke St., Edgartown, MA 02539; 508-627-3791; edgartown seafood.com) from May until Jan.

Maison Villatte, 267 Main St., Falmouth, MA 02540; (774) 255-1855; Bakery Cafe. Authenticity is the watchword at this truly French bakery from Boris Villatte, who was co-owner of **PB Boulangerie** (see p. 258). Now the Upper Cape can also get flaky croissants, crusty baguettes, and delicate *macarons*. There are about 20 seats where folks plop down to tuck into pastries and hot drinks, or sandwiches and quiches later in the day. Weeks after opening in fall 2012, the bakery was selling 1,000 croissants and several hundred loaves of bread per day. In addition to classic baguettes and sourdough country white loaves, Villatte bakes a broad line of grainy, rustic breads using rye, spelt, and buckwheat—made with a sourdough starter incorporating whole grains and stoneground organic whole wheat.

Marion's Pie Shop, 2022 Main St. (Route 28), Chatham, MA 02633; (508) 432-9439; marionspieshopofchatham.com; Bakery. For a half-century, this little roadside shop has been providing fabulous baked goods to both loyal locals and amazed vacationers whose motel rooms have microwaves for reheating. Breakfast muffins and coffee cakes are delicious, as are the fruit and pumpkin pies, but the real stars are the savory pies in 6- and 9-inch sizes: chicken (with or without carrots and peas); beefsteak with baby carrots and pearl onions; clams with sautéed onions and clam broth thickened with fresh bread crumbs; hamburger (ground beef and beef gravy); and seafood (lobster, shrimp, scallops, and cod in a sherry-butter-cream sauce). Open Feb through Dec.

Murdick's Fudge, 21 N. Water St., Edgartown (Martha's Vineyard), MA 02539; (508) 627-8047; 5 Circuit Ave., Oak Bluffs, MA 02557; (508) 693-2335; Union St., Vineyard Haven, MA 02568; (508) 693-7344; murdicks.com; Chocolatier. A box of Murdick's fudge is a tradition for most people who summer on (or even visit) Martha's Vineyard. The company is more than a century old and still uses the same basic recipes of butter, sugar, and all-natural ingredients. Buy by the piece or the box. (A box gets you a handy knife for splitting it up.) You can work off some of the calories at Murdick's Run the Chop Challenge in early July. Proceeds from the 5-mile road race benefit local youth. Open Apr through Dec.

Nantucket Roasters, 15 Teasdale Circle, Nantucket, MA 02584; (508) 228-6862 or (800) 432-1673; nantucketcoffee.com; Coffee. Wes Van Cott has been roasting coffee beans on Nantucket since the spring of 1993 under the slogan, "Don't get burnt, get roasted!" (a not-so-sly dig at a certain West Coast roaster often accused of disguising mediocre beans with dark roasts). Look for such rarities as Tanzania peaberry. Roasted beans (whole or in three different grinds) are available by phone or mail order or through the website—or you can taste the goods at the company's coffee shop, **The Bean,** at 29 Centre St. in Nantucket (508-228-6215).

Nauset Fish & Lobster Pool, 38 Rte. 6A, Orleans, MA 02653; (508) 255-1019; **and Sir Cricket Fish & Chips;** (508) 255-4453; **Fishmonger.** The market justifiably calls itself the "Home of the King-Size Lobster." Indeed, many of the crustaceans swimming in the icy water of its tanks are around 8 pounds. (They once sold a 33-pounder.) In addition to big lobsters, Nauset Fish has fresh finfish, clams, mussels, oysters, frozen dinners and chowders, cooked prepared lobster and crab meat, and shucked clams. Sir Cricket is the attached take-out fish shack, with just a few seats for indoor dining. English-style fish-and-chips, in honor of owner Ron Harrison's English grandfather, is the flagship of the menu, but you can also order fried clams, lobster rolls, fish sandwiches, and crab cakes. Sir Cricket is cash only.

Net Result, 79 Beach Rd., Vineyard Haven (Martha's Vineyard), MA 02568; (508) 693-6071 or (800) 394-6071; mvseafood.com; **Fishmonger.** This operation is the largest distributor of seafood on Martha's Vineyard. Operated by the Larsen family, Net Result expanded recently with an on-premises take-out counter and picnic tables where you can enjoy steamed lobster, fried clams, crab cake sand-

wiches, and other briny delights. There is even a sushi counter. Net Result also packs up cooked fish for takeout and will ship fresh fish and shellfish overnight to anywhere in the continental United States.

Pain D'Avignon, 15 Hinckley Rd., Hyannis, MA 02601; (508) 771-9771; french-bread.com; **Bakery Cafe.** Back in 1992, four friends—three ex-Yugoslavs and a French Canadian—found themselves thrown together on Cape Cod by unpredictable world politics. So they opened an Old World bakery that makes some of the finest breads—try the signature pecan and raisin loaf—in eastern Massachusetts. Dense without being heavy, Pain D'Avignon breads can be the centerpiece of a meal rather than an afterthought. They're widely available at gourmet shops, health food stores, convenience stores, and some supermarkets. The bakery-cafe carries the full line, along with sandwiches, salads, pizza, coffee, pastries, Italian oils and vinegars, French mustards and pâtés, high-quality cheeses, and organic juices. In the evening, the cafe shows its bistro aspirations with plates like beef bourguignon or risotto with Chatham cod and lobster—and the wonderful breads, of course.

Provincetown Portuguese Bakery, 299 Commercial St., Provincetown, MA 02657; (508) 487-1803; Bakery. Even amid the crowds on Commercial Street, it's hard to miss this shop, where one of the bakers often stands in the window frying sweet dough in hot oil to make Portuguese *malassadas*. Step inside and you're transported to Portugal with the hefty white bread and rolls, the bakery's justly famous cakelike sweet bread called *massa cevada,* and *trutas,* a southern Portuguese pastry with a brandied filling of sweet potatoes, lemon, and sugar in a shell-shaped crust. Savory treats are also available, including croissants with linguiça and cheese and the Portuguese extravaganza sandwich of linguiça and cheese in a Portuguese roll, topped with a fried egg. One of Cape Cod's oldest bakeries, Provincetown Portuguese is open from Easter to late Oct.

Something Natural, 50 Cliff Rd., Nantucket, MA 02554; (508) 228-0504; somethingnatural.com; Bakery. Some of Nantucket's best restaurants buy their breads from Something Natural, but you can get the whole wheat, pumpernickel, oatmeal, rye, six-grain, and Portuguese loaves straight from the source. The bakery also sells a wide variety of cookies and pastries and makes sandwiches and salads to eat on-premises or for takeout. Open May to mid-Oct.

Stage Stop Candy, 411 Main St. (Route 28), Dennisport, MA 02639; (508) 394-1791; stagestopcandy.com; Chocolatier. When  you enter this candy shop in the historic Jonathan P. Edward House, Raymond Hebert or his wife, Donna, might greet you at the door with a tray of chocolates to sample. Grandson of the founder of the Hebert candy empire in central Massachusetts (see p. 75), Raymond took his grandfather's recipe books when he moved to Cape Cod in the early 1980s to open his own candy shop. Following his grandfather's entrepreneurial example, he decided to add "a Cape Cod thing" and set out to perfect a cranberry cordial with whole berries. He picked berries in a wild bog, started experimenting, and "got lucky," as he puts it. "We got it right on the third try." The cordials, which resemble chocolate-covered cherries but are not as sweet, remain one of Stage Stop's leading sellers, along with Hebert's exquisitely smooth truffles. Cranberries also take the place of nuts in the Heberts' cranberry caramel patties, with white, dark or milk chocolate.

Straight Wharf Fish Store, Straight Wharf, Harbor Square, Nantucket, MA 02584; (508) 228-1095; Fishmonger. Nantucket's fishing fleet is small, but the offshore location and the nearby shoals guarantee an incredible range of fish. This shop carries all varieties of finfish, as well as clams, oysters, lobsters, and crab, and its own bluefish pâté and various marinades. You can also order sandwiches, swordfish and tuna steak, lobster rolls, crab cakes, seafood gumbo, and raw-bar items (clams, scallops, and oysters) to go from late morning to early evening from mid-May through mid-Oct.

Sweet Inspirations Chocolate Shop, 26 Centre St., Nantucket, MA 02554; (508) 228-5814; nantucketchocolatier.com; Chocolatier. During the winter, Sweet Inspirations ships out boxes of its signature Cranberry Creations (chocolate covered cranberries) and a lot of Sailor's Valentine gift tins of exquisitely hand-crafted truffles, caramels, chocolate whales, and sea-salt dusted almonds enrobed in rich chocolate. During the summer, you'll have to come and pick them up yourself, since Sweet Inspirations doesn't ship in warm weather.

Truro Vineyards of Cape Cod, 11 Shore Rd. (Route 6A), North Truro, MA 02652; (508) 487-6200; trurovineyardsofcapecod .com; Wine, Beer & Spirits. This small winemaking operation is a pioneer (since 1991) in the art of growing European wine grapes in the sandy soils of the outer peninsula. Boasting Cape Cod's first successful *vinifera* plantings, the winery grows its own Cabernet Franc, Chardonnay, and Merlot grapes and purchases others from Massachusetts, New York, and California. The grounds are a real showcase, and visitors are encouraged to stroll through the vineyards and peek in on activities in the state-of-the-art winery. The Cabernet Franc, with an austere, light-claret expression of the fruit, is the food-friendly flagship wine. Open late May through mid-Oct.

Farm Stands & PYOs

Bartlett's Ocean View Farm, 33 Bartlett Farm Rd., Nantucket, MA 02554; (508) 228-9403; bartlettsfarm.com. The Bartlett family has been farming what they claim is the largest and oldest family-owned farm on the island since the early 1800s, when William Bartlett sailed over from Marblehead and started plowing the land. Dorothy and John Bartlett continue the tradition, growing flowers, vegetables, tomatoes, lettuces, and greenhouse plants. The Farm Market carries their own produce as well as fruit and dairy products, some from other local producers. You can pick up milk, cheese, and eggs, as well as farm-fresh salads, breakfast snacks, pies and other baked goods, and prepared entrees. Check the website for a schedule of farm dinners. The market closes for a couple of weeks in Jan.

Cape Abilities Farm, 458 Main St. (Route 6A), Dennis, MA 02638; (508) 778-5040; capeabilities.org. This highly productive farm employs about 80 persons with disabilities to grow a wide variety of fruits and vegetables. The farm's greenhouses keep producing fresh tomatoes and lettuce well into October, when every other farm is reduced to selling just pumpkins and squash. (Cape Abilities has those too.) The stand is open July to Christmas Eve.

Coonamessett Farm, 277 Hatchville Rd., East Falmouth, MA 02536; (508) 563-2560; coonamessettfarm.com. Ronald and Roxanna Smolowitz run this 20-acre farm and "research enterprise," as Ron calls

it. Coonamessett grows a panoply of vegetables and fruits in the fields (tomatoes, strawberries, raspberries, garden greens, and so on). The farm stand is open to all, but the Smolowitzes ask people to become members (for the day or the season) in order to pick fruits, veg-etables, herbs, and flowers and to enjoy visiting with the farm animals. Popular Wednesday night Jamaican buffets and Friday night farm buf-fets start in July and are open to all, as is the lunchtime cafe (open July and Aug). In addition to produce, the shop also sells the farm's own jams and salad dressing as well as alpaca yarn and knit items. Open May through late Dec.

Eileen Blake's Pies, 515 State Rd., West Tisbury (Martha's Vineyard), MA 02575; (508) 693-0528. Old-fashioned baker Eileen Blake began selling pies from her front yard on Martha's Vineyard in the early 1970s, making up to 135 pies a day from scratch during the frenetic week leading up to Thanksgiving. Her daughter Mary Ellis now continues the tradition. One of the Blake specialties is burgundy pie, which is filled with a mixture of blueberries and cranberries sweetened with brown sugar and spiked with a teaspoon of nutmeg. Mary also makes apple, strawberry rhubarb, pumpkin, pecan, blueberry peach, blackberry peach, and lemon chess pies, as well as a Toll House pie full of chocolate and walnuts. Look for the gazebo along State Road near Cronig's Market and the Coop Bank. Open Apr through Thanksgiving. During the off-season, Ellis sells half- and full-size pies at **Reliable Market** (36 Circuit Ave., Oak Bluffs; 508-693-1102). For the Blakes' recipe for **Burgundy Pie,** see p. 308.

Morning Glory Farm, 290 W. Tisbury Rd., Edgartown (Martha's Vineyard), MA 02539; (508) 627-9003; morninggloryfarm.com. Jim and Debbie Athearn farm 55 acres of fruits and veg-etables and operate Martha's Vineyard's largest and most comprehensive farm stand, selling their own vegetables and berries, baked goods, sweet corn, and huge heads of tender lettuce.  The stand also carries fruit from other Mas-sachusetts growers, as well as cheese, peanut butter, crackers, and herbal remedies. The soup and salad bar is a great option for a quick and healthy lunch. Open May through Dec.

Tony Andrews Farm, 394 Old Meetinghouse Rd., East Falmouth, MA 02536; (508) 548-4717; tonyandrewsfarmstand.com. There are plenty of choices at this pick-your-own organic farm with 23 acres under cultivation. The season begins with strawberries and lettuce in June and progresses through spinach, peas, peppers, and tomatoes in summer before winding down with squashes and pumpkins in the fall. The farm stand also has other vegetables and cut flowers, as well as fruit from area orchards, local cider, eggs, jams, honey, and breads. In the course of the season you might find wax beans, lima beans, broccoli, cauli-flower, lettuces, peppers, white zucchini, pumpkins, Silver Queen corn, tomatillos, swiss chard, parsley, eggplant, Japanese eggplant, cucumber,

LEARN TO COOK

Green Briar Nature Center and Jam Kitchen, 6 Discovery Hill Rd., East Sandwich, MA 02537; (508) 888-6870; thorntonburgess.org. Back in 1903, Ida Putnam began making jams and jellies and operated a tearoom here, turning over the operation to Martha Blake in the early 1950s. Now owned by the Thornton Burgess Society, the building is a throwback to old Cape Cod. The existing jam kitchen, with 20 propane burners on a long table, dates from 1917. Burgess, the prolific author of such children's books as *The Mother West Wind Stories,* lived in Sandwich until age 18 and often visited the jam kitchen in his youth. Recalling those days, he wrote to Ida Putnam in 1939, "It is a wonderful thing to sweeten the world which is in a jam and needs preserving." The jam kitchen runs two-hour Wednesday evening and Saturday morning jam-making workshops for adults or for families from late March through October. All supplies for making jams and preserves are supplied and participants take home four to six full jars. The gift shop also sells the jam kitchen products—chutneys, relishes, salsas, marmalades, jams, and jellies, including (of course) the classic jelly of Cape Cod, beach plum.

Highfield Hall, 56 Highfield Dr., Falmouth, MA 02541; (508) 495-1878; highfieldhall.org. This Italianate mansion is an arts and cultural center for Falmouth, and its programs include cooking classes on everything from making European-style breads or Mexican quesadillas, to creative uses for leftovers.

shell beans, several kinds of squash, cabbage, kale, strawberries, and rhubarb. There's always a surprise, as owner Geoffrey Andrews likes to experiment with new crops and varieties each year. Farm stand open mid-June through Oct.

Farmers' Markets

Falmouth Farmers' Market, Peg Noonan Park, Main Street, Falmouth. Thurs from noon to 6 p.m., late May through Dec.

Falmouth/Green Harvest Farmers' Market, Barnstable County Fairgrounds, 1220 Nathan Ellis Hwy. (Route 151), East Falmouth. Tues from noon to 4 p.m., June through mid-Nov.

Hyannis/Mid Cape Farmers' Market, 486 Main St., Hyannis. Wed from 2 to 6 p.m., June through Oct.

Nantucket Farmers' & Artisans' Market, Upper Cambridge and North Union Streets, Nantucket. Sat from 9 a.m. to 1 p.m., June through mid-Oct.

Nantucket Farmers' & Artisans' Market, The Muse parking lot, 44 Surfside Rd., Nantucket. Tues from 3:30 to 6:30 p.m., July and Aug.

Orleans Farmers' Market, Old Colony Way, Orleans Center. Sat from 8 a.m. to noon, mid-May to mid-Nov.

Provincetown Farmers' Market, Ryder Street at Town Hall, Provincetown. Sat from 11 a.m. to 4 p.m., mid-May to mid-Nov.

Sandwich Farmers' Market, Village Green across from fish hatchery, Sandwich. Tues from 9 a.m. to 1 p.m., June through Oct.

Sandwich Winter Farmers' Market, Scenic Roots, 349 Rte. 6A, Sandwich. Every other Sun from 11 a.m. to 2 p.m., early Nov through late Mar.

West Tisbury Farmers' Markets, Grange Hall, State Road, West Tisbury, Martha's Vineyard. Wed (mid-June through Aug) and Sat (June through early Oct) from 9 a.m. to noon.

West Tisbury Winter Farmers' Market, The Agricultural Society, 35 Panhandle Rd., West Tisbury, Martha's Vineyard. Every other Sat from 10 a.m. to 1 p.m., mid-Oct through Dec.

Recipes

We always find that re-creating recipes in our own kitchen is a good way to bring the taste of travel back home. So we are grateful to the chefs and growers who provided these recipes that highlight local flavors and reflect Bay State food traditions. We have adapted the recipes for home kitchens and standardized their presentation. Any errors are our inadvertent introductions rather than the fault of our sources.

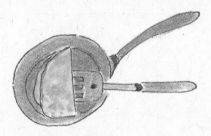

Berkshire Apple Pancake

The Red Lion Inn has been hosting travelers just about since tourism was invented. This breakfast favorite takes advantage of two of the Berkshires' greatest local treasures: its wonderful apples and its golden maple syrup.

Serves 6.

3 apples, peeled and cored
Lemon juice
3 eggs, beaten
3 cups all-purpose flour
1½ tablespoons baking powder
¾ teaspoon salt
5 tablespoons sugar

2 cups milk
¾ teaspoon vanilla extract
¾ teaspoon ground cinnamon
5 tablespoons unsalted butter
¼ cup firmly packed light brown sugar
Warm pure maple syrup, for serving

Preheat oven to 450°F.

Coarsely chop 2½ of the apples. Slice the remaining ½ apple into thin spirals for garnish. Brush the spirals with lemon juice to prevent them from darkening and set aside.

Mix together the eggs, flour, baking powder, salt, sugar, milk, vanilla, cinnamon, and chopped apples in a large mixing bowl. Stir until well combined, although the batter will remain lumpy.

Melt the butter in a 10-inch cast-iron skillet. Pour the batter into the skillet and arrange the reserved apple spirals on top.

Bake the pancake for 15 minutes. Reduce oven temperature to 350°F and bake for 40 minutes more, or until a toothpick inserted in the center comes out clean. Remove the skillet from the oven and let pancake stand for 5 minutes.

Sprinkle the brown sugar over the top of the pancake, cut it into wedges, and serve with maple syrup.

Adapted recipe courtesy of the Red Lion Inn in Stockbridge (p. 11)

Classic New England Oyster Stew

*Clam chowder may be the star of all the contests, but Massachusetts has an
equally venerable tradition of making oyster stew. This version is slightly lighter
(no heavy cream) to suit modern tastes.*

Serves 4–6.

½ pound chopped bacon
1 cup chopped shallots
2 teaspoons chopped garlic
1 pound shucked oysters
3 tablespoons butter
2 tablespoons flour
2 teaspoons sea salt

½ teaspoon black pepper
¼ teaspoon cayenne pepper
¼ cup chopped leeks
1 quart light cream
24 ounces milk
Additional salt and pepper to
taste

In a 4-quart saucepan, cook bacon over medium heat until brown
and cooked through. Remove bacon and set aside on paper towels
to drain, leaving the fat in the pan.

Sauté the shallots and garlic in the fat until tender. Next, add
the oysters and their liquor and cook for 2 minutes. Add the
butter and stir until it is melted.

Sprinkle in the flour and gently stir until well blended. Cook this
mixture for about 1 minute to make a light roux. Finally, stir in the
reserved bacon, sea salt, black pepper, cayenne pepper, leeks, cream,
and milk.

Bring stew to a boil, then reduce to a simmer and cook, stirring frequently,
until desired thickness, about 5 minutes. Season to taste with salt and pepper.

Adapted recipe courtesy of Turner's Seafood Grill & Market in Melrose (p. 105).

Guido's Gazpacho

This chilled summer vegetable soup is a great way to enjoy the Berkshires' produce in a bowl.

Serves 6–8.

1 zucchini, diced

1 yellow squash, diced

1 each red, yellow, green, and orange pepper, diced

1 large Vidalia onion, diced

1 small red onion, diced

2 stalks celery, diced

1 English cucumber, diced

½ cup chopped fresh cilantro

2 tablespoons chopped basil

Juice of 1 lime

Juice of 1 lemon

⅛ teaspoon ground cumin

1 quart tomato or vegetable juice

1 tablespoon Worcestershire sauce

1 tablespoon balsamic vinegar

1 teaspoon Spike seasoning, a low-salt blend of herbs available at most organic food stores

⅛ teaspoon ground white pepper

2 cloves garlic, minced

Combine all ingredients in a large bowl. Allow to marinate for 2 to 3 hours in the refrigerator. Serve with a dollop of plain yogurt or sour cream.

Adapted recipe courtesy of Guido's Quality Fruit & Produce
of Pittsfield and Great Barrington (p. 17).

Kale Soup

This beefy, beany version of the classic Portuguese soup caldo verde *mates kale, cabbage, and sausage for a hearty fall or winter meal.*

Serves 8.

1½ pounds linguiça or chouriço

½ pound shredded beef shank meat or chuck roast (optional)

2 teaspoons crushed red pepper

1 medium onion, sliced

2 teaspoons salt

2 bunches of kale, shredded, or 4 boxes of frozen kale

1 head of cabbage, shredded

1–2 (16-oz.) cans kidney beans

6 potatoes, peeled and diced

Place linguiça or chouriço (and shank meat or chuck roast, if using) in a large stew pot or dutch oven.

Add red pepper, onion, and salt. Add water to cover. Bring to a boil and simmer until meat is almost done (about 30 minutes).

Add kale, cabbage, and kidney beans to broth.

When kale is about half-cooked (about 10 minutes), add potatoes and cook an additional 30 minutes.

Adapted recipe courtesy of Bob Gaspar
of Gaspar's Sausage Company Factory Outlet in North Dartmouth (p. 236).

Verrill Farm Corn & Tomato Tart

This recipe is a perennial favorite. Jennifer Verrill Faddoul recommends using Sweet 100 cherry tomatoes, which are a small variety best left whole. Other cherry tomato varieties can be substituted, she says. We've found that larger tomatoes tend to make a watery tart. (If using standard tomatoes, peel, chop, and drain well before using.) For variations on the tart, add chopped bacon or chopped jalapeño peppers.

Serves 6.

Tart Crust

2½ cups flour
8 ounces (2 sticks) butter

1 teaspoon salt
¼ cup water

This recipe makes three single pie shells. Use a 9- to 10-inch ceramic pie plate or a tart pan.

Preheat oven to 375°F.

Pulse flour, butter, and salt in food processor until mixture resembles corn kernels.

Add water and pulse until mixture forms a ball.

Divide dough into three parts, roll out, and place in three pie pans. Freeze two for future use.

Cover edges of pastry with aluminum foil to prevent burning. Bake in 375°F oven for 10 to 15 minutes. Remove from oven when the crust is very lightly browned and the surface of the dough is set.

Remove foil, let crust cool, and add filling.

Tart Filling

½ cup chopped onion
1 clove garlic, chopped
3 tablespoons olive oil
5 ears corn, uncooked, kernels removed
Salt and pepper to taste
¼ cup shredded smoked cheddar

½ pint Sweet 100 cherry tomatoes
3 scallions (green and white parts), chopped
2 eggs
½ cup milk
½ cup cream

Preheat oven to 375°F.

Sauté onion and garlic in olive oil until translucent. Add corn kernels and cook 5 to 10 minutes. Add salt and pepper to taste and remove pan from heat.

Put half of corn mixture in cooked pie shell. Layer shredded cheese on top. Add remaining corn mixture. Place cherry tomatoes and scallions on top.

Whisk eggs, milk, and cream with a pinch of salt and pour over tart.

Bake for 30 minutes or until filling is set.

Adapted recipe courtesy of Verrill Farm in Concord (p. 217).

Rice, Lobster & Cucumber Salad

Chrissi Pappas, proprietor of Ipswich Shellfish, hails from Thessaloniki in Greece. This refreshing salad blends the flavors of her native cuisine with sweet North Shore lobster.

Serves 4:

1 cup white basmati rice
¾ cup chopped fresh dill
¾ cup thinly sliced scallions
½ cup lemon juice
¼ cup olive oil
Salt and pepper to taste
1½ pounds lobster meat, chopped, tail meat reserved

1 head romaine or Bibb lettuce
1 large English cucumber, peeled and chopped in ½-inch dice

Heat 1½ cups lightly salted water in a saucepan with a tight-fitting lid. When water begins to simmer, stir in rice. Continue stirring until water comes back to a simmer. Place lid on pan and reduce heat. Cook rice for 16 minutes, then remove from heat. Let stand 5 minutes before removing lid. Remove rice to a bowl to cool before proceeding.

In a large bowl, whisk together dill, scallions, lemon juice, olive oil, and salt and pepper.

Stir in cooked rice until well coated with dressing.

Reserving tails, add lobster meat to rice and gently toss to coat.

Line a serving dish with lettuce leaves and mound rice on top. Garnish with reserved lobster tails and chopped cucumber.

Recipe courtesy of Ipswich Shellfish Fish Market in Ipswich (p. 112).

Summer Vegetable Pasta with Arugula Pesto

This versatile pasta dish can be served warm as an entree or cold as a side salad. Chef Todd Heberlein finds that corn stock really accentuates the flavors of the summer harvest and suggests having it on hand to use in any dish that calls for chicken stock.

Serves 4–6.

1 pound Israeli couscous or pearl pasta
Corn stock (recipe below)
4 to 5 ears of corn, cut from cob, cobs reserved
2 diced zucchini

2 diced summer squash
½ pint grape tomatoes, halved
Olive oil
Salt and pepper to taste
Arugula pesto (recipe below)

Cook couscous in water or corn stock according to package directions and allow to cool.

Preheat oven to 425°F.

Add corn, zucchini, squash, and tomatoes to a large bowl. Lightly coat with olive oil, then add salt and pepper to taste. Place on a sheet pan or two in a flat layer. Roast in oven until lightly browned and tender, about 6 to 8 minutes. Allow to cool.

Toss together couscous, roasted vegetables, and arugula pesto. Adjust salt and pepper. Enjoy hot or cold.

Arugula Pesto

½ pound baby arugula
⅔ cup roasted pistachios
¾ cup Romano cheese, grated

1 tablespoon chopped garlic
1 cup olive oil
Salt and pepper to taste

Working in two batches, divide ingredients into two halves. Add first half to food processor and puree. Scoop into bowl and repeat with second half. Salt and pepper to taste as needed.

Corn Stock

Makes 1–2 gallons.

4 to 5 corn cobs, kernels removed
1 yellow onion, chopped
2 carrots, peeled and chopped
2 celery stalks, chopped
3 cloves garlic

Few sprigs each of fresh thyme and parsley
2 bay leaves
Pinch of salt and pepper
Water

Put all ingredients in a large stockpot and add enough water to cover by 2 inches. Bring to a boil and then reduce to a simmer for 2 hours. Strain.

Corn stock can be made using only cobs, without the other vegetables, but amount of water will need to be adjusted to make sure there is enough stock for cooking couscous or pasta.

Adapted recipe courtesy of Chef Todd Heberlein
of Volante Farms in Needham (p. 244).

Pasta with Tomato Sauce, Broccoli & Goat Cheese

This is an easy variant of a classic summer pasta with vegetables. Cooking the broccoli with the pasta saves a preparation step, and the goat cheese creates a creamy sauce without masking the summery flavors of the fresh vegetables and basil.

Serves 4.

1 tablespoon olive oil

2–3 large cloves garlic, minced or pressed

2 pounds fresh tomatoes, peeled, seeded, and diced, or 1 (28-ounce) can tomatoes, seeded and diced

¼ teaspoon sugar

Salt to taste

1 tablespoon slivered fresh basil

Freshly ground pepper to taste

12 ounces fusilli, penne, or other pasta

1 pound broccoli, broken into florets, stems peeled and chopped

3 ounces (about ⅓ cup) goat cheese, crumbled

Bring a large pot of water to boil while you make the tomato sauce.

Heat the olive oil in a large, heavy-bottomed nonstick skillet over medium-low heat, then add the garlic. Cook, stirring, just until it begins to color, 30 seconds to 1 minute, then add the tomatoes, sugar, and salt.

Raise the heat to medium, bring to a simmer, and cook, stirring often, 15 to 20 minutes, or until the tomatoes have cooked down, smell fragrant, and are beginning to stick to the pan. Remove from the heat and stir in the basil and pepper. Adjust the salt.

When the water reaches a rolling boil, add 2 to 3 teaspoons salt and the pasta. Stir until the water comes back to a boil. Cook the pasta for 6 minutes, then add the broccoli. Continue cooking another 4 minutes, stirring occasionally, until the pasta is done but still firm to the bite (al dente).

Drain the noodles and broccoli together when the pasta is al dente, and toss with the tomato sauce and the goat cheese. Divide at once among four warm plates.

Adapted recipe courtesy of Westfield Farm in Hubbardston (p. 82).

New England Lobster Bake

Chef Peter Davis of Henrietta's Table at the Charles Hotel is a champion of farmers, fishermen, and other local food producers and he draws on several different purveyors for this authentic lobster bake.

Serves 4

8 medium red-skinned
    potatoes
4 pieces of cheesecloth, cut
    into 18-inch squares
4 (1½-pound) live lobsters
4 ears of corn, unhusked

2 pounds steamer clams
Fresh seaweed from seashore,
    to cover bottom of pan
1 pound butter (4 sticks/
    2 cups)
2 lemons, halved

Preheat oven to 350°F.

Boil the potatoes for 5 minutes, then allow them to cool.

On a piece of cheesecloth, place 1 lobster, 1 ear of corn, 2 parboiled potatoes, and ½ pound of clams. Fold the cheesecloth to form a sack and tie shut. Repeat with the remaining ingredients to form 4 sacks.

Place the seaweed in the bottom of a heavy-bottomed pan large enough to hold the 4 lobster sacks. Add 1 cup water. Place the sacks on top of the seaweed and cover the pan with aluminum foil.

Place the pan over a hot stove or char-grill for 10 minutes. Remove and put into the oven for about 15 minutes, or until the lobster is cooked (antennae separate easily when pulled).

While the sacks are cooking, melt the butter over low heat.

Remove the sacks from the pan and serve with melted butter and lemon halves.

Adapted recipe courtesy of Chef Peter Davis of Henrietta's Table in Cambridge (p. 142).

Cape Cod Crab Cakes

This spicy and colorful version of crab cakes comes from one of the Cape's leading fishmongers. If panko crumbs are not available, substitute unseasoned white bread crumbs.

Serves 4.

3 tablespoons clarified butter

4 teaspoons olive oil

1 tablespoon finely diced onion

1 tablespoon finely diced red pepper

1 tablespoon finely diced yellow pepper

1 tablespoon finely diced celery

2 tablespoons chopped parsley

1 cup panko bread crumbs

¼ cup mayonnaise

1 egg, beaten

1½ teaspoons Dijon mustard

1 tablespoon lemon juice

1 teaspoon Creole seasoning

2 teaspoons Worcestershire sauce

1–2 dashes Tabasco sauce

1 pound shredded crabmeat

Salt and pepper to taste

Heat about 1 tablespoon clarified butter and 1 teaspoon of olive oil in a sauté pan. Sauté the onions, peppers, and celery until the onion is opaque.

Add the parsley and sauté for 30 seconds; remove from the heat.

In a large bowl, combine the panko, mayonnaise, egg, cooled vegetables, mustard, lemon juice, Creole seasoning, and Worcestershire and Tabasco sauces. Mix very well. Add the crabmeat and mix in gently.

Form into 8 cakes, each ¾ inch thick. Heat remaining 2 tablespoons butter and 3 teaspoons oil in a pan. Fry the crab cakes on each side until golden brown. Serve with additional Worcestershire and Tabasco sauces and lemon wedges.

Adapted recipe courtesy of Chatham Fish & Lobster in Chatham (p. 268).

Pork Tenderloin with Maple Glaze

Tangy cider vinegar, sweet maple syrup, and the herbal scent of sage make this version of roast pork an especially local treat.

Serves 8.

2 (12- to 14-ounce) pork tenderloins

2 teaspoons dried sage leaves

Salt and pepper to taste

1 tablespoon butter

6 tablespoons pure maple syrup

6 tablespoons apple cider vinegar

2 teaspoons Dijon mustard

Rub pork with sage and sprinkle with salt and pepper. Melt butter in a large sauté pan and brown pork over medium-high heat, turning occasionally until brown on all sides, about 6 minutes.

Reduce heat to medium-low, cover, and cook pork, turning occasionally, about 15 minutes more, or until a meat thermometer shows an internal temperature of 150°F. Remove pork to platter.

Whisk 5 tablespoons maple syrup, 4 tablespoons cider vinegar, and 2 teaspoons mustard in bowl.

Put the remaining 2 tablespoons of vinegar in the sauté pan, bring to a boil, and scrape up browned bits.

Return pork to pan, add syrup-vinegar-mustard mixture, and glaze pork for 2 minutes. Lower heat and cook for 2 more minutes.

Remove pork from pan and slice. Add the remaining tablespoon of maple syrup to the glaze remaining in pan. Stir and warm, then spoon glaze over the pork slices.

Adapted recipe courtesy of Boisvert Farm and North Hadley Sugar Shack in Hadley (p. 55).

Braciola

This old-time Italian-American favorite has a slight Sicilian twist with the addition of raisins. The butchers at the shop that provided the recipe will even pound the beef for you on request.

Serves 4.

1 pound top round steak
6 ounces mozzarella cheese
6 teaspoons butter
⅓ cup grated Parmesan cheese
2 cloves garlic, minced
¼ cup raisins

Salt and pepper to taste
2 tablespoons olive oil
1 (32-ounce) jar spaghetti sauce (or your own home-made tomato sauce)

Cut the steak into 4 to 6 pieces and pound each piece until thin with a mallet or the side of a cleaver. Place a slice of mozzarella cheese and 1 teaspoon of butter on each piece, then sprinkle each piece with Parmesan cheese, garlic, and raisins, and season with salt and pepper.

Roll each piece tightly and tie securely with string. Heat olive oil in a medium skillet over medium high heat. Sauté each roll in the oil for 5 to 10 minutes, or until browned on all sides.

Place rolls in tomato sauce and simmer for 1½ hours or until tender. Remove from sauce, cool slightly and remove the strings before serving.

Adapted recipe courtesy of Haverhill Beef Co. in Haverhill (p. 111).

Honey Pumpkin Tea Bread

This is the taste of fall. If you'd like, you can substitute mashed steamed pumpkin for the canned pumpkin.

Makes 12 slices.

2 cups all-purpose flour
1 teaspoon baking soda
½ teaspoon salt
½ teaspoon ground cinnamon
½ teaspoon ground ginger
½ teaspoon grated nutmeg
½ cup (1 stick) unsalted butter, at room temperature

1 cup honey
1 cup canned pumpkin (not pumpkin pie filling)
2 eggs, at room temperature
2 teaspoons lemon juice
1 teaspoon vanilla extract

Preheat oven to 350°F. Position rack in center of oven. Generously butter a 9 x 5-inch metal loaf pan and set aside.

Sift flour, baking soda, salt, cinnamon, ginger, and nutmeg into a medium bowl. Set aside.

In a large bowl, combine butter and honey and beat with an electric mixer at medium speed for 2 minutes or until smooth. Add the pumpkin; beat for 1 minute or until well combined. Beat in eggs one at a time, beating each for 1 minute. Stir in lemon juice and vanilla extract.

Add the sifted dry ingredients. With the mixer on low, beat until just incorporated. Increase mixer speed to medium and beat for 2 minutes or until the batter is smooth, scraping down the sides of the bowl as necessary with a rubber spatula.

Spread batter in prepared pan. Bake about 65 minutes, or until a cake tester or wooden skewer inserted into the middle of the loaf comes out clean. Cool the bread on a wire rack for 10 minutes, then remove from pan and continue cooling on the rack for 30 minutes before cutting.

Adapted recipe courtesy of Dunbar Tea Shop in Sandwich (p. 270).

Chèvre Pound Cake

This cake becomes even better after a couple of days and also freezes well. It is delicious topped with blueberries muddled with blueberry jam.

Serves 12.

½ pound unflavored fresh goat cheese, at room temperature

3 cups unsalted butter, at room temperature

2 cups sugar

6 eggs

1½ teaspoons vanilla

3 cups all purpose flour

Preheat oven to 325°F. Butter and flour a 10-inch tube or bundt pan.

With a hand mixer on medium speed, beat cheese and butter together until smooth. Add in sugar slowly while continuously beating, until mixture is light and fluffy. Add eggs one at a time, beating after each addition, then add in vanilla.

Fold flour gently into mixture until incorporated. Pour batter into pan and bake for 1¼ hours. Do not overbake. Use an instant-read thermometer to check for an internal temperature of 200°F.

Allow cake to cool in pan for 10 minutes, then turn it out onto a cooling rack. Serve slightly warm with sliced seasonal fruit of choice, lightly sweetened if desired.

Adapted recipe courtesy of The Concord Cheese Shop in Concord (p. 203).

Honey & Thyme Roasted Pears

Ashmont Grill offers these pears as a light dessert. We like to serve them with a small scoop of vanilla ice cream.

Serves 4.

8 to 10 small pears
2 tablespoons olive oil
2 tablespoons honey
½ cup white wine

1 tablespoon cider vinegar
8 sprigs of thyme
Salt and pepper

Heat oven to 425°F. Peel the pears, cut into quarters, and remove seeds. Gently toss pears with all other ingredients. Season to taste with salt and pepper.

Pour pears into a shallow baking dish that fits them comfortably. Roast in oven about 20 minutes until edges are lightly browned and pears are cooked through.

Adapted recipe courtesy of Ashmont Grill in Dorchester (p. 127).

Lemon Blackberry Pound Cake

Chef-Owner Eunice Feller at Bread & Chocolate Bakery Cafe puts a summer seasonal twist on this classic pound cake.

Makes 12–16 slices.

- 1 cup (2 sticks) unsalted butter, at room temperature
- 3 cups sugar
- 3 cups cake flour
- ½ teaspoon baking soda
- ½ teaspoon salt
- 6 large eggs, at room temperature
- 1 tablespoon lemon zest
- 3 tablespoons lemon juice
- 8 ounces sour cream
- 3 pints fresh blackberries, slightly crushed
- Powdered sugar

Preheat oven to 325°F. Butter and flour a large bundt pan.

Using an electric mixer, beat butter and sugar at high speed in a large bowl for 5 minutes. Sift together flour, baking soda, and salt. Set aside.

When butter and sugar mixture is light and fluffy, add eggs one at a time, beating well after each addition. Then beat in lemon zest and lemon juice.

Reduce mixer speed to low. Add flour mixture and beat until just mixed. Scrape down bowl and beat in sour cream until just mixed. Gently fold in crushed blackberries by hand.

Spoon batter into prepared pan and bake 50 to 60 minutes, or until a toothpick inserted near center of the cake comes out clean. Cool cake in pan on a rack for 15 minutes, then invert rack over cake and reinvert cake onto rack. Let cool, then dust with powdered sugar.

Adapted recipe courtesy of Bread & Chocolate Bakery Cafe
in Newton Highlands and Newtonville (p. 202).

Easy Vanilla Wafers

Charles H. Baldwin & Sons is justifiably proud of its vanilla extract, and this recipe for a classic cookie shows off the vanilla at its finest. Jackie Moffatt recommends draping the cookies over a wooden dowel or the handle of a wooden spoon immediately after removing them from the cookie sheet to give them a pretty curved shape.

Makes about 36 cookies.

¼ cup (½ stick) unsalted butter, room temperature

⅓ cup vanilla sugar (recipe follows)

¼ cup egg whites (whites from two large eggs)

⅓ cup unbleached all-purpose flour

Pinch of salt

Preheat oven to 400°F. Generously butter a large heavy cookie sheet.

Beat butter and vanilla sugar in a medium bowl until light and fluffy. Beat in egg whites. Gradually mix in flour and salt (batter will be soft).

Drop batter by level teaspoonfuls onto prepared cookie sheets, spacing cookies 3 inches apart.

Bake until cookie edges are golden brown and centers of cookies are still pale, about 7 minutes. Transfer cookies to racks and cool completely.

Vanilla Sugar

Jackie Moffatt adds that this sugar is also good for sweetening whipped cream.

Makes 2 cups.

2 cups sugar

1 vanilla bean, cut into small pieces

Process sugar and vanilla bean in food processor until vanilla bean is very finely minced. Strain sugar to remove any large pieces of vanilla bean. Store sugar in airtight container.

Adapted recipe courtesy of Charles H. Baldwin & Sons in West Stockbridge (p. 27).

Chocolate Stout Cake

We all know how well red wine and chocolate go together, but who would have guessed that deep, dark beer would meld so nicely with rich cocoa to make a robust, moist, chocolate-covered cake? This recipe replicates the three-layer version at Barrington Brewery & Restaurant in Great Barrington, the most popular dessert on the menu.

Serves 8–12.

Cake

- 2 cups stout (such as Guinness)
- 2 cups (4 sticks) unsalted butter
- 1½ cups sweetened cocoa powder (preferably Dutch-process)

- 4 cups all-purpose flour
- 4 cups sugar
- 1 tablespoon baking soda
- 1½ teaspoons salt
- 4 large eggs
- 1⅓ cups sour cream

Icing

- 2 cups whipping cream

- 1 pound bittersweet (not unsweetened) or semi-sweet chocolate, chopped

For the cake

Preheat oven to 350°F. Butter three 8-inch round cake pans with 2-inch-high sides. Line with parchment paper. Butter paper.

Bring stout and butter to a simmer in a large heavy saucepan over medium heat. Add cocoa powder and whisk until mixture is smooth. Cool slightly.

Whisk flour, sugar, baking soda, and salt in a large bowl to blend.

Using electric mixer, beat eggs and sour cream in another large bowl to blend.

Add stout-chocolate mixture to egg mixture and beat just to combine. Add flour mixture and beat briefly on slow speed. Using rubber spatula, fold batter until completely combined.

Divide batter equally among prepared pans. Bake cakes until tester inserted into center of cakes comes out clean, about 35 minutes. Turn cakes out onto a rack and cool completely.

For the icing

Bring cream to a simmer in a medium heavy saucepan. Remove from heat.

Add chopped chocolate and whisk until melted and smooth. Refrigerate until icing is spreadable, stirring frequently, about 2 hours.

Place one cake layer on plate. Spread ⅔ cup icing over.

Top with second cake layer. Spread ⅔ cup icing over.

Top with third cake layer. Spread remaining icing over top and sides of cake.

Adapted recipe courtesy of Barrington Brewery & Restaurant in Great Barrington (p. 4).

Burgundy Pie

Martha's Vineyard pie maker extraordinaire, the late Eileen Blake, once cautioned, "A recipe is only a rough guide. You have to make it your own." This combination of fruits that are abundant on the Vineyard makes a rich, deeply colored pie. Her daughter Mary Ellis makes her crusts with all-purpose King Arthur flour and Crisco shortening but can't give an actual recipe. "It's all in the feel," she says.

Makes one 9-inch pie.

- **2 cups fresh or frozen blueberries**
- **2 cups fresh or frozen cranberries (halved if using fresh)**
- **1 cup firmly packed light brown sugar**
- **¼ cup all-purpose flour**
- **1 teaspoon freshly ground nutmeg**
- **1 teaspoon salt**
- **Dough for a double-crust 9-inch pie**
- **2–3 tablespoons unsalted butter**
- **1 egg, beaten with 1 teaspoon water to form a glaze**

Preheat the oven to 400°F. Have on hand a 9-inch pie pan.

In a bowl, combine the blueberries, cranberries, brown sugar, flour, nutmeg, and salt; toss until well combined.

Divide the pie dough into two parts, one slightly larger than the other. Using as little additional flour as possible, roll out the larger piece of dough and use it to line the pie pan.

Spoon the filling into the lined pan, then dot filling liberally with butter.

Roll out the remaining dough until it is large enough to cover the pie. Set it on the filling. Fold and crimp the overhang to seal it. Brush the surface with the egg mixture, and cut a few slashes to vent.

Bake the pie for about 50 minutes, or until the crust is golden. Let cool to room temperature before serving.

Adapted recipe courtesy of Eileen Blake's Pies in West Tisbury (p. 278).

Mulled Cider

Everyone loves the aroma (and flavor) of mulled cider. The key to successful mulling is extremely low heat, to keep from cooking the little bits of apple pulp still present in good fresh cider.

Makes 8 cups.

½ gallon fresh apple cider
3–4 cinnamon sticks
2 teaspoons whole cloves
2 teaspoons allspice

1–2 tablespoons orange juice concentrate (optional)
1–2 tablespoons honey (optional)

Pour ½ gallon or more of apple cider into a large steel or enamel saucepan. Simmer for 1 hour over very low heat, stirring occasionally. Do not let cider boil!

Just before serving, add cinnamon, cloves, allspice, and orange juice concentrate and honey (if using).

Adapted recipe courtesy of Clarkdale Fruit Farms in West Deerfield (p. 55).

Appendices

Appendix A:
Eateries by Cuisine

Codes for Corresponding Regional Chapters:
(BERK) The Berkshires
(C&I) Cape Cod and the Islands
(CENT) Central Massachusetts
(CV) Connecticut Valley
(METRO) Metropolitan Boston
(NE) Northeastern Massachusetts
(SE) Southeastern Massachusetts
(SUB) Suburban Boston

Asian
Blue Ginger, (SUB), 189
Jae's Asian Bistro, (BERK), 8
Moksa, (METRO), 148
Pearl, The, (C&I), 259
Spice Dragon, (BERK), 12

Barbecue
Blackstrap BBQ, (NE), 92
Blue Ribbon Bar-B-Q, (SUB), 190
Redbones Barbecue, (METRO), 154
Smokestack Urban Barbecue,
    (CENT), 69

Brazilian
Brazilian Grill, (C&I), 252

Cambodian
Elephant Walk, (SUB), 192,
    (METRO), 138

Caribbean
Miami Restaurant, (METRO), 148

Casual American
Armsby Abbey, (CENT), 65
Black Cat Tavern, (C&I), 251
Black Dog Tavern, (C&I), 251
Blue Moon Diner, (CENT), 66
Bobby's Burger Palace, (NE), 93
Boulevard Diner, (CENT), 71
Brick Wall Bistro, (CV), 31
Casey's Diner, (SUB), 191
Charlie's Diner Bar & Grill,
    (CENT), 67
Charlie's Sandwich Shoppe,
    (METRO), 132
Coney Island Lunch, (CENT), 67

Deluxe Town Diner, (SUB), 191
5 South Main, (SE), 225
Four Sisters Owl Diner, (NE), 96
Freestones City Grill, (SE), 226
Gould Farm Roadside Store & Cafe,
(BERK), 6
Gypsy Joynt Cafe, (BERK), 7
Inna's Kitchen, (SUB), 195
Jack's Hot Dog Stand, (BERK), 8
Kelly's Roast Beef, (NE), 98
Mac's Shack, (C&I), 255
Mark's Deli, (NE), 101
Miss Florence Diner, (CV), 38
Miss Worcester Diner, (CENT), 71
Moran Square Diner, (CENT), 68
Mr. Bartley's Gourmet Burgers,
(METRO), 148
Nancy's Airfield Cafe, (NE), 101
Nor'East Beer Garden, (C&I), 257
Parkway Diner, (CENT), 71
Ruggie's Breakfast & Lunch,
(C&I), 260
Scratch Kitchen, (NE), 103
Shawmut Diner, (SE), 229
Strip-T's, (SUB), 197
Twigs Cafe, (CENT), 70
Wahlburgers, (SE), 232
Willow Rest, The, (NE), 105
Worcester Art Museum Cafe
(CENT), 71
Zaftig's Delicatessen, (METRO), 160

Chinese
CK Shanghai, (SUB), 191
Dumpling Cafe, (METRO), 136
East by Northeast, (METRO), 137
East Ocean City, (METRO), 137
Q Restaurant, (METRO), 153
Sichuan Gourmet, (SE), 230

Continental
Blantyre, (BERK), 5
Vienna Restaurant & Historic Inn,
(CENT), 70

Cuban
El Oriental de Cuba, (METRO), 138
Gustazo Cuban Cafe, (SUB), 194

Eclectic
Via Lago Cafe & Catering, (SUB), 199

French
AKA Bistro, (SUB), 188
Aquitaine, (METRO), 126
Beacon Hill Bistro, (METRO), 129
Bistro Les Gras, (CV), 31
Bistro Zinc, (BERK), 5
Chez Albert, (CV), 33
Chez Henri, (METRO), 133
Chillingsworth, (C&I), 254
Clio, (METRO), 133
Elephant Walk, (SUB), 192,
(METRO), 138
Hamersley's Bistro, (METRO), 141

Butcher Shop, (METRO), 130

Cafe Paprika, (SE), 224

Oleana, (METRO), 150

Rendezvous, (METRO), 155

Rialto, (METRO), 155

Mexican

Olé Mexican Grill, (METRO), 150

Middle Eastern

El Basha, (CENT), 67

New American

Abba, (C&I), 250

Allium Restaurant + Bar,
(BERK), 3

Alta Restaurant & Wine Bar,
(BERK), 3

Ashmont Grill, (METRO), 127, 302

Back Eddy, The, (SE), 223

Baker's Oven Bistro, (CV), 30

Bell & Anchor, (BERK), 4

Bia Bistro, (SE), 223

Biltmore Bar & Grille, The,
(SUB), 189

Blue Ginger, (SUB), 189

Blue, Inc., (METRO), 129

Bramble Inn, (C&I), 252

B Street, (SUB), 189

Cape Sea Grille, (C&I), 253

Catalyst, (METRO), 132

Chillingsworth, (C&I), 254

Church Street Cafe, (BERK), 6

Clio, (METRO), 133

Coco, (CV), 33

Craigie on Main, (METRO), 133

Duckworth's Bistrot, (NE), 95

East Coast Grill, (METRO), 137

80 Thoreau, (SUB), 192

EVOO Restaurant, (METRO), 138

51 Lincoln, (SUB), 193

Firefly New American Bistro,
(BERK), 6

Fireplace, The, (METRO), 139

Flora, (SUB), 193

Food 101 Bistro, (CV), 34

Franklin Cafe, (METRO), 140

Franklin Cape Ann, (NE), 96

Franklin Southie, (METRO), 140

Glass Onion, (C&I), 254

Gramercy Bistro, (BERK), 7

Hamersley's Bistro, (METRO), 141

Harvest, (METRO), 141

Henrietta's Table, (METRO), 142, 296

Herb Lyceum at Gilson's Farm, The,
(NE), 97

Hope and Olive, (CV), 35

John Andrews/A Farmhouse
Restaurant, (BERK), 9

J's at Nashoba Valley Winery,
(CENT), 68

L'Espalier, (METRO), 145

Local, The, (SUB), 196

Local 149, (METRO), 145

Magpie Woodfired Pizzeria, (CV), 35

Market Restaurant, The, (NE), 101

Menton, (METRO), 147
Mezze Bistro + Bar, (BERK), 9
No. 9 Park, (METRO), 149
Nudel Restaurant, (BERK), 10
Oak Long Bar + Kitchen,
    (METRO), 150
Old Inn on the Green, (BERK), 10
Òran Mór Bistro, (C&I), 258
Oro, (SE), 226
Paul & Elizabeth's, (CV), 38
Red Lion Inn, (BERK), 11, 285
Red Pheasant Inn, (C&I), 259
Red Rock Bistro, (NE), 102
Salt Kitchen & Rum Bar, (NE), 103
Scargo Cafe, (C&I), 260
Scarlet Oak Tavern, (SE), 229
Seven Sisters Market Bistro, (CV), 40
Sonoma, (CENT), 69
Southfield Store, (BERK), 12
Steel & Rye, (SE), 231
Stonehedge Inn, (NE), 104
Strip-T's, (SUB), 197
Ten Tables, (C&I), 261
Tiny's, (C&I), 262
Toppers, (C&I), 262
Trade, (METRO), 158
Tremont 647, (METRO), 158
Tryst, (SUB), 198
T.W. Kitchen, (METRO), 159
Upstairs on the Square, (METRO), 160

Peruvian
Taranta, (METRO), 156

Polish
Cafe Polonia, (METRO), 131
Pulaski Club (Polish American
    Citizens Club), (CV), 39

Portuguese
Antonio's Restaurant and Cafe,
    (SE), 223
Atasca Restaurant, (METRO), 127
Ceia Kitchen + Bar, (NE), 94
Cinderella Restaurant, (SE), 225
Mimo Restaurant, (SE), 226
Sagres Restaurant, (SE), 229

Salvadoran
Topacio, (METRO), 159

Scottish
Haven, The, (METRO), 142

Seafood
B&G Oysters, (METRO), 128
Barking Crab, (METRO), 128
Blount Clam Shack and Soup Store,
    (SE), 224
Bookstore & Restaurant, (C&I), 251
Brine, (NE), 93
Cape Sea Grille, (C&I), 253
Clam Box of Ipswich, (NE), 100
Cru, (C&I), 254
Daily Catch, (METRO), 134
East Ocean City, (METRO), 137
Home Port Restaurant, (C&I), 255

Hope and Olive, (CV), 35
Local 149, (METRO), 145
Oleana, (METRO), 150
Organic Garden Cafe, (NE), 102
Paul & Elizabeth's, (CV), 38
People's Pint, (CV), 39

Q Restaurant, (METRO), 153
Spice Dragon, (BERK), 12

Vietnamese
Pho Pasteur, (METRO), 152

Appendix B: Dishes, Specialties & Purveyors

Codes for Corresponding Regional Chapters:

(BERK) The Berkshires
(C&I) Cape Cod and the Islands
(CENT) Central Massachusetts
(CV) Connecticut Valley

(METRO) Metropolitan Boston
(NE) Northeastern Massachusetts
(SE) Southeastern Massachusetts
(SUB) Suburban Boston

Offshore Ale Company, (C&I), 258

Paper City Brewing, (CV), 50

People's Pint, (CV), 39

Salem Beer Works, (NE), 102

Wachusett Brewing Company,
(CENT), 81

Watch City Brewing Company,
(SUB), 200

Burgers

Bell & Anchor, (BERK), 4

Bobby's Burger Palace, (NE), 93

Brew City Grill and Brew House,
(CENT), 66

Brick Wall Bistro, (CV), 31

Firefly New American Bistro,
(BERK), 6

High Horse Brewing + Wicked
Fancy Dining, (CV), 34

Lee's Place Burgers, (SUB), 208

Mr. Bartley's Gourmet Burgers,
(METRO), 148

Nor'East Beer Garden, (C&I), 257

PB Boulangerie Bistro, (C&I), 258

Scratch Kitchen, (NE), 103

Ten Tables, (C&I), 261

Wahlburgers, (SE), 232

Butcher

Chicopee Provision Company,
(CV), 44

Gaspar's Sausage Company Factory
Outlet, (SE), 236, 288

Haverhill Beef Co., (NE), 111, 299

Meat House, The, (SUB), 209

Meat Market, The, (BERK), 18

Pekarski's Sausage, (CV), 50

Rainbow Turkey Farm, (SE), 238

Savenor's, (METRO), 176

T.F. Kinnealey, (SUB), 207

Cheese

Bloomy Rind, (SE), 233

Chase Hill Farm, (CV), 44

Concord Cheese Shop, The, (SUB),
203, 301

Cricket Creek Farm, (BERK), 16

Crystal Brook Farm, (CENT), 73

Formaggio Kitchen, (METRO), 169

Mozzarella House, (NE), 113

Pecorino, a Country Cheese Shop,
(CENT), 78

Rawson Brook Farm, (BERK), 19

Robinson Farm, (CENT), 79

Rubiner's Cheesemongers & Grocers, (BERK), 20

Smith's Country Cheese, (CENT), 80

South End Formaggio, (METRO), 169

Wasik's, the Cheese Shop, (SUB), 215

Westfield Farm, (CENT), 82, 294

Chocolatier

Catherine's Chocolate Shop,
(BERK), 13

Chatham Candy Manor, (C&I), 267

Chocolate Springs Cafe, (BERK), 15

Colonial Candies, (CENT), 75

Dante Confections, (NE), 109

Dorothy Cox's Chocolates, (SE), 236

Eaton Farm Confectioners,
  (CENT), 73

Harbor Sweets, (NE), 110

Heavenly Chocolates, (CV), 47

Hebert Candies, the Candy
  Mansion, (CENT), 75

L.A. Burdick Chocolates,
  (METRO), 173

Mrs. Nelson's Candy House,
  (NE), 114

Murdick's Fudge, (C&I), 273

Prides Crossing Confections,
  (NE), 116

Priscilla Hand Made Candies,
  (CENT), 79, (SUB), 210

Richardson's Candy Kitchen, (CV), 51

Serenade Chocolatier, (METRO), 177

Stage Stop Candy, (C&I), 276

Sweet Inspirations Chocolate Shop,
  (C&I), 276

Taza Chocolate, (METRO), 179

Tuck's Candies, (NE), 117

Turtle Alley Chocolates, (NE), 118

Ye Olde Pepper Candy Company,
  (NE), 119

Coffee

Barrington Coffee Roasting Company, (BERK), 4, 307

Caffè Vittoria, (METRO), 164

Elmer's Store, (CV), 45

George Howell Coffee, (SUB), 206

Nantucket Roasters, (C&I), 273

RAO's Coffee Roasting Company,
  (CV), 51

Ride Studio Cafe, (SUB), 211

Tunnel City Coffee Roasters,
  (BERK), 20

Dining Cars

Blue Moon Diner (CENT), 66

Boulevard Diner, (CENT), 71

Casey's Diner (SUB), 191

Charlie's Diner Bar & Grill, (CENT), 67

Four Sisters Owl Diner, (NE), 96

Lanna Thai Diner, (NE), 99

Miss Florence Diner, (CV), 38

Miss Worcester Diner, (CENT), 71

Moran Square Diner, (CENT), 68

Parkway Diner, (CENT), 71

Shawmut Diner, (SE), 229

Fishmonger

Amaral's Market, (SE), 233

Cape Quality Seafood, (SE), 235

Captain Marden's Seafoods,
  (SUB), 202

Catch of the Day Seafood Market &
  Grill, (C&I), 266

Chatham Fish & Lobster, (C&I),
  268, 297

Courthouse Seafood Fish Market
  and Restaurant, (METRO), 167

Appendix C: Massachusetts Food Events

Boston Wine Expo, wine-expos.com. Seminars, cooking demonstrations, and, of course, tastings headline the largest consumer event of its kind in New England. Held at Seaport World Trade Center in January/February.

Dinner in a Country Village, osv.org. Beginning in January and running through March, Old Sturbridge Village in Sturbridge hosts open hearth dinners. Costumed interpreters direct the proceedings, but the guests do the chopping, mixing, and basting, using early-19th-century tools and techniques.

Super Hunger Brunch, gbfb.org/superhungerbrunch. Around four dozen top Boston-area restaurants offer special brunches one weekend in January to benefit the hunger alleviation programs of the Greater Boston Food Bank.

Winter Restaurant Week, bostonrestaurantweek.com. More than 100 high-class restaurants from Boston and the surrounding region offer special fixed-price menus at lunch and dinner during March.

Cape Cod Restaurant Week, capecodrestaurantweek.com. May is a great time to check out some of Cape Cod's best restaurants before the busy summer season gets in full swing. Participants offer three- or four-course fixed-price menus.

Nantucket Wine Festival, nantucketwinefestival.com. More than 100 wineries and restaurants participate in tastings at Nantucket homes, as well as special wine dinners and seminars. The capper is a grand tasting at the 'Sconset Casino.

Quaboag Valley Asparagus & Flower Festival, asparagusfestival.blogspot.com. Dutch immigrant Diederik Leertouwer lived in West Brookfield from 1794 to 1798. Local legend has it that Leertouwer imported asparagus from his homeland and was the first to plant it in this country. Wild asparagus continues to grow in the area and a few farms also cultivate it. This spring festival on the Town Common in West Brookfield features homegrown and homemade agricultural products and a generally festive atmosphere, including maypole dancing for children and lots of homemade foods.

Strawberry and Asparagus Supper, firstchurchhadley.org. The harvest season gets under way with this popular supper featuring famous Hadley asparagus along with baked ham, potato salad, rolls, strawberry shortcake, and ice cream. Two seatings at the First Congregational Church of Hadley are by advance reservation.

World's Largest Pancake Breakfast, spiritofspringfield .org. This pancake breakfast with live entertainment stretches along Main Street between State and Bridge Streets in Springfield. It was named a "Local Legacy" by the Library of Congress.

June

Lavender Festival, lavenderland.com. The hill towns around Greenfield have blossomed into one of North America's premier lavender-growing regions over the last few years. This annual event at Johnson Hill Farm in Buckland features local vendors selling wool, lotions, and other products. You can also participate in culinary and craft herbal workshops, wind your way through a lavender-lined stone labyrinth, and purchase lavender plants.

Nashua River Brewers Festival, beersforgood.com. Celebration of regional craft beers benefits local charities and takes place at Riverfront Park in Fitchburg.

Scooper Bowl, jimmyfund.org. One of the largest ice cream festivals in the country kicks off the summer season in style—and benefits the Jimmy Fund at the same time. The event takes place on Boston's City Hall Plaza.

Strawberry Festival, russellorchards.com. Russell Orchards in Ipswich celebrates the first sweet crop of summer. Homemade strawberry shortcake is the star of this event, along with other food samples and wine tastings, live folk music, and hayrides. Pick-your-own strawberries in season.

Summertime Polish Feast, olphchurchnb.org. Tents on the lawn of Our Lady of Perpetual Help Church in New Bedford offer arts and crafts and live entertainment, but the real focus is on authentic Polish food. On Sunday there's also a polka mass.

A Taste of the Vineyard, mvpreservation.org. The top restaurants and caterers of Martha's Vineyard turn out to offer samples of their cuisine and beverages to benefit the Martha's Vineyard Preservation Trust in Edgartown.

July

Annual Clambake, lloydcenter.org. The Lloyd Center for the Environment serves up "an old-fashioned, mouthwatering clambake  with all the fixings" to raise funds to support its programs. The event is held at Lloyd State Park in Dartmouth. It's a bit of a splurge but supports a worthy cause.

Annual Indian Pow Wow, mashpeewampanoagtribe.com. The Wampanoags host tribes from all over North America, who gather to celebrate their heritage. Among the highlights at this event in Mashpee are native foods, including a Cape Cod clambake.

Boston Harborfest, bostonharborfest.com. This festival celebrating the maritime history of Boston wouldn't be complete without a "chowderfest" competition among Boston restaurants and caterers.

Festival Betances, iba-etc.org. Annual Puerto Rican festival on Plaza Betances in Boston's South End emphasizes food, as well as music, dancing, and sports, as residents of the Villa Victoria housing complex re-create an authentic village celebration. It honors Emeterio Betances, an abolitionist and champion of Puerto Rican independence.

Pilgrim Breakfast, plymouthantiquariansociety.org. Servers in Pilgrim-era costume deliver cod cakes, homemade baked beans, corn bread, muffins, and juice to diners at outdoor tables on the lawn of the Harlow Old Fort House in Plymouth. Strolling entertainers sing, tell riddles, and generally make merry, 17th-century style.

Religious Festivals, northendboston.com. Big signs proclaim "Mangia!" as Italian-Americans gather to honor the patron saints of their home country and feast on sausages, cannoli, pizza, and Italian ices. The celebrations take place most weekends in July and August in Boston's North End.

August

Adams Agricultural Fair, adamsfair.com. One of the most rural of the Massachusetts agricultural fairs is held at Bowe Field in Adams. The fair is known for its rabbit and poultry competitions and its demonstrations of sheepdog herding skills. That's not to say that it lacks the whole panoply of pies, pickles, and produce along with hot rods, chain-saw sculpture, tractor pulls, and country music. You can see it all while walking around with handheld country-fair food.

Bolton Fair, boltonfair.org. A farmers' market and a chicken barbecue are just two of the highlights of this agricultural fair, established in 1874 and held at the Fairgrounds in Lancaster. The "best apple pie" competition is one of the most spirited, but bakers also compete for best cookies, cakes, brownies, and candy.

Caribbean-American Festival, bostoncarnival.org. The parade along Blue Hill Avenue in Boston is the most colorful part of this celebration. But many visitors eagerly anticipate the food court that is set up in front of the Franklin Park Zoo. Expect curried goat, conch fritters, fried plantains, jerk chicken, pigeon peas and rice, and Bahamian coco—a dish of codfish and coconut milk.

Feast of the Blessed Sacrament, portuguesefeast.com. Four Madeiran immigrants who wanted to re-create the religious festivals that were so common in the villages of their home island founded the Feast of the Blessed Sacrament in 1915. Today, its organizers claim it is the world's largest Portuguese feast and the largest ethnic festival in New England. More than 300,000 people attend for the continuous live entertainment and the Portuguese food specialties, including *carne de espeto* (a form of barbecue), stewed codfish, marinated fresh tuna, *carne guisada* (stewed beef), stewed rabbit, fresh fava beans, sausages, and fried pastries. Activities take place at Madeira Field in New Bedford.

Gloucester Waterfront Festival, castleberryfairs.com. A pancake breakfast on Saturday and a gala lobster bake Sunday afternoon anchor this celebration of Gloucester that takes place at Stage Fort Park. Musicians play the whole time and artists and artisans display their wares.

Martha's Vineyard Agricultural Livestock Show & Fair, mvas.vineyard.net. Sample the baked goods, admire the prize fruits and vegetables, and purchase some of the preserves at this old-fashioned country fair at the West Tisbury Fairgrounds on Martha's Vineyard.

Massachusetts State Chili Cook-Off, appleseed.org. About 50 competitors offer their best in the categories of red chili, green chili, and salsa. Visitors are encouraged to taste. The event is held at Bentley Field in Winchenden.

Red Fire Farm Tomato Festival, redfire farm.com. Cooking demonstrations, workshops, and an afternoon of tomato tasting celebrate the harvest at Red Fire's farm in Granby.

Summer Restaurant Week, bostonrestaurantweek.com. More than 100 high-class restaurants from Boston and the surrounding region offer special fixed-price menus at lunch and dinner.

Tanglewood Wine & Food Classic, bso.org. The grounds of Tanglewood in Lenox, the summer home of the Boston Symphony Orchestra, have always been associated with great picnics. For one weekend it turns to the pleasures of the complete table with wine and food seminars, meet-the-chef and meet-the-winemaker events, a gala dinner and wine auction, and the Saturday "Great Tasting" with hourly cooking demos.

Three-County Fair, 3CountyFair.com. This annual agricultural fair that stretches into early September has been a mainstay in the Northampton calendar since 1818, making it one of the oldest continuous fairs in the country. The Polish festival at the fair invariably blends oompah and dance music with the Polish-American cuisine of the Connecticut Valley's farmers. Other highlights include the New England championship horse-pulling competition and Thoroughbred racing.

Ware Grange Fair, facebook.com/WareGrange164. If you're particularly good at pickling or growing champion green beans or basil, this is your chance to vie for recognition. Any resident of Massachusetts is eligible to enter the fair competition and need not be a Grange member. Categories include vegetables, fruit, herbs, eggs, canned goods, poultry, and farm crops. An old-fashioned ham and bean supper caps the festivities held at the fairgrounds on Belchertown Road in Ware.

September

Agricultural Exhibition, osv.org. Old Sturbridge Village in Sturbridge hosts this early-19th-century forerunner of today's community agricultural fairs featuring exhibitions of livestock and produce. Home gardeners show off their heirloom vegetables, flowers, and herbs—antique varieties only.

Bourne Scallop Fest, bournescallopfest.com. Buzzards Bay is renowned for its scallops, and this long-standing annual celebration of the harvest features grilled, fried, and baked scallop dishes along with crafts, entertainment, a parade, and children's games. It is held at Buzzards Bay Park in Buzzards Bay.

Eastern States Exposition, thebige.com. Held at the fairgrounds in West Springfield, the Big E is New England's counterpart to the giant state fairs of the Midwest. It features multiple stages of famous-name performers, a big-top circus, a rodeo, and what seems like miles of food vendors serving almost anything that can be eaten off a stick, in a bun, or dipped in ketchup. In fact, the hoopla is so overwhelming that you could forget to visit the extensive agricultural exhibits and the 4-H livestock judging. The fair's signature food, the Big E Cream Puff, is sold inside the New England Center.

Hancock Shaker Village Country Fair, hancockshaker village.org. A deliberate throwback to New England's agricultural heyday of the mid-19th century, this old-time country fair features the largest exhibit of heritage breed livestock in the Northeast. Heirloom vegetables and fruits are offered for sale, and your mouth will no doubt water at the pie-judging contest. Some of the top practitioners of traditional crafts demonstrate blacksmithing, woodworking, basket-making, and other country skills. Don't miss the round barn at this beautifully restored Shaker site in Pittsfield.

Mahrajan Lebanese Festival, (978) 685-7233. St. Anthony's Church parking lot in Lawrence is the site for this cultural festival, which includes live Lebanese and American music, belly dancing performances, and tables of such Lebanese delicacies as falafel, kebabs, kibbe, spinach pies, and hummus.

North Quabbin Garlic and Arts Festival, garlicandarts.org. This homegrown country fair and arts show celebrates garlic in every form. About two dozen farms and vendors participate, offering everything from fresh garlic to seed garlic to barbecue sauce. The festival includes an art show and games. The highlight is the garlic-eating contest. Location changes, so check website.

What the Fluff? Festival, somervilleartscouncil.org. A cooking contest and colorful events in Union Square celebrate the invention of Marshmallow Fluff in Somerville.

October

Annual Applefest, wachusett.com. The entire Wachusett area is major apple country, and this fall festival at Wachusett Mountain Ski

Area is a cross between an agricultural fair and an Oktoberfest. Look for apple pies and cider as well as sausages, German music, craft exhibitions, a farmers' market, and pie-baking and pie-eating contests.

Boston Vegetarian Food Festival, bostonveg.org. Organized to promote "vegetarian and earth-friendly eating," this popular festival features about 80 vendors offering samples of everything from vegan chocolate peanut butter brownies to soy cheesecake and hemp-sprouted bread to seaweed caviar. It's held at the Reggie Lewis State Track Athletic Center in Roxbury.

Brookfield Apple Country Fair, applecountryfair.com. This fund-raiser to send the local sixth grade class to environmental summer camp has two major draws: a raffle for a community-made quilt and a massive bake sale of apple pies. There's also a pie-judging contest, live music, and more than 70 local craftspeople and vendors selling their wares on Brookfield Common.

Church bazaars. Bostonians of Armenian, Lebanese, and Greek descent know that church bazaars are the best place to find the foods that their grandmothers used to make. From October into November, you're also likely to rub elbows with dedicated foodies at some of the most popular fairs, including St. James Armenian Apostolic Church (465 Mount Auburn St., Watertown, MA 02472; 617-923-8860); St. George Orthodox Church (Emmonsdale Road, West Roxbury, MA 02132; 617-323-9861), Our Lady of the Cedars of Lebanon (61 Rockwood St., Jamaica Plain, MA 02130; 617-522-0225), and St. Stephen's Armenian Apostolic Church (bazaar held at Armenian Cultural and Educational Center, Nichols Avenue, Watertown, MA 02472; 617-924-7562).

Cranberry Harvest Celebration, cranberryharvest.org. Held during the height of the harvest season, this festival is sponsored by the Cape Cod Cranberry Growers' Association and A. D. Makepeace

Company (the world's largest cranberry grower), which welcomes visitors to its operation in Wareham.

Essex Clamfest, visitessexma.com. Essex has been famous for its clams for more than three centuries, and a chowder-tasting competition is at the heart of this annual celebration at Memorial Park, which also features arts and crafts, games, and live entertainment.

Topsfield Fair, topsfieldfair.org. Established in 1818, the Topsfield Fair proclaims itself America's oldest continuously operating country fair. It's notable for several cooking contests, a beer-making competition, and its beekeeping and honey exhibit. The New England Giant Pumpkin Contest, held on opening day, is the World Series and Super Bowl rolled into one for the horticultural subculture of giant pumpkin growers. The 2012 winner set a new record of 2,009 pounds.

Wellfleet OysterFest, wellfleetoysterfest.org. The Atlantic bluepoint oysters of Wellfleet are famed throughout the Northeast as some of the finest cold-water oysters of the region. This festival brings out restaurateurs to show off their oyster dishes, lets champion shuckers compete against one another to separate the bivalves from their shells, and even pits local restaurants against one another. You won't leave hungry.

November

Chocolate Dessert Buffet and Silent Auction, sponsored by AIDSCARE/Hampshire County; (413) 586-8288, ext. 5. Pioneer Valley bakeries and restaurants donate chocolate cakes, desserts, and cookie plates for sampling during the event, which benefits support programs for county residents living with HIV/AIDS. Held at Clarion Hotel Conference Center in Northampton.

Cider Days in Franklin County, ciderdays.org. The rural apple growers in the hill towns west of Greenfield welcome the public for self-guided tours of Franklin County orchards, tastings of sweet and hard ciders and local cheeses, demonstrations of cider pressing, and workshops. Many activities center on downtown Shelburne Falls, where apple growers in some of the most remote areas bring their often unusual varieties for display and sale. Area restaurants feature apples and cider on their menus.

Thanksgiving Dinner at Plimoth Plantation, plimoth .org. Our modern Thanksgiving grows out of several earlier traditions, including the harvest festival, the commemoration of the Pilgrims' landing at Plymouth, and their Thanksgiving feast the following spring. Thanksgiving as we celebrate it today developed in the Victorian period, as an elaboration of the day of national Thanksgiving first proclaimed by Abraham Lincoln in 1863. The living history museum Plimoth Plantation offers several versions of Thanksgiving dining, each of which makes a nod to the changing traditions around the holiday. The "Victorian Thanksgiving Dinner" is a sit-down feast in Victorian dress with period singers. The museum also offers a classic Thanksgiving dinner buffet menu as well as a la carte dining without reservations on Thanksgiving Day. The buffet and Victorian dinners tend to sell out by mid-October.

December

Cambridge School of Culinary Arts Holiday Bake Sale, cambridgeculinary.com. Bake sale of creations by current faculty and students (and items donated by CSCA alumni and area businesses) benefits Share Our Strength, a not-for-profit organization dedicated to ending childhood hunger in America.

Index

Hebert Candies, the Candy
Mansion, 75
Henrietta's Table, 142, 296
Herb Lyceum at Gilson's Farm,
The, 97
Herrell's, 48
Highfield Hall, 280
High Horse Brewing + Wicked Fancy
Dining, 34
Hilltop Steak House, 100
Hingham Farmers' Market, 246
H Mart, 110
Holden Farmers' Market, 89
Holyoke Donahue Elementary
School Farmers' Market, 61
Holyoke Farmers' Market, 61
Holyoke Open Square Farmers'
Market, 61
Holyoke Peoples Bank Farmers'
Market, 61
homebrewing, 76
Home Port Restaurant, 255
Hong Kong Supermarket, 170
Hope and Olive, 35
How on Earth, The Store, 237
Hungry Ghost Bread, 48
Hungry Mother, 143
Hutchins Farm, 216
Hyannis/Mid Cape Farmers'
Market, 281
Hyland Orchard, 86

I
Iggy's Bread of the World, 171
Il Capriccio, 194
Il Casale, 195

Il Pastificio, 111
Inna's Kitchen, 195
IOKA Valley Farm, 21
Ipswich Farmers' Market, 123
Ipswich Shellfish Fish Market,
112, 291
Istanbul'lu, 143
Ithaki, 97

J
Jack's Hot Dog Stand, 8
Jae's Asian Bistro, 8
Jamaica Plain Community Servings
Farmers' Market, 184
Jamaica Plain Farmers' Market, 184
Jamaica Plain/Loring-Greenough
Farmers' Market, 184
James Hook + Co., 171
Jasper White's Summer Shack, 143
John Andrews/A Farmhouse
Restaurant, 9
J.P. Licks, 171
J's at Nashoba Valley Winery, 68
J. T. Farnham's, 97

K
Kam Man Market, 172
Kane's Donuts, 112
Karl's Sausage Kitchen & European
Market, 113
Katz Bagel Bakery, 113
Kelly's Roast Beef, 98
Keltic Krust, 207
Kimball Fruit Farm, 120
KO Catering and Pies, 172
KO Prime, 144